God Will Be All in All

God Will Be All in All

Theology through the Lens of Incarnation

Anna Case-Winters

WESTMINSTER
JOHN KNOX PRESS
LOUISVILLE · KENTUCKY

First edition
Published by Westminster John Knox Press
Louisville, Kentucky

21 22 23 24 25 26 27 28 29 30—10 9 8 7 6 5 4 3 2 1

Unless otherwise indicated, Scripture quotations are from the New Revised Standard Version of the Bible, copyright © 1989 by the Division of Christian Education of the National Council of the Churches of Christ in the U.S.A., and are used by permission.

BWHEBB, BWHEBL, BWTRANSH [Hebrew]; BWGRKL, BWGRKN, and BWGRKI [Greek] PostScript® Type 1 and TrueType fonts Copyright ©1994–2015 BibleWorks, LLC. All rights reserved. These Biblical Greek and Hebrew fonts are used with permission and are from BibleWorks (www.bibleworks.com). The only BibleWorks font used in this book is BWHEBB.

Book design by Sharon Adams
Cover design by Allison Taylor

Library of Congress Cataloging-in-Publication Data
Names: Case-Winters, Anna, 1953– author.
Title: God will be all in all : theology through the lens of incarnation / Anna
   Case-Winters.
Description: First edition. | Louisville, Kentucky : Westminster John Knox Press, 2021. |
   Includes index. | Summary: "In this volume, Anna Case-Winters demonstrates that
   the doctrine of the incarnation of God in Christ is not simply one belief among
   others; it is the cornerstone on which all other Christian convictions are built"—
   Provided by publisher.
Identifiers: LCCN 2021038146 (print) | LCCN 2021038147 (ebook) |
   ISBN 9780664267025 (paperback) | ISBN 9781646982196 (ebook)
Subjects: LCSH: Incarnation. | Theology, Doctrinal.
Classification: LCC BT220 .C24 2021 (print) | LCC BT220 (ebook) |
   DDC 232.1—dc23
LC record available at https://lccn.loc.gov/2021038146
LC ebook record available at https://lccn.loc.gov/2021038147

Contents

viii   *Contents*

Acknowledgments

There are many to whom I owe a great debt of gratitude for their part in this endeavor. I first want to express appreciation for McCormick Theological Seminary. I am grateful to the Board of Trustees for granting the yearlong sabbatical that made it possible to undertake and complete a project of this scope. The seminary has been generous in granting time and resources for continuing in research, writing, and reflection. My colleagues here are a gift to me. They know why theology matters and care about what it causes people *to do*. We share a commitment to a world-engaged, transformative theology. Their dedication and camaraderie lift my heart. We are blessed to have students who are a wonderfully diverse and amazing group of people. They are willing to delve deeply into the really big questions, and they pursue them with tenacity and openness. They have taught me so much. It is a privilege to be part of this teaching/learning community.

In working on the manuscript, I received invaluable assistance from the Director of the JKM Library, Barry Hopkins who facilitated my research and biblical scholar Thehil Singh who advised and assisted in my work with Hebrew and Greek terminology. Special thanks are due to Westminster John Knox and especially to Robert Ratcliff, Editor-in-Chief; Daniel Braden, Senior Managing Editor; and Bob Land, copyeditor. My manuscript received a close and careful reading. The corrections and suggestions offered greatly improved upon the original, and I am most grateful.

Our adult children (plus two significant others in our expanding family) continue to be a source of delight and refreshment along the way as I continue these endeavors. Jenny, Matt, Mike, Claire, and Danny have kindly taken interest in my work through the years and have encouraged me along the way. Dreaming of a different kind of world for this new generation is a large part of what motivates me to do theology aimed at transformation. I am pleased to see that we have raised kids who want to change the world. I hope they will.

My husband of forty-five years, R. Michael Winters III, is my foremost partner in this and every good endeavor. He has offered lively interaction with this project chapter by chapter and excellent advice and editing on the first draft. His many years in pastoral ministry bring an invaluable perspective to this work. For his eager partnership in all things and his love that upholds my life, I am more grateful than words can express.

Introduction

A central conviction of Christian faith is that "God is *with* us." One of the ways this is manifest most clearly is when the "Word became flesh" in Jesus of Nazareth (John 1:14). This book inquires into what this means and explores the provocative questions—ancient and contemporary—this affirmation of divine incarnation as such has evoked.

Christians have even claimed that, in the person of Jesus of Nazareth, God's presence is seen in a decisive and distinctive way. Early Christians struggled to understand how it could be that "God was in Christ." What could that mean? What changes for us when we look through the lens of Incarnation in Jesus of Nazareth? Does it change the way we think about who God is? Is the focus of the Christ event sharpened when we view it through the lens of divine incarnation in a wider sense? How might divine incarnation cause us to rethink who we are as human beings—embodied as we are? How might divine incarnation inform our understanding of what we are called to do?

Attention to the implications of incarnation may help us address hard questions that arise to challenge our affirmation that God is with us: How can we say "God is with us" when there is so much suffering and evil around us and within us? Who is the "us" when we affirm that God is with us? Does saying that God is with "us" in Christ mean only us Christians, and automatically entail a Christian exclusivism? Does "God with us" even mean only us human beings? What about divine presence in the wider natural world? Widening our view, what if we, on planet Earth, are not alone in the cosmos? Is God present with others out there, too? What is the depth and scope of incarnation? How wide is the divine embrace?

Traditional and contemporary Christian theological resources are primary conversation partners here. Scripture, historic creeds and confessions, and insights from theologians through the centuries illumine the questions we are exploring. Reformed theologians figure prominently in this mix. Contemporary theologians are informing this work broadly, and from a range of perspectives: process-relational theology, religion and science conversations, ecojustice theologies, ecumenical and interfaith engagement, and emancipatory movements of our time, particularly liberationist and feminist/womanist resources.

Chapter 1 revisits the traditional symbol of Chalcedon and the christological controversies it was navigating. Unfortunately, the resolution it expressed, "truly God and truly human . . . two natures in one person," has seemed to many contemporary believers to be paradoxical at best and contradictory at worst. Many Christians end up settling for a "Christology from above," deemphasizing the human, or a "Christology from below," deemphasizing the divine. Both alternatives are problematic. If, on the one hand, we do not see a "true human being" in Jesus the Christ, then his life cannot serve as a model for our own. We might be moved to worship him (as divine), but we cannot really be expected to follow him. If, on the other hand, we do not see "true God" in him, then our view of who God is and how God is related to us cannot really be shaped by what we see in him. The ancient saying "If this is God, then thus is God" cannot hold. There are perplexities here that need a considered response.

The next step is to offer possibilities arising from exploring key biblical texts, reframing incarnation in the dynamic relationality of the Trinity, and opening a window on what process-relational theology could bring to the present perplexities.

In chapter 2, we ask the question of how the Incarnation in Jesus of Nazareth changes the way we think about God. It is possible that the implied contradiction in affirming "truly God and truly human" is a misunderstanding of our own making. We come to the Incarnation with a preconceived notion of what God is like—one that makes a problem of the Incarnation. What if, instead, we began with the reality of the Incarnation and let that reshape our understanding of what God is like? This approach introduces a new way of seeing that may help us to articulate more coherently the genuine union between divine and human in the Incarnation. Beginning with the Incarnation opens the way to seeing that God *is really in the world*, though always more than the world. This shifts the discourse for us, revealing the deeper reality of divine presence (incarnation) in all things. If that is the nature of God's relation to the world, then the Incarnation in Jesus of Nazareth is not a contradiction or an exception to God's ordinary way of being. It is rather an exemplification of who God is. This book uses Incarnation (capital "I") in reference to the Incarnation in Jesus the Christ and incarnation (lowercase "i") when referring to the wider reality of God's union with all things. Shifting away from "substance" thinking to dynamic relational ways of thinking as exemplified in Trinitarian relations makes an important difference in how we understand God. God is internally related to all things that are.

Chapters 3 and 4 ask how the Incarnation changes the way we think about what it is to be human. Chapter 3 asks, who are we? Chapter 4 asks, what are we called to do? When looking through the lens of the Incarnation, we see more deeply into who we are as human beings. We gain a better understanding of what it is to be made in the image of God as we consider the one "who *is* the image of God" (2 Cor. 4:4; 3:18–4:6). We also see in the Word made flesh a divine embrace of embodiment and material reality. This embrace is already apparent in the creation of the natural world in Genesis. The first human becomes a living being formed from the dust of the ground and the breath of God. Human beings are "at home in the cosmos." Our reality is enfleshed, "incarnate." We are embodied beings who are embedded in a larger web of life. Biblical, theological, scientific, and practical resources are drawn in here to illumine who we are as human beings.

The question of chapter 4, "What are we called to do?," is given an implicit answer when we understand who we are. We are *created* and therefore we are one among the many, of the same substance with all else that is created. We are meant to live together in a convivial community of creation. As creatures in the image of God—the one who creates—human beings have a calling to exercise our own creativity, we are *co-creators* with God. God is love, and we who are in God's image reflect that image best by loving as God loves. Human beings have heightened capacities for freedom and rationality. With these gifts comes a heightened responsibility for creativity and care in relation to the rest of creation. Here we pose the question, "Why do human beings not do better at fulfilling this human vocation?" A brief exploration of the "human problematic" follows. The conclusion of the chapter is that, among other things, incarnation means that *bodies matter*. We conclude that "incarnational ethics" would call us to advocacy and action in the places where bodies are vulnerable. From the many possibilities, we illustrate with issues of disability and racism.

Chapter 5 asks, how does the Incarnation change the way we think about the Christ event? Contemporary challenges have arisen around the central place of the cross in framing what God was doing in Christ. Some charge that it amounts to a glorification of suffering and sacrifice. In responding, this chapter suggests repositioning the major moments of the Christ event—birth, life and ministry, cross, and resurrection—within the frame of Incarnation. Incarnation is the wonder of Word made flesh. There is a sense in which the Incarnation all by itself is sufficient for God's saving work. In this chapter, we trace a theological trajectory from ancient times until the present that sees God's saving work precisely here—in the union of God with the creation. The chapter explores various understandings of God's saving work as they are associated with moments in the Christ event: (1) with the birth of Jesus—the Word made flesh and *theosis* (union of the divine with the creation); (2) with the life and ministry of Jesus—Christ the exemplar; the one on whom the Spirit came to rest; (3) with the death of Jesus—the sacrificial metaphor, the juridical metaphor; and (4) with resurrection of Jesus—the *Christus Victor* metaphor. The chapter concludes with an invitation to reclaim the cross—not as a glorification of suffering but as "a scene of dangerous remembrance, empowering resistance, and emancipatory hope."

Three questions are taken up in chapter 6. All pertain to the issue of what we mean by "us" when we say, "God is with us." It is a matter of how we understand the scope of divine incarnation. How wide is the divine embrace? The questions include: (1) Does God with "us" mean only us Christians? Do Christian claims about the Incarnation lock us into an unavoidable exclusivism? Does the Incarnation in Jesus of Nazareth mean that God's self-revelation has happened *only* in him and not in other times and places? (2) In the face of the hard realities of our current eco-crisis, does God with "us" mean only us human beings? Is the claim of Incarnation irreducibly anthropocentric? (3) Science is daily discovering new exoplanets in what we think of as zones habitable for life. What if we should discover that there are other forms of life out there in the wider cosmos? Does incarnation mean that God is with them too?

Chapter 7 asks the troubling question: How can we say that "God is with us" in the face of so much suffering and evil? Natural disasters and the pandemic certainly raise this question in our day under the category of what is commonly called "natural evil." Under the category of "moral evil" we might name the oppression, injustice, and violence pervasive in the contemporary context. Much of human history can be characterized as a slaughter of the innocents. In what way is God "with us" in all this suffering and evil? What is the nature of divine presence and activity in world process? It would seem that God is *not* with us in the way of a dominating, controlling power that overrules us or natural processes through external intervention that unilaterally determines what happens in world process. Here again the incarnational lens helps us reconstruct our idea of what divine power looks like. In the life and ministry of Jesus and in his death on the cross, God is with us in the way of compassionate resistance in the face of evil and saving solidarity in the face of suffering. In the resurrection of Jesus we see God is with us as life-giving power in the face of all that is death dealing. The real question in our situation is not whether God is with us but whether we are *with God* in the work of compassionate resistance, saving solidarity, and life-giving power.

Chapter 1

Truly God and Truly Human

Two Natures in One Person: Perplexities and Possibilities

Perplexities

The traditional christological symbol of Chalcedon (451)—"truly God and truly human . . . two natures in one person"—has seemed to many contemporary believers to be paradoxical at best and contradictory at worst. The apparent tension has in practice led to distortions in christological understandings. Facing the seeming incoherence in the Chalcedonian affirmation, many Christians end up settling for either a Christology "from above," deemphasizing the "truly human," or a Christology "from below," deemphasizing the "truly God." These options risk Docetism on the one hand and adoptionism on the other. Both alternatives are problematic. In Docetism God only *appears* to be human[1]—a kind of divine deception. In adoptionism Jesus, the Son of God, is an ordinary human being who, because of his obedience to God, is "adopted" to divine status (whether at his baptism, resurrection, or ascension).[2]

Another set of problems arises regarding the affirmation of "two natures in one person." How can divine and human natures—presumed to be utterly different—be joined in one person? Efforts to make sense of

---

1. Docetism is the view that the human, fleshly form seen as Jesus of Nazareth was mere semblance without any true reality. The root of the word means "to seem" (Greek: δοκείν [*dokein*]). God was present but the human form itself was a kind of illusion—God only seeming to be human and not truly human. This way of thinking was rejected at the Council of Nicaea in 325.

2. This approach in effect denies that in Jesus we see the incarnation of the divine Logos, who from the beginning has been in union with God. Jesus is the "Son of God" in the sense of being created/begotten by God at some point in time and thus does not share in the divine essence or equality with God. This view entails a subordinationism such as Arius articulated, a view that was also rejected at the Council of Nicaea in 325.

7

this have generally created problematic resolutions that fall down either on the side of emphasizing "two natures" or on the side of emphasizing "one person." Calvin took the former route while Luther took the latter. Attempts to articulate a unity-in-difference have lacked plausibility. For example, the proposal of a *communicatio idiomatum* (communication of the divine and human attributes within the one person) has seemed to many like a trick with smoke and mirrors and not a resolution at all. An unfortunate byproduct of the proposal of the communication of the attributes is a habit of parceling them out. As Joseph Bracken observes, "It was necessary to distinguish within Jesus between that which was divine in him (the second person of the Trinity) and that which was merely human."[3] The capacity for suffering, notably, was assigned to the merely human.

The resolutions attempted created their own problems theologically and practically. The result is a level of incoherence that has threatened the religious viability of these christological affirmations.[4] People choose either a high Christology or a low Christology and cannot hold together, "truly God and truly human . . . two natures in one person."

The practical outworking of making a choice between divine and human in the person of Jesus the Christ is of real religious consequence. On the one hand, if we do not see "true human being" in him, then his life cannot serve as a model for our own. If God's presence in him is ontologically different from God's presence in the rest of us, then we cannot be expected to be like him.[5] In the ancient church, especially in the East, union of human and divine is the relation for which we are created and the destiny to which we are drawn. The primary purpose of the incarnation is to help us realize this destiny.[6] In this way of thinking, to be "truly human" includes and does not exclude union with God. The stark separation of human and divine in modern and popular thinking loses sight of this union and thereby makes a contradiction of the incarnation. Treating God's presence in Jesus as ontologically different from God's presence in us makes such a separation between us and Jesus that we

3. Joseph Bracken, *Society and Spirit: A Trinitarian Cosmology* (Selinsgrove, PA: Susquehanna University Press, 1991), 28.

4. What follows here was first presented in my article "Incarnation: In What Sense Is God Really 'with Us'?," *European Journal for Philosophy of Religion* 11, no. 1 (Spring 2019): 19–38.

5. Bracken, *Society and Spirit*, 28.

6. Athanasius of Alexandria, *On the Incarnation of the Word*, trans. John Behr (Popular Patristics Series 44; Yonkers, NY: St. Vladimir's Seminary Press, 2011), sec 5.3, p. 167.

cannot see him as "like us." If he is not like us in every way, one consequence is that we cannot be expected to be like him.

We might be moved to worship him (as divine), but we cannot really be expected to follow him. The "reign of God" that Jesus preached ceases to be the focus of our attention, as a kind of "cult of Jesus" takes its place. He becomes a mere object of devotion rather than a companion in seeking and working for the reign of God.[7] If we do see "true human being" in him, then he can be an exemplar for us, and the calling to follow in his way would be viable and compelling. Ethical implications and obligations would come to the fore. Karl Barth urged that the full humanity of Jesus be claimed. In fact, he put the matter provocatively and insisted that the question is not whether Jesus is human but whether *we* are. This is the case because only in Jesus do we see what a "true" human being looks like. The true human being is one who lives in the fullness of covenant relation with God, undistorted by sin. Being in right relation with God, the true human being will be in right relation to all else.[8] Jesus opens up this true humanity for us. It becomes a future possibility and destiny, however imperfectly it may be realized in our situation of sinfulness. These insights illustrate the theological importance of the affirmation of "truly human."

On the other hand, if we do not see "true God" in Jesus the Christ, then does the term "incarnation" even apply? If we do not see "true God" in him, then our view of who God is and how God is related to us and to the world cannot be significantly shaped by what we see in him. Some of our deepest theological insights cannot authentically be affirmed if we do not see "true God" in Jesus the Christ. For example, the compassion and the vulnerable, suffering love we see there are not reliably revelatory of the heart of God. What Jesus does and teaches tells us who he is, but does not tell about God's nature and activity in world process. We cannot really acknowledge, as Barth did, that because of Jesus Christ, we know about the "humanity of God."[9] The deeper implication of the incarnation—that God is in, with, and for the world—is lost. Many claims central to Christian faith are grounded in the belief that in the incarnation

---

7. Choan-Seng Song, *Jesus and the Reign of God* (Minneapolis: Fortress, 1993), 17.

8. Karl Barth, *Church Dogmatics*, III/2, *The Doctrine of Creation*, trans. Geoffrey W. Bromiley (Edinburgh: T. & T. Clark, 1956), 222–25.

9. Karl Barth, *The Humanity of God* (Richmond, VA: John Knox Press, 1960), 49–51. "When we look at Jesus Christ we know precisely that God's deity includes and does not exclude His humanity. . . . His deity encloses humanity in itself. . . . In his divinely free volition and election, in his sovereign decision, God is *human*."

we see "true God." If this is not the case, then the ancient saying "if this is God, then thus is God" cannot hold.

There are ways of addressing the apparent contradiction in affirming "truly God and truly human . . . two natures in one person." The remaining chapters suggest some approaches to untangling the knots that make an absurdity of the incarnation. This chapter offers an overview of biblical, theological, and philosophical elements that shape the orientation of the remaining work. The first section reviews a few key biblical texts that may illumine the incarnational affirmation claimed at Chalcedon. These particular texts are some to which we return from time to time in the remainder of the book. The second section argues that incarnation is better understood when framed in a thoroughgoing Trinitarian theology that takes dynamic relationality as fundamental. The final section in this chapter enumerates several key insights from process-relational theology. Because of the priority of relationality in process thought, these insights reinforce what has been argued about the advantages of understanding incarnation in connection with the dynamic relationality of the Trinity. The following chapters revisit these insights at greater length.

Possibilities

Many biblical texts illumine alternative understandings that could address the apparent perplexities cited above. Here we explore four texts by way of example.

Biblical Explorations: Insights from Four Key Texts

Philippians 2:5–11, Kenotic Christology: "He was in the form of God."
A key text that has been influential for interpreting the meaning of incarnation is a passage from an early Christian hymn that Paul employs in Philippians 2:5–11 as an example to the believers in the church at Philippi.

> Let the same mind be in you that was in Christ Jesus,
> who, though he was in the form of God,
>   did not regard equality with God
>   as something to be exploited,
> but emptied himself,
>   taking the form of a slave,
>   being born in human likeness.

And being found in human form,
   he humbled himself
   and became obedient to the point of death—
   even death on a cross.
Therefore God also highly exalted him
   and gave him the name
   that is above every name,
so that at the name of Jesus
   every knee should bend,
   in heaven and on earth and under the earth,
and every tongue should confess
   that Jesus Christ is Lord,
   to the glory of God the Father.

The history of theological interpretation of this passage has been rich. One problem, though, recurs. The passage has regularly been used as a springboard into discussions of divine and human attributes and how the divine Logos "emptied himself" of divine attributes in order to become fully human in Jesus of Nazareth. The theological overlay upon the text has reinforced the problematic tendency to parcel out divine and human attributes, as discussed earlier, under the topic of "perplexities." Inability to suffer, for example, was a presumed divine attribute. Since Jesus suffered on the cross, that attribute of divinity must have been "emptied." So also with many other divine attributes. This way of thinking risks undermining the Chalcedonian affirmation that Jesus is "fully God." It makes it seem as if the God parts were emptied out in order for God to become human in Jesus of Nazareth.

Perhaps more to the point, this theological overlay may not be the best interpretation of this biblical text in its own right. Sorting out what had to go in order for God to become human is not really central to the text. In its context, the hymn is brought forward to enjoin the believers at Philippi to live life together working for the common good instead of living selfishly. It is prefaced with these words: "be of the same mind, having the same love, being in full accord and of one mind. Do nothing from selfish ambition or conceit, but in humility regard others as better than yourselves. Let each of you look not to your own interests, but to the interests of others" (Phil. 2:2–5). An alternative interpretation suggests itself from this contextual frame. What the passage enjoins is humility, unselfishness, and self-giving. Perhaps "self-giving" is a less misleading interpretation than "self-emptying."

What happens in Jesus the Christ may not be so much an "emptying" of what is divine as an exemplification of who God is—a self-giving God. A well-articulated theology of the cross, for example, contends that the epitome of divine power is seen precisely in the vulnerable, suffering love we see on the cross.[10] Because "self-emptying" can be theologically misleading, as if God is no longer fully God in the incarnation, I prefer "self-giving" as the better alternative. Biblical scholar Michael Gorman points out that *kenosis* as a "divestiture" of something would be quite foreign to Paul's purposes in this passage and that self-giving has the advantage of being a relational term, which is more fitting.[11] In this connection Thomas Oord has pointed out that self-emptying as a metaphor may be problematic. It sounds as if God is like a container whose contents can be poured out. Since this passage centers relations, relational terms are more fitting in the context of this passage. The language of "self-giving" serves better. Oord speaks of "essential *kenosis*" as the self-giving, other-empowering love of God that is essential to who God is.[12]

Perhaps the "parceling out the attributes" approach to this ancient hymn is a result of a theological/philosophical presupposition that divine and human attributes are polar opposites that cannot really be held together in dynamic relational unity. Chapter 2 calls this fundamental presupposition into question.

John 1:1–3, 14—Logos Christology: "And the Word was God."
The Gospel of John, written later than the Synoptic Gospels, has greater theological complexity. It goes further in its eloquent articulation of early intimations of an incarnational understanding of how it is that "God is with us" in the person of Jesus of Nazareth. "In the beginning was the Word, and the Word was with God, and the Word was God. He was in the beginning with God. All things came into being through him, and without him not one thing came into being. . . . The Word [Greek: λόγος (*logos*)] became flesh and lived among us" (John 1:1–3, 14).

Three elements prominent here are important for the understanding of incarnational theology advocated in what follows:

10. See particularly Jürgen Moltmann, *The Crucified God*, 40th anniversary ed. (Minneapolis: Fortress, 2004).
11. Michael J. Gorman, *Inhabiting the Cruciform God: Kenosis, Justification, and Theosis in Paul's Narrative Soteriology* (Grand Rapids: Eerdmans, 2009), 22.
12. Thomas Jay Oord, *The Uncontrolling Love of God: An Open and Relational Account of Providence* (Downers Grove, IL: InterVarsity Press, 156).

1. The Word is fully identified with God: "the Word was God."
2. The Word is preexistent and does not begin with the Incarnation in Jesus of Nazareth.
3. The Word is active in creation as the one through whom "all things came into being."

The deep connection of the incarnate One with the whole of creation—all things—is made explicit here.

Niels Gregersen's work on "deep incarnation" envisions the nature of God's Incarnation in Jesus of Nazareth in ways that emphasize incarnation in the larger natural world—not limited to human beings as such. He proposes that incarnation "reaches into the depths of material existence."[13] The point is well made with the observation that the text uses the flesh (Greek: σάρξ [*sarx*]) in John 1:14. This is a much broader concept than "the Word became human" would have been. *Sarx* is the Greek term that would be used to translate the Hebrew term for "all flesh" (Hebrew: כל-בשׂר [*kl - bśr*]). It can even be used to indicate the whole of material reality. In this way "the eternal Logos embraces the uniqueness of the human but also the continuity of humanity with other animals, and with the natural world at large."[14]

This insight comes into play more fully in chapter 5 as we question whether divine Incarnation in Jesus of Nazareth must necessarily be anthropocentric. Perhaps it need not be. Incarnation has to do with "all flesh" and by extension the material world out of which all things come.

Colossians 1:15–20—Cosmic Christology: "In him all things hold together."
Another passage comparable to John 1 and to Logos Christology is Colossians 1:15–20, usually identified with "cosmic Christology." These are different texts from different contexts, but they share some fundamental assumptions. The Colossians text reads as follows:

> He is the image of the invisible God, the firstborn of all creation; for in him all things in heaven and on earth were created, things visible and invisible, whether thrones or dominions or rulers or powers—all things have been created through him and for him. He himself is before all things, and in him all things hold together. He is the head

13. Niels H. Gregersen, "Deep Incarnation: Why Evolutionary Continuity Matters in Christology," *Toronto Journal of Theology* 26, no. 2 (2010): 173–88, 174.
14. Gregersen, "Deep Incarnation," 174.

of the body, the church; he is the beginning, the firstborn from the dead, so that he might come to have first place in everything. For in him all the fullness of God was pleased to dwell, and through him God was pleased to reconcile to himself all things, whether on earth or in heaven, by making peace through the blood of his cross.

This text speaks of the incarnation in this way: "in him all the fullness of God was pleased to dwell." As in the text from John there is a connection with this Incarnate One and the One in whom all things were created and all things hold together. This understanding, later called "cosmic Christology," is prominent in notable theologians of the early church such as Justin Martyr, Irenaeus, and Clement of Alexandria. Twelfth- and thirteenth-century theologians, Bonaventura in particular, supported a cosmic Christology, and this view is the predominant perspective in Eastern Orthodox theology to this day.[15]

An essential implication of this understanding is that the incarnation is cosmic in scope—not limited to human beings. As Joseph Sittler reminds us, for Irenaeus, "The Incarnation and saving work of Jesus Christ meant that the promise of grace was held out to the whole of nature and henceforth nothing could be called common or unclean."[16] Notably, medieval Franciscan theology traces out the logical implications of this text to insist that incarnation is no afterthought or emergency measure on God's part to deal with human sin. The incarnation lies in the primordial creative intent of God, and it is related to the whole of creation prior to any role in redeeming humankind. The goal of all creation is to be found in its relation with God—its union with God (*theosis*).

The incarnation is redemptive precisely because this union with God—intended for all—is manifest in Jesus of Nazareth. Notable in this text is the affirmation that "in him all the fullness of God was pleased to dwell" (Col. 1:19). In the next chapter of Colossians this is reiterated with an addition: "For in him the whole fullness of deity dwells bodily, *and you have come to fullness in him*" (Col. 2:9–10). There is an explicit connection between the "fullness of deity" in him and our coming to fullness in him.

15. Zachary Hayes, "Christ and the Cosmos," in *The Epic of Creation: Scientific, Biblical, and Theological Perspectives on Our Origins*, ed. Karl Peters, Thomas Gilbert, Marjorie Davis, and Philip Hefner (Chicago: Zygon Center for Religion and Science, 2004), 25.

16. Joseph Sittler, "Called to Unity," in *Creation and the Future of Humanity* (Chicago: Lutheran School of Theology, 2000), 52.

This resonates with Irenaeus's claim that "He became as we are that we might become as he is."[17]

Thus, when the symbol of Chalcedon expresses who the Christ is understood to be—"truly God, truly human," it is expressing that union with God that is intended for all things. God is bringing to completion what God has begun in creation. Themes of fulfillment and consummation take center stage. "God creates so that a (final) life-giving synthesis of God and world might be realized."[18] God will be all in all (1 Cor. 15:28) in a redemption, reconciliation, reunification, and reconstitution of all things.

Luke 4—Spirit Christology: "The Spirit of the Lord is upon me."
There is yet another way to think about how "God is with us" in the incarnation. A thoroughgoing Trinitarian framing of incarnation cannot be about the first and second person of the Trinity, passing over the Spirit's role. A robust understanding of the presence and activity of the Spirit in the life of Jesus of Nazareth is essential. Is there a sense in which the divine incarnation in Jesus of Nazareth is a working of the Holy Spirit in him? Could this be a way of thinking about how "in him all the fullness of God was pleased to dwell" (Col. 1:19)? In the Gospel of Luke, the accounts of Jesus' life and ministry make regular reference to the Spirit. In the annunciation to Mary, she is told that she will bear a son. When she asks how this can be, she is told "the Holy Spirit will come upon you." (1:35). In his baptism the Spirit descends upon him bodily (3:22). In the account of his temptation, it is the Spirit who leads him into the wilderness (4:1). When he returns from the wilderness he is "filled with the power of the Spirit" (4:14). At pivotal moments the activity of the Spirit is prominent.

This is also true at the inauguration of his ministry. Luke 4:14–21 recounts the story in this way:

> Then Jesus, filled with the power of the Spirit, returned to Galilee, and a report about him spread through all the surrounding country. He began to teach in their synagogues and was praised by everyone.
>
> When he came to Nazareth, where he had been brought up, he went to the synagogue on the sabbath day, as was his custom. He

---

17. Irenaeus, *Against Heresies*, vol. 5 preface, in *Ante-Nicene Fathers*, ed. Philip Schaff (1885; repr., Grand Rapids, Eerdmans, 2001), 1:526.
18. Hayes, "Christ and the Cosmos," 25.

stood up to read, and the scroll of the prophet Isaiah was given to him. He unrolled the scroll and found the place where it was written:

> "The Spirit of the Lord is upon me,
>   because he has anointed me
>   to bring good news to the poor.
> He has sent me to proclaim release to the captives
>   and recovery of sight to the blind,
>   to let the oppressed go free,
> to proclaim the year of the Lord's favor."

And he rolled up the scroll, gave it back to the attendant, and sat down. The eyes of all in the synagogue were fixed on him. Then he began to say to them, "Today this scripture has been fulfilled in your hearing."

The central content of the text is decisive for understanding the life and ministry of Jesus, content covered more fully in chapter 4. What we note at this juncture is that the Spirit is spoken of as upon him, filling him, and directing him. Notably, the Spirit fills others as well. In fact, the text Jesus reads from at this inauguration of his ministry is an ancient one, from Isaiah 61:1–2. "The Spirit of the Lord GOD is upon me" was Isaiah's experience (61:1) before it was Jesus' experience. In the rest of the Gospel of Luke multiple persons are said to be directed by the Spirit or full of the Spirit: Zechariah, Elizabeth, John, Mary, and others. It is apparent that being filled with the Holy Spirit is not something that distinguishes Jesus from other human beings but rather something that makes him like us. The Spirit that was in him is in us, too.

A more extended exploration of the Spirit in biblical texts would reveal accounts of the pervasive presence of the Spirit in the whole creation. In the beginning of creation, the Spirit of God hovers over the face of the deep. The terms here translated as "Spirit" (Hebrew: רוח [*rwḥ*] and Greek: πνεῦμα [*pneuma*]) have the connotation of wind or breath: that which enlivens all living things. The Nicene Creed even identifies the Spirit as "giver of life."

It makes a difference for how we think about the Incarnation if we understand the Spirit of God as, in some sense, the means by which God comes to dwell fully in Jesus of Nazareth. Furthermore, if the Spirit may be said from time to time to fill others and even the whole of creation, this may help us to untie the knots of perceived contradiction of Chalcedon's affirmation of "truly God and truly human." God's presence in Jesus of Nazareth does not have to be seen as the exception, but can be seen as the chief exemplification of the presence of God's Spirit in all persons and pervading the whole of creation.

Theological Understandings: Trinitarian Framing of Incarnation

The Christian vision of God has a distinctive shape—its Trinitarian form. This larger frame should shape our understanding of incarnation. Fundamental to the Trinitarian vision of God is relationality. God in God-self, in the inter-Trinitarian life (*ad intra*), is already a Being-in-Relation. Inter-Trinitarian relations may be envisioned as a communion of love. What God is, in God's own life *ad intra*, God is also *ad extra* in relation to the whole of creation, including human beings. Perhaps the image of God in human beings is precisely this property of "Being-in-Relation." I argue this last point more fully in chapter 3.

Relationality is of paramount importance for better understanding the language of truly God and truly human, two natures in one person. Other insights particular to Trinitarian theology may also help in this regard. A very brief exploration of Trinitarian thinking will be undertaken here with particular attention to its connections with incarnational theology. Christological controversies on the way to Chalcedon will also be very briefly reviewed. The argument here is that Trinitarian and relational approaches alleviate some of the presumed difficulties in affirming "truly God, truly human . . . two natures . . . in one person."

How does the understanding of God in Christian tradition come to take Trinitarian form? This distinctive Christian vision of God has multiple sources: biblical, experiential, and theological. In part, the doctrine of the Trinity is an inference from Scripture. Throughout the Bible there are intimations of a "threefoldness" in God. This, in later theological reflection, comes to be referred to as the "three persons" of the one God. In the Hebrew Bible, God, the Holy One of Israel, is envisioned not only as Creator but also the One who redeems Israel out of bondage and as One whose Spirit inspires and speaks through the prophets. Early Christian writings already contain Trinitarian formulations. What has become known as the apostolic benediction reads, "The grace of the Lord Jesus Christ, the love of God, and the communion of the Holy Spirit be with all of you" (2 Cor. 13:13). In the Great Commission, there is the injunction to "'Go therefore and make disciples of all nations, baptizing them in the name of the Father and of the Son and of the Holy Spirit'" (Matt.

28:19). The roots of Trinitarian thinking are certainly there in Scripture, though generations of theological reflection continue to inquire into how this is best understood and articulated.

There is a sense in which the Trinitarian vision is also a dimensioning of our experience of God in the life of faith. The fundamental sense that "God is with us" is nuanced in three distinguishable—though not separable—ways. God is affirmed as the source and origin of all things—the Creator God who elects to be *"with us"* in relationship. This is not a God who dwells aloof from the world in splendid isolation, but a God who is *in relation* to all things and makes space within the divine life for genuine "others" to live and move and have their being. We also experience God as one who is *"for us."* In the Christ event, God shows saving solidarity with us in the places of our brokenness and suffering. God in Christ demonstrates redemptive resistance to death-dealing principalities and powers—including the systems and structures that diminish the fullness of life God intends for all. We also experience God as being *"in us"*—closer to us than breathing—a life-giving power that guides, inspires, comforts, and calls us into the future that God intends. As we trace the experiences of the vivifying presence of the Holy Spirit, the liberating story of Jesus of Nazareth, and the generative mystery of the Creator God, our experience of God does indeed take a threefold shape.

Another important element in our Trinitarian vision comes from the history of theological reflection on Scripture and our experience of God. Theologically, it was important to answer the question of how these *three* experiences are all experiences of the *one* God. How, for example, can we say that God is "one"—the strong conviction of monotheistic faiths—while also affirming that in Jesus the Christ, it is God with whom we have to do. Further reflection was needed to give voice to the monotheistic vision of a God in the face of this threefold experience. More broadly, there were insights that seemed (to some) to be contradictory and to need sorting out. For example, on the one hand, there was the intuition of divine transcendence (that God is above/beyond/before all things). On the other hand, there was the intuition of divine immanence in the world—that God is closer to us than breathing. Our thought and our words stretch to communicate at one and the same time divine ultimacy and divine intimacy. The God who is above all (*ad intra*) is also in all and through all (*ad extra*). God is the source of all that is, God is incarnate in Jesus of Nazareth, and God is enlivening and indwelling all things in the Spirit.

To this general threefold shaping the Greek-speaking church in the East and the Latin-speaking church in the West brought different languages and different understandings of the Trinity. Painting in broad strokes, the Latin-speaking West tended to emphasize unity as fundamental and see the threefoldness as God's "modes of being"—one God in different roles. They tended to employ psychological analogies such as the "mind," which includes memory, intellect, and will. The Greek-speaking East, on the other hand, emphasized the threefold nature of God and tended to use social analogies illustrating the idea that there are three persons in God who have a shared character or essence. To some extent the differences were already embedded in the differences of language. Latin terms were one *substantia* (material ground) and three *personae* (masks). The Greek terms were *ousia* (shared essence) and *hypostases* (self-subsisting substances). For the West, the material ground was a unity that could be expressed in three different ways. By analogy, I am one person, but I am daughter to my parents, wife to my husband, and mother to my children. For the East, there were three who were self-subsisting yet sharing in one essence.

A point of abiding agreement between East and West was relationality. The relation conceived was marked by equality, mutuality, inter-being, and dynamism. God's internal life was viewed as a "communion of love." This inter-Trinitarian relation was expressed in Latin as *circumincessio*—the metaphor being "sitting around" a table together, in communion. In Greek the term used was *perichoresis*—the metaphor being "dancing around," a dynamic, interactive engagement.

This Trinitarian vision allows us to see dynamic communion in the divine life. In the inter-Trinitarian relation, there is unity and co-inherence without any diminution of the persons of the Trinity. This decisively relational Trinitarian vision lays a better foundation for understanding how God can be "in Christ" in the incarnation. Consistently framing "truly God and truly human . . . two natures in one person" within this dynamic, relational Trinitarian framework would go a long way toward resolving the presumed contradiction of the Chalcedonian affirmation.

A complex and controversial history led up to the affirmation of Chalcedon. Tracing a bit of that history may help to illumine the result achieved there. The conclusion reached at Nicaea, that Jesus was *homoousias* (of the same substance) with God, gave a kind of answer but also bequeathed a question: How can a human being be "of one substance" with God and still be a human being? Is it as if two different substances (divine and human) are occupying the same body? In the wider discussion, problematic approaches arose to achieving resolution to this question. Some of these proposals were already present at the Councils of Nicaea (325) and

Constantinople (381). In general, two schools of thought were emerging: one coming out of Antioch that emphasized the divine and human natures, and the other coming out of Alexandria that emphasized their union in one person. There were some extremes from each school that the Council of Chalcedon explicitly excluded. A shorthand description of four excluded extremes is as follows:[19]

- *Confusion* (Eutyches, Alexandrian school). There were two natures before the incarnation but only one after, with a complete union of human and divine. Chalcedon counters by saying there are "unconfusedly" two natures.
- *Transmutation* (Arius). Jesus is a passible/mutable being (therefore not God since God is deemed to be impassible and immutable). Chalcedon counters by asserting that Christ is "unchangeably" and "truly God."
- *Division* (Nestorius, Antiochene school). No union of divine and human is possible. A kind of double personality inhabits the one body. Chalcedon counters with the claim that Christ is "indivisibly" "one person."
- *Separation* (Apollinaris, Alexandrian school). There is a human body with a divine mind/soul. The divine Logos took the place of the human mind/soul of Jesus. There is a kind of separation between the human body and the divine Logos that is operating in and through it. Chalcedon counters by insisting that Christ is "inseparably" and "truly human."

Chalcedon's conclusions on these four extremes are emphasized in bold in the fuller statement of the Symbol of Chalcedon:

> We, then, following the holy Fathers, all with one consent, teach men to confess one and the same Son, our Lord Jesus Christ, the same perfect in Godhead and also perfect in manhood; **truly God and truly man**, of a reasonable [rational] soul and body; consubstantial [coessential] with the Father according to the Godhead, and consubstantial with us according to the Manhood; in all things like unto us, without sin; begotten before all ages of the Father accord-

19. Terms in quotation marks here are those found in Philip Schaff, ed., *The Creeds of Christendom: With a History and Critical Notes*, vol. 2, *The Greek and Latin Creeds*, with translations (Grand Rapids: Baker, 1931), 62.

ing to the Godhead, and in these latter days, for us and for our salvation, born of the Virgin Mary, the Mother of God, according to
the Manhood; one and the same Christ, Son, Lord, Only-begotten,
to be acknowledged in **two natures, *inconfusedly, unchangeably,
indivisibly, inseparably;* the distinction of natures being by no
means taken away by the union, but rather the property of each
nature being preserved, and concurring in one Person** and one
Subsistence, not parted or divided into two persons, but one and the
same Son, and only begotten, God the Word, the Lord Jesus Christ,
as the prophets from the beginning [have declared] concerning him,
and the Lord Jesus Christ himself has taught us, and the Creed of
the holy Fathers has handed down to us.[20]

In the final analysis, the Chalcedonian Definition did not "define" so
much as it marked boundaries excluding extremes. In a sense, Chalcedon
put up signs that said, "This road closed," in those extreme directions.
Sarah Coakley concurs with this assessment and has spoken of Chalcedon as an "ontologically regulatory but apophatic statement."[21] On the
one hand it cannot be taken strictly metaphorically as it intends to be
speaking truly about how God was in Christ. On the other hand, it cannot be taken literally and it proceeds mostly by the way of negation. For
example, it insists that two natures are *not* confused, the two natures are
not separated. It does not fill in much in the way of positive content.

The resulting statement did not completely resolve the differences
between Antiochene and Alexandrian tendencies. Those differences have
continued to reassert themselves through the centuries. What it did do
was carve out a space that both could inhabit within the prescribed boundaries. This is a significant achievement even if the fault lines between
these two prominent views remain.

Philosophical Insights: Process-Relational Orientation

What if the controversy-generating question was misdirected in the first
place? Two philosophical and theological assumptions were at work that are
at the root of the question: (1) that "substance" is what is real/fundamental

20. Schaff, *Creeds of Christendom*, 62.

21. Sarah Coakley, "What Does Chalcedon Solve and What Does It Not? Some Reflections
on the Status and Meaning of the Chalcedonian 'Definition,'" in *The Incarnation: An Interdisciplinary Symposium on the Incarnation of the Son of God*, ed. Stephen T. Davis, Daniel Kendall,
and Gerald O'Collins (Oxford: Oxford University Press, 2002), 143.

and therefore the best way to frame the discussion of how God is in Christ, and (2) that divine and human are utterly different—a binary opposition. Both of these assumptions are challenged briefly and elaborated here.

What if divine and human are not rightly thought of as "substances"? A process-relational rethinking could assist with some of the difficulties theologians in earlier times struggled with so mightily. LeRon Shults in good humor speaks of "a theological addiction to substances," what he calls "substance abuse."[22] A shift to *relational* thinking in place of substance thinking could remove a barrier to understanding how God can be "in Christ."

What if divine and human are not binary opposites and therefore not absolutely mutually exclusive? The problem arises in the way we have delineated divine attributes. We will contend with the unfounded assumption that divine attributes must be derived in opposition to attributes of the world (a world that God has created) and in opposition to attributes of human beings (who are created in the image of God). This assumption sets up binary oppositions: the world is temporal, God is eternal; the world is changing, God is unchanging; human beings are mortal, God is immortal, and so on. If these attributes could be seen in *relation* rather than in opposition, this would also make a significant difference.

Relationality is emerging as a central concept for better understanding how "truly God, truly human, two natures in one person" can be affirmed without contradiction. This was illustrated in the earlier reframing of incarnation in dynamic-relational Trinitarian terms. In a similar way, we may now see how process-relational theology helps communicate dynamic relationality. The shift from thinking in terms of substance to terms of relation also makes it possible to see divine and human not as a binary opposition of different substances. Instead we think in terms of dynamic relationality between these, which proves a rich resource alongside the biblical/theological/experiential resources more commonly employed. Because the philosophical resources may be less familiar to the reader, I also add a personal note here as a help to understanding how this approach enters the picture and what it has to offer.

I write as a philosophically interested theologian with a deep appreciation of process philosophy in particular.[23] Process thought has offered a

22. F. LeRon Shults, *Christology and Science* (Grand Rapids: Eerdmans, 2008), 7.

23. This section of the chapter was first presented at the 2015 Tenth International Whitehead Conference held in Claremont, California, on "Seizing an Alternative: Toward an Ecological Civilization." Proceedings of the philosophical work group have since been published in a collected volume, including my article, "Coming Down to Earth: A Process-Panentheist Reorienta-

lifeline in an ongoing quest to find a more "adequate" concept of God—one more promising than prevalent classical and popular alternatives. Of course, God is and remains a Holy Mystery incomparably greater than all our best visions and concepts of God. Nevertheless, it is important to articulate concepts that at least gesture in good directions. Whitehead spoke of the "brief Galilean vision" that has "flickered uncertainly through the ages."[24] My belief is that this vision is more credible, more religiously viable, and more morally adequate than what many popular and traditional presentations of it have offered. Process thought critiques and clears away some of the theological overlay that obscures the deeper vision available to us from the life and ministry of Jesus of Nazareth. As a theological conversation partner, process thought has been a welcome source of correction and new illumination—a breath of fresh air for me as a theologian. The dynamism in process approaches and the centrality of relationality have much to offer to the discussion at hand. Engagement with the process philosophy in the work of theology is a bit of an adventure of ideas.[25] I believe such adventures are warranted and even essential to progress in theology. As Victor Lowe has pointed out, "Theology, like metaphysics, is dead when it ceases to be a continuing business."[26]

Process-relational theology developed out of theological engagement with the philosophy of Alfred North Whitehead. Whitehead's philosophy contributed new understandings coming out of the sciences of the era, such as evolutionary biology and relativity theory. He believed that process and relations are the heart of reality. He goes beyond the common assumption that reality is "in process" to say that reality *is* process. All things flow. The final real things are not things (substances) at all but processes. Furthermore, everything that is, is related to everything else. In this sense, all things are utterly connected, socially constituted, co-inhering, and mutually influencing.

---

tion to Nature," in *Conceiving an Alternative: Philosophical Resources for an Ecological Civilization*, ed. David Conner and Demian Wheeler (Claremont, CA: Process Century Press, 2017). The current presentation also incorporates earlier work from my article "God Will Be All in All: Implications of the Incarnation," included in a festschrift for Joseph A. Bracken, *Seeking Common Ground*, ed. Marc Pugliese and Gloria Schaab (Milwaukee: Marquette University Press, 2012).

24. Alfred North Whitehead, *Process and Reality: An Essay in Cosmology*, corrected ed., ed. David Ray Griffin and Donald W. Sherburne (1929; repr., New York: Free Press, 1978), 342.

25. Alfred North Whitehead, *Adventures of Ideas* (New York: MacMillan Co., 1933).

26. Victor Lowe, *Understanding Whitehead* (Baltimore: Johns Hopkins University Press, 1962), 92.

Process approaches can help toward a more coherent affirmation of the insights of Chalcedon through several distinctive contributions. At this point, we take up only the two mentioned above. The first is the shift from substance thinking to process thinking. This shift could help to untie some of the theological knots around how divine and human natures can both be present in one person. In the historical christological controversies, the Chalcedonian formulation of "truly God and truly human . . . two natures . . . in one person" seems to have been interpreted through the lens of "substance metaphysics." If divine and human are like two different substances, then for the divine Logos to be present in Jesus of Nazareth, some "part" of his human nature must necessarily be displaced.[27] How can two substances occupy the same space? How can they be both unconfused and inseparable?

Process thinking provides a more workable alternative than substance thinking. Process theologian Joseph Bracken has demonstrated how a creative rethinking in this direction advances the present discussion.[28] The incarnate One may be thought of as co-constituted by divine and human processes, just as God and the world are "interpenetrating fields of activity."[29] There can be a co-presence of two processes in the same space; for example, gravity and electromagnetism can operate in the same space. One might think of two natures in one person analogously. Similarly one may think in terms of "God immanent in the world and the world immanent in God without loss to the independent status of either God or the world."[30] When recast in terms of divine process and world process, there emerges a more coherent way to understand the divine-human relationality and the possibility of truly human and truly divine being noncontradictory.

The second contribution has to do with the way we understand the attributes of God. Whitehead's vision of God and the world provides a meaningful critique and promising alternative to some problematic elements in classical theism.[31] In brief, the classical derivation of divine attributes saw God as eternal, unchanging (immutable), and unable to

27. John Cobb and David Ray Griffin, *Process Theology: An Introductory Exposition* (Philadelphia: Westminster Press, 1976), 104.

28. Bracken, *Society and Spirit*, 48–57.

29. Joseph Bracken, *The One and the Many: A Contemporary Reconstruction of the God-World Relationship* (Grand Rapids: Eerdmans, 2001), 159.

30. Bracken, *One and the Many*, 159.

31. Whitehead, *Process and Reality*.

suffer (impassible). This was in opposition to all that is temporal, change-able, and capable of suffering. Problems with this view arise if we ask questions such as, How can a God who is eternal act in a temporal world? How can an unchangeable God respond to what happens in world pro-cess? What does it mean to pray to a God that cannot respond? How do we make sense of the affirmation that "God is love" if God does not suffer when God's beloved suffer? The derivation of the divine attributes seems to lose the sense of God as Being-in-Relation. Process takes divine relationality as primary.

Charles Hartshorne, one of the foremost interpreters of Whitehead, pointed out that classical theism was also working from some philosophi-cal presuppositions.[32] These were assumptions about what perfection must entail. Conclusions reached philosophically included that it is more "perfect" not to be subject to time or change or suffering. Hartshorne sug-gests an altogether alternative approach. Divine attributes should rather be derived in terms of their religious viability. What is most worshipful? What is most worthy of emulation? A different kind of question yields a different set of attributes. Attributes entailed in creative-responsive love are the ones that will come to the fore. They transcend the binaries that classical theism envisioned. For example, God does not have to be chang-ing or unchanging. God can be both—and will be each in the way in which it is most excellent to be so. For example, God may be unchanging in faithfulness but changing in the sense of responding (faithfully) to us and our changing world.

Perhaps, with substance thinking and opposition thinking challenged, the whole conversation can shift. These ways of thinking made a contra-diction of the christological affirmations of Chalcedon. What is clear is that early Christian tradition held an abiding sense that, in the person of Jesus of Nazareth, it is God with whom we have to do. Some texts articu-late this sense of the matter: "in him the whole fullness of deity dwells bodily" (Col. 2:9); "in Christ God was reconciling the world" (2 Cor. 5:19). The christological questions shift. Who was this man? What was his relation to God, and how does that impact our relation with him and with God and with one another? Jesus' life was revolutionary in what he proclaimed and how he lived. Love of God and love of neighbor were fundamental. This led him to challenge the systems and structures that

---

32. See Charles Hartshorne, *The Divine Relativity: A Social Conception of God* (New Haven, CT: Yale University Press, 1948).

were oppressive and death-dealing for those around him. His ministry was characterized by solidarity and redemptive resistance to all that would hurt or destroy God's beloved children.

In the dynamic relations between this man and God, there are reconciliation, redemption, and salvific power for us. Can we find better ways of understanding this dynamic relation? The problems of the christological affirmation can be addressed in a manner similar to the differences that arose around Trinitarian thinking. What is required is a shift to dynamic, relational approaches. If the human being is in God's image and God is a Being-in-Relation, it is possible to think about the human and the divine together relationally rather than as two different substances occupying the same space. Thus union need not require a division of labor or a parceling out of attributes or a kind of hybrid existence that is neither truly divine nor truly human. Relationality is essential for thinking about God in Trinitarian terms and for thinking about Jesus the Christ as "truly God and truly human . . . two natures in one person." The incarnation in Jesus the Christ, situated in a Trinitarian-relational frame, admits of greater coherence conceptually and greater depth and scope in its implications than when treated in isolation. This framing continues to inform all that follows.

Conclusion

The seeming incoherence of the Chalcedonian affirmation has proven perplexing and has resulted in christological controversies. Many Christians end up making a choice. They either end up settling for a "Christology from above," deemphasizing the human, or a "Christology from below," deemphasizing the divine. Both alternatives are problematic. If, on the one hand, we do not see a "true human being" in Jesus the Christ, then his life cannot serve as a model for our own. We might be moved to worship him (as divine), but we cannot really be expected to follow him. If, on the other hand, we do not see "true God" in him, then our view of who God is and how God is related to us cannot really be shaped by what we see in him. Without this, the ancient saying "If this is God, then thus is God" cannot hold.

In the face of the apparent contradiction, theologians are inclined to just throw up their hands and say, "Mystery." While the doctrine of God is mystery through and through, we misplace the mystery when we use this term to cover over contradictions we have ourselves created. This first chapter has attempted to show prospects for finding more coherent alternatives. A brief exploration of biblical texts, Trinitarian theology, and process-relational philosophy has offered possible ways forward. We continue to access these resources through the book to deepen understanding of the implications of the incarnation. Our overriding question is, what does incarnation mean, and what difference does it make? In particular, we pursue the difference it makes for how we think about God, human beings, the Christ event, and the sense in which God is "with us."

Chapter 2

How Does Incarnation Change the Way We Think about God?

Incarnation fundamentally changes the way we think about God. God's relation to the world is shown to be not only transcendent but also immanent.[1] We learn that there is both ultimacy and intimacy in the God-world relation. Denis Edwards puts it this way: "God is a dynamic Being-in-relation. God makes space within the divine relations for a dynamically unfolding universe and for the evolution of life in all its diversity and interconnectedness."[2]

Some visions of God have pictured a distant, aloof, unmoved deity, who exists in splendid isolation from the world. Such a vision cannot readily accommodate incarnation. Looking through the lens of incarnation causes us to see God's relation to the world very differently. In Christian tradition, we think of divine incarnation in Jesus of Nazareth as the emblematic expression of God being "with us." Once we have seen

1. A preliminary presentation of this chapter was given as an invited lecture for an international conference sponsored by Regensburg University and the School of Philosophy in Munich on "The Nature of God—Advancing and Challenging Classical Theism," July 27–August 7, 2017. It was later published as "Incarnation: In What Sense Is God Really 'with Us'?" *European Journal for Philosophy of Religion* 11, no. 1 (Spring 2019): 19–38. Earlier reflections appear in "Coming Down to Earth: A Process-Panentheist Reorientation to Nature," in *Conceiving an Alternative: Philosophical Resources for an Ecological Civilization*, ed. David Conner and Demian Wheeler (Claremont, CA: Process Century Press, 2017), 99–114. Still other parts came together in a festschrift written for Joseph Bracken, "God Will Be All in All: Implications of the Incarnation," in *Seeking Common Ground*, ed. Marc Pugliese and Gloria Schaab (Milwaukee: Marquette University Press, 2012), 119–30.

2. Denis Edwards, *The God of Evolution: A Trinitarian Theology* (New York: Paulist Press, 1999), 126. Other books by Edwards include *Jesus and the Cosmos* (New York: Paulist Press, 1991), and *Breath of Life: A Theology of the Creator Spirit* (Maryknoll, NY: Orbis Books, 2004).

God in him, we are moved to explore the deeper implications. If this is how God is with us, then surely God's presence must always, already have been profound and pervasive. While we maintain divine transcendence—God is more than the world—through the lens of the Incarnation we now see an *immanent* transcendence. We are pushed to reconsider ways of thinking and talking about God that imply fundamental separation between God and the world. What changes in the Incarnation is not who God is, but how we come to know God.

The presence of God—that is already in, with, and under all things—is manifest, in the fullness of time, in the Incarnation in Jesus of Nazareth. In this chapter we articulate what changes in our thinking about God when we look through the lens of the Incarnation. In turn we work toward a more coherent and religiously viable understanding of our affirmation that "God is with us" in the Incarnation. These two steps are mutually reinforcing: from the standpoint of the Incarnation we discern that "God is with us" in dynamic relationality with the world. If we see that this is how God is with the world, then the Incarnation in Jesus of Nazareth is more coherently conceivable. Some significant insights shaped by process-relational theology (enumerated below) can help us elaborate relationality in general and God's relation to the world in particular. These provide a new way of seeing that is more adequate to the task at hand.

- Seeing the attributes of God in terms of "transcendent-immanence" rather than choosing only the attributes of transcendence and rejecting the attributes of immanence.
- Seeing the relation between God and the world as "internal" to God (affecting God) rather than "external" to God (not affecting God).
- Seeing that God and the world are in interactive creativity rather than marking an absolute divide between "Creator" and "created."
- Seeing "all things in God and God in all things," even as we affirm that God is more than all these.
- Seeing the value and interconnectedness of all things.

Each of these changes illumines the dynamic relationality between God and the world that we have come to know in looking through the lens of the Incarnation. Each also helps us to articulate divine incarnation as an authentic possibility rather than an incoherent contradiction. I address them in turn to illustrate.

God's Transcendent-Immanence

In chapter 1 we explored the significant difference it makes to think of reality in *process* terms rather than in substance terms. In this chapter we show the difference it makes to see reality as fundamentally relational rather than seeing relations as something into which agents and objects, which are otherwise independent, may or may not enter. Relationality is essential. It is not just an option or an attribute particular to some and not others. Everything is utterly connected to everything else.

With this second shift of thinking in play, we have two profound insights into reality offered by process-relational theology. Reality is process; all things flow, and everything that is, exists in *relation* to everything else. In this dynamic relational process, all things are utterly connected, co-constituted by their relations, and therefore mutually influencing. These two insights make it possible to untie some of the theological knots around how the divine nature and human nature can be present in one person.

We also discussed issues with the derivation of divine attributes that constructed a binary opposition between divine attributes and human attributes. That made a problem for understanding how to coherently affirm "truly God and truly human . . . two natures in one person." I draw out this insight in more detail here because divine attributes are very much to the point as we discuss how the Incarnation changes the way we think about God.

Process approaches invite us to see divine attributes differently. In the interest of upholding divine transcendence, classical theism derived divine attributes *over against* the attributes of the natural world. On the one hand, this way of negation (not this, not that), the apophatic reserve, is fitting. God is *not* the world and *not* anything in the world. However, what began as an apophatic reserve has hardened into a binary opposition. In effect, God has been *structured out* of the natural world, and the world has been desacralized. This approach has had the effect of making the affirmation of truly divine and truly human unimaginable. The binary opposition falls out somewhat like this:

God	*World*
Eternal	Temporal
Unchanging (immutable)	Changing
Not subject to suffering (impassible)	Subject to suffering
Necessary being	Contingent being

A welcome alternative to this way of thinking is found in Whitehead's "dipolar theism,"[3] later interpreted by Charles Hartshorne as a kind of "dual transcendence."[4] Rather than setting up metaphysical polarities and assigning one pole to God and the other to the world, divine perfection is reconceived as embracing both poles, manifesting each attribute in the way in which it is most excellent to do so. God can be both unchanging in the sense of divine (loving) faithfulness and changing in the sense of divine (loving) responsiveness. Faithfulness and responsiveness are both ingredients in the Christian vision of God as loving. Divine transcendence and divine immanence can be maintained together. For this reason, I prefer to hold them together by calling this "transcendent-immanence" rather than adopting Whitehead's or Hartshorne's terminology.

God's incarnate presence in the world is less problematic from this beginning point of transcendent-immanence than it was from the classical derivation of divine attributes. Consequently the Incarnation of Jesus of Nazareth can be seen in a new light. Though profound and mysterious, the Incarnation is not absurd or even contradictory.

God and the World: Mutual Indwelling and Mutual Influence

A question of some importance in this discussion is whether and how God is affected by relation with the world. Process-relational theology assumes that God's relation to the world is "internal" rather than "external." In classical theism, it was assumed that while the world is *internally* related to God (and therefore can be affected by God), this relation is not reciprocal. God is only *externally* related to the world and can affect the world without being affected by it. This way of thinking led to a persistent belief that God cannot suffer (divine impassibility). The moments of suffering in the life of Jesus are not understood to be moments of suffering in the divine life. When it comes to the passion narratives and particularly the cross, theologians took care to make clear that it was the "human nature" and not the "divine nature" that suffered. The idea that God (in Christ) actually suffered on the cross (patripassionism, from the Latin *patri* [father] and *passio* [suffering]) was declared heretical. Patripassionism was in fact the nickname given to modalism by its opponents. Modalists so identified the Father and the Son that it could be said that

---

3. Alfred North Whitehead, *Process and Reality* (1929; repr., New York: Macmillan, 1978), 345.

4. Charles Hartshorne, "The Dipolar Conception of Deity," *Review of Metaphysics* 21, no. 2 (December 1967): 273–89.

the Father was born, suffered, and died. Both modalism and these logical outworkings of it were resisted. Tertullian suggested instead that the Father "co-suffered" in the sense of having compassion for the Son. This came to be the orthodox view. Prevailing ideas about divine perfection excluded the possibility of patripassionism. To admit capacity to suffer seemed to be admitting an imperfection. This is true in part because it admits capacity to change, which was already excluded from the divine attributes (as classically derived).[5] God is unchanging (immutable).

This way of thinking has lately been reconsidered. We see a seismic shift in thinking in twentieth-century theology on this question of whether God can suffer. This new view was compellingly presented in Jürgen Moltmann's *The Crucified God*. Contemporary theology has largely followed Moltmann's reading and rejected the impassibility of God. Joseph Sittler put it starkly: "Unless you have a crucified God, you don't have a big enough God."[6] One generation's heresy is another's orthodoxy.

Process thinkers such as Charles Hartshorne already questioned the assumption that God cannot suffer on the basis of the religious conviction that God is love. Love suffers when the beloved suffers. Divine perfections should be derived from their religious viability rather than in some other way. Hartshorne's innovation was to suggest "worshipfulness" as a good beginning point and standard.[7] A God worthy of worship must be worthy of admiration, respect, love without limits, and human imitation. We are invited to ask whether a God who does not suffer when the world God so loves is suffering would really be "worshipful." Would such a God be truly "with us" in our suffering? If one takes "God is love" and "God is with us" seriously, then thinking in terms of internal rather than external relations is more religiously viable. The process insistence that God is internally—and not just externally—related to the world lays aside divine impassibility in preference for a God who can be consistently thought of as a God of love.

Embracing God's relation with the world as an internal relation also opens up new prospects for thinking about mutual indwelling. Through

---

5. The logic of why change is an imperfection was sometimes articulated in this way: Something that changes either changes for the better (in which case it was not originally perfect) or it changes for the worse (in which case it is not now perfect). Another element was the association of this view with monarchical modalism, the view that the unity of God was such that Father, Son, and Holy Spirit are not persons as much as modes of expression of the divine unity.

6. Joseph Sittler, *Grace Notes and Other Fragments* (Minneapolis: Augsburg, 1981), 228.

7. Charles Hartshorne, *The Divine Relativity: A Social Conception of God* (New Haven, CT: Yale University Press, 1948), 41.

internal relations, everything that exists is co-constituted with the divine. Divine reality includes and does not exclude material reality. With this new orientation, new possibilities open up for understanding the Incarnation. We now have a way of seeing how God can be "in" a human being without compromising that person's humanity. In the fullness of this internal relation, humanity is brought to perfection.[8]

By extension, internal relation implies that, in this sense, God is already "all in all" (1 Cor. 15:28). This is not something deferred to the eschaton.[9] One may speak even now of the "indwelling presence" (Hebrew: שׁכינה [škynh]) of God in the world or of God's "glory" (Hebrew: כבוד [kbwd]) appearing in our midst. Mayra Rivera puts it this way: "Glory is the trace of the divine relationship woven through creaturely life and its relationships. It is the cloudy radiance of the ungraspable excess that inheres in ordinary things—something that manifests itself, that gives itself."[10]

Creator-Created-Creativity

In another helpful step, process thought reconsiders the traditional assumption of an absolute divide between "Creator" and "created." Insistence upon an "infinite qualitative distinction" between Creator and created is yet another reason any joining of divine and human has been difficult to imagine. This is yet another binary opposition of attributes applied to God and the world. In its place, Whitehead introduces the category of *creativity* as a capacity shared by God and the world, though in different measure. God is supremely creative—the chief exemplification of creativity—and the leader of the creative advance. This does not require that God be thought of as having a monopoly on creativity.[11] One might say that the Creator has created a creative world. The universe is itself a creative process. All being is "becoming." Human beings, and other beings as well, might be thought of as "created, co-creators."[12]

8. Marjorie Suchocki, "Spirit in and through the World," in *Trinity in Process: A Relational Theology of God*, ed. Marjorie Suchocki and Joseph Bracken (New York: Continuum International, 1996), 60.

9. Catherine Keller, *Cloud of the Impossible: Negative Theology and Planetary Entanglement* (New York: Columbia University Press, 2015), 52.

10. Mayra Rivera, "Glory: The First Passion of Theology?," in *Polydoxy: Theology of Multiplicity and Relation*, ed. Catherine Keller and Laurel C. Schneider (London: Routledge, 2011), 177.

11. Whitehead, *Process and Reality*, 21.

12. Philip Hefner coined this very helpful description in his book *The Human Factor: Evolution, Culture, and Religion* (Minneapolis: Fortress, 1993). An exploration of this idea is set forward in chapter 3.

Whitehead envisions God as both the Ground of Order and the Ground of Novelty. In this way, God provides the conditions of the possibility of creativity. Nothing exists *apart from* the exercise of divine creativity, yet the creation is not devoid of its own creativity. The habitual stark separation between Creator and created does not fit a world with its own creativity exercised in its semiautonomous unfolding. The God who is "with us" creates *with us*. God's interaction with the world is always an "interaction," a mutual dynamic creativity.

Whitehead goes further and puts the matter somewhat provocatively: "It is as true to say that God creates the World as that the World creates God."[13] This is a logical outworking of interactive creativity. It also follows upon conclusions made in the previous section. If God's relation to the world is *internal*, then what happens in world process affects God.

One way to imagine how this works is as follows: Moment to moment in the becoming of the world, God receives what happens in the world into the divine life. This is a kind of creative impact of the world upon God. God exercises creativity in offering back to the world novel possibilities for good. In this dynamic we see how God may both create and be created in dynamic internal relation with the world. God's creative interaction with the world is not a matter of external intervention from the outside, but rather a matter of *acting with and within the world*. This interactive creativity is amplified as we explore more deeply the conviction that God is in the world and the world in God.

God in All Things and All Things in God

Perhaps the most decisive step of interrelating God and the world in process-relational theology is panentheism. Panentheism, simply put, is the view that "God is in all things and all things are in God" (from the Greek terms: πάν [all things], έν [in], θεος [God]). Panentheism is to be distinguished from pantheism. For pantheism, God is the world and the world is God. Transcendence collapses into immanence. The "en" in pan*en*theism makes a world of difference. Perhaps the best metaphor for this understanding is the one Augustine offers in his *Confessions*:

> I visualize you, Lord, surrounding [creation] on all sides and permeating it, but infinite in all directions, as if there was a sea everywhere, and stretching through immense distances, a single sea which had

---

13. Whitehead, *Process and Reality*, 348.

within it a large but finite sponge, and the sponge was in every part filled from the immense sea. This is the way in which I supposed your finite creation to be full of you, infinite as you are, and said: "Here is God and see what God has created. God is good and is most mightily and incomparably superior to these things."[14]

Panentheism affirms "God immanent in the world and the world immanent in God without loss to the independent status of either God or the world."[15] God is in the world and the world is in God, yet God is more than the world. Arthur Peacocke defines panentheism similarly as "the belief that the Being of God includes and indwells all things in the cosmos, while not being reducible to these things."[16] God is *really present* "in, with, and under" all things while simultaneously transcending them. We may speak of transcendent-immanence or even immanent-transcendence in God's relation to the cosmos. With this step all else falls into place. Incarnation of the divine is cosmic in scope. God enfolds the world in God's own being.[17]

Among the panentheisms on the horizon, process panentheism may hold the most promise in articulating the depth of divine relation to the world. It does not so easily fall into *pantheism* on the one hand or *pancosmism* on the other.[18] In pantheism, there is no distinction between God and the world; the world is "simply divine." In pancosmism, the world is all there is. There is no reality we might name as God; there is only the world and its processes. In distinction from these two extremes, process panentheism takes a genuinely relational approach that presupposes differentiation. Both the alterity (otherness) of the world and the transcendence of God are preserved in process panentheism.

14. Augustine, *The Confessions*, trans. Henry Chadwick (Oxford World Classics; New York: Oxford University Press, 1998), 7.115.

15. Joseph Bracken, *Society and Spirit: A Trinitarian Cosmology* (Selinsgrove, PA: Susquehanna University Press, 1991), 159.

16. Arthur Peacocke, *Paths from Science towards God: The End of All Our Exploring* (Oxford: One World, 2004), 51.

17. Following Nicholas of Cusa, it is best to think of this as an enfolding rather than an enclosure. His panentheism "destabilizes any picture of a container-God" (Keller, *Cloud of the Impossible*, 113).

18. For example, the emanationist panentheism of Sallie McFague's proposal ("the world as God's body") may be leaning toward pantheism. Gordon Kaufman's proposal that God is the (nonagential) "serendipitous creativity in the bio-historical process" leans toward pancosmism. For the full argument, see Anna Case-Winters, *Reconstructing a Christian Theology of Nature: Down to Earth* (Burlington, VT: Ashgate, 2006), 19–43.

Resisting pantheism, panentheism insists that the world is not divine; it is not "God's body." Alterity is essential, or else there is no relation with a genuine other, only a divine self-relation. The world, dependent as it is on God as the Ground of Order and Ground of Novelty, nevertheless has its own semiautonomous unfolding. Within the boundaries of what is past and what is possible, those who are coming to be have their own part to play in how the past will be incorporated and how the possible will be embraced. Without this, what happens in the world would only be God's own doing. It would be meaningless to speak of either freedom or ethical responsibility.

Resisting pancosmism, panentheism insists that God is not reducible to world process, even though God is pervasively present in world process. God is not just the "serendipitous creativity in the bio-historical process." God transcends the world even while indwelling and enfolding world process. Transcendence, in a process-relational framework, is not a matter of separation but a matter of supreme relation. God is *supremely related* to all that is. For this transcendent relationality, Hartshorne coined the term "surrelativity."[19] This is a transcendence that includes and does not exclude relations with genuine others.

Process panentheism proves helpful for the Chalcedonian affirmation of "truly God, truly human." If God is (already) in all things, there is no essential contradiction in saying God was "in" Jesus of Nazareth. The world's presence in God and God's presence in the world are already the reality. The Incarnation makes visible this deeper reality. What happens in the man, Jesus of Nazareth, is emblematic of what is *already the case* about the whole of creation.

For Christian theology, this view unveils—among other things—the deeper meaning of incarnational theology. Whitehead offered, "The world lives by its incarnation of God in itself."[20] Arthur Peacocke, who also speaks from a panentheist perspective, expressed the meaning of the Incarnation in this way:

> The incarnation can thus be more explicitly and overtly understood as the God *in whom the world already exists* becoming manifest in the trajectory of a human being who is naturally in and of that world. In that person the world now becomes transparent, as it were, to the God in whom it exists: The Word which was before *incognito*,

19. Hartshorne, *Divine Relativity*, 88.
20. Alfred North Whitehead, *Science and the Modern World* (New York: Macmillan, 1926), 149.

implicit, and hidden, now becomes known, explicit, and revealed. The epic of evolution has reached its apogee and consummation in God-in-a-human-person.[21]

In this sense, when we speak of "the Incarnation" we are describing an instance of transparency to a deeper reality—a place where the light shines through. The meaning of the Christian theology of incarnation has not yet been tapped for its deeper significance in conveying God's pervasive presence in world process (incarnation in all things). This presence of God in all things has implications for how we value material reality.

In Jesus of Nazareth there is a responsiveness to divine initial aims, such that in him we are able to see the divine intention. Looking at what God does in him, we get a glimpse of what God is doing everywhere and always. We see that God is in, with, and for the world. God's intentions and actions for each and for all become transparent in Jesus the Christ. As Allan Galloway put it, "Once we have encountered God in Christ, we must encounter God in all things."[22] This necessarily reshapes how we think about the natural world as well as how we think about God.

The Intrinsic Value and Vital Interconnectedness of All Things

Whitehead's "philosophy of organism" helps us to see the value and interconnectedness of all things. In a sense it shifts to a more ancient way of viewing the world. Part of our problem in the current eco-crisis is a shift in metaphors for understanding the nature of the world. The primary metaphor for thinking about the world in medieval times was as an organism. In the scientific revolution a fundamental shift occurred that gave way to a mechanical model. Value and interconnection are more easily conveyed in thinking of the world as an organism than in thinking of the world as a mechanism. With a mechanism, one pictures some mechanical object that is composed of independent parts. A mechanism can be taken apart and reassembled with nothing lost. Not so with an organism.

Jürgen Moltmann has pointed out that one of our difficulties has been an "objectification of nature" and a "subjectification of the human

21. Arthur Peacocke, "Articulating God's Presence in and to the World Unveiled by the Sciences," in *In Whom We Live and Move and Have Our Being: Panentheistic Reflections on God's Presence in a Scientific World*, ed. Philip Clayton and Arthur Peacocke (Grand Rapids: Eerdmans, 2004), 154.

22. Allan Galloway, *The Cosmic Christ* (New York: Harper Brothers, 1951), 250.

being."[23] In this configuration, the human being has a monopoly on spirit and stands with God on the other side of the great divide between the spiritual and the material, the subjects and the objects. The human being is, in a sense, lifted out of the natural world as a "spiritual creature" in a "material world." Accompanying this shift is the habit of assigning intrinsic value to subjects and only instrumental value to objects. This way of thinking is in part responsible for the cavalier and exploitative treatment of the natural world.

Whitehead's "philosophy of organism" has the benefit of returning "organism" thinking to our worldview. The world is no longer a mechanism that humans inhabit and oversee. There is no devaluation of the rest of creation in relation to human beings. In Whitehead's system, "Value is inherent in actuality itself."[24] Every actual entity has capacity for inwardness, subjectivity, and relationality. This may come in varying different degrees with varying capacities for sentience, but everything should be granted subject status. Everything has both subject status in itself (in its coming to be) and object status (in its effects on others). This is a radically different picture that Whitehead has introduced. It breaks down the divide between subjects and objects; the spiritual-material dichotomy dissolves. The human being no longer has a monopoly on spirit or a monopoly on intrinsic value. As John Cobb in good humor insists, "Process theology does not commit monopoly."[25] The huge distinction drawn between the human being and the rest of nature disappears; we are all together in this Earth community. As Thomas Berry repeatedly observes, "The universe is a communion of subjects rather than a collection of objects."[26]

Granting value and subject status to all things proves to be of pivotal importance in our chapter 5 discussion of the current eco-crisis. Incarnation makes a difference in how we view the rest of the world of nature and also how we might live in relation to the other subjects we encounter. One treats a communion of subjects very differently than a collection of objects.

Another important contribution of the "philosophy of organism" is the way it conveys the vital interconnectedness of all things. All things

23. Jürgen Moltmann, *God in Creation: A New Theology of Creation and the Spirit of God* (San Francisco: Harper and Row, 1985), 25.

24. Whitehead, *Process and Reality*, 100.

25. John Cobb, "Seizing an Alternative: Toward an Ecological Civilization" (Keynote Address, Tenth International Whitehead Conference, Claremont, California, June 2015).

26. Brian Swimme and Thomas Berry, *The Universe Story from the Primordial Flaring Forth to the Ecozoic Era: A Celebration of the Unfolding Cosmos* (San Francisco: Harper, 1992), 243.

are said to be co-constituted by their social world. We are not separate but internally joined with all others who inhabit our world. Whitehead said of his whole philosophy of organism that it is "mainly devoted to the task of making clear the notion of 'being present in another entity.'"[27] This clarity will help in understanding what we are affirming when we say, "God was *in Christ*, reconciling the world unto himself" (2 Cor. 5:19 KJV, emphasis added).

We have our being together, not separately. The notion of the autonomous individual is a false report on experience. All things are utterly connected. This is the case despite their seeming autonomy. There are many ways this could be illustrated. We draw here from experience, science, Scripture, and theology.

Experientially, there are multiple instances where what appears to be separate and individual turns out to be connected when we look more deeply. One illustration from the world of nature is a beautiful stand of quaking aspens in south central Utah. This stand of aspens occupies 106 acres of land. Looking at it, one sees many, many lovely trees. As it happens, the identical genetic markers of these trees reveal that it is a clonal colony of an individual male quaking aspen. Scientists have named it "Pando" (Latin for "I spread out"). It is also known as "the trembling giant." It weighs six million kilograms, making it the heaviest known organism. It has one root system, which is eighty thousand years old—among the oldest known living organisms.[28] Here is one instance where what appears to be a collection of individuals turns out to be one organism when we look more deeply.

There are interesting instances in the sciences of deep connections that are unexpected. A surprising discovery in contemporary physics discloses a dynamic of profound interconnectedness at the subatomic level. It seems that two particles that have contact in the same quantum system continue to influence one another no matter how far they are subsequently separated. Even just *measuring* one particle affects the other particle. This happens instantaneously and thus is not thought to be a matter of one "communicating" with the other. Quantum mechanics calls this "nonlocality," "nonseparability," or "entanglement." Though these particles appear to be separate, some kind of connection resides below the apparent separation. It is a remarkable instance of a cosmology

27. Whitehead, *Science and the Modern World*, 50.
28. Wikipedia, s.v. "Pando (tree)," https://en.wikipedia.org/wiki/Pando_(tree).

of "each in each and all in all." As Catherine Keller puts it in *Cloud of the Impossible*, this is one more case where "separateness is a sham."[29]

The possibility that what appears to be separate may in fact be vitally connected is not a strange idea for Christian tradition. There are biblical texts and theological perspectives that take vital interconnectedness as fundamental. In Scripture, for example, we have texts like Acts 17, a passage that tells of Paul's address to the Athenians in the Areopagus. There he offers a vision of God as the one in whom "'we live and move and have our being'" (v. 28). We are together in the life of God. Another text, John 17, should be mentioned. This text has come to be known as Jesus' "high priestly prayer." Here he prays that his followers may be one: "'As you, Father, are in me and I am in you, may they also be in us'" (17:21). Earlier in this Gospel, there appears a metaphor of Jesus' relation with his followers as being like that of a vine and its branches. "Abide in me as I abide in you. Just as the branch cannot bear fruit by itself unless it abides in the vine, neither can you unless you abide in me. I am the vine, you are the branches. Those who abide in me and I in them bear much fruit, because apart from me you can do nothing" (John 15:4–5). All these texts, and many others that could be referenced, hold out a vision of vital connection, of our abiding in God and in one another.

Insights of a long line of theologians and mystics through the centuries provide resources for thinking about how we are all "in" God. Nicholas of Cusa speaks of God as "equally enfolding and unfolding all things."[30] All are "enfolded" in God, and there we are joined to one another. We are utterly connected.

Theologians working out Trinitarian theology gave much attention to the mutual indwelling of the persons of the Trinity. They used language of "interpenetration" and "co-inherence" to describe inter-Trinitarian life. Each person of the Trinity is "in" the other two. The persons are not confused, but neither are they separated. As set forth in chapter 1, the relationality of the Trinity can be expressed in various ways. The multiple approaches all attempt to describe a dynamic of mutual indwelling,

---

29. Keller, *Cloud of the Impossible*, 128.

30. Nicholas of Cusa, *Selected Spiritual Writings*, trans. H. Lawrence Bond, Classics of Western Spirituality 89 (New York: Paulist Press, 1997), 255. To say that all things are enfolded in God and unfolded from God is to say (1) that all things are present in God as God and not as contracted and finite and that God is present in all things but not as God is in Godself, and (2) that God is all things but only as they are enfolded in God, and although God is present in all things God is not all things as each created thing originated and unfolded from God.

of each person of the Trinity being in the others without diminishment of any.

One of the most prominent metaphors in Christian ecclesiology is an image of vital interconnectedness—the church as the "body of Christ." As Paul observes, "Now you are the body of Christ and individually members of it. . . . For just as the body is one and has many members, and all the members of the body, though many, are one body, so it is with Christ. . . . If one member suffers, all suffer together with it; if one member is honored, all rejoice together with it" (1 Cor. 12:27, 12, 26). Here again, organism thinking rather than mechanism thinking prevails.

Thich Nhat Hanh, in his book *Living Buddha, Living Christ*, illustrates the vital interconnection with the image of a flower:

> When we look into the heart of a flower, we see clouds, sunshine, minerals, time, and the earth, and everything else in the cosmos with it. Without the clouds there could be no rain, and there would be no flower. . . . In fact, the flower is made entirely of non-flower elements; it has no independent, individual existence. It "inter-is" with everything else in the universe.[31]

This quality of "inter-being" is a profound understanding of relationality and vital interconnectedness. When we see the nature of inter-being, barriers between ourselves and others fall away. We are perhaps less likely to live lives turned in on ourselves as if we are separate individuals independent of all others. Pursuing selfish interests makes no sense if we know we are truly, profoundly connected to one another.

Even the way we think about and care for our own bodies may change when we understand our vital interconnectedness. We may exercise even greater care realizing that what affects us affects others as well. We also recognize that our bodies are a gift. We did not make ourselves. Christian tradition has voiced this conviction in many ways. We are not our own; we belong to God. We are part of a larger body, the body of Christ. Our bodies are themselves temples of the Holy Spirit. In addition to these biblical and theological affirmations, we know experientially that we did not arrive here all by ourselves. We gratefully acknowledge that we belong to our parents, grandparents, and ancestors who gave life forward and nurtured it. We would not be here without them and their life-giving care. We also belong to the Earth from which they and we have drawn

---

31. Thich Nhat Hanh, *Living Buddha, Living Christ* (New York: Riverhead Books, 2007), 11.

our daily sustenance. Our life is a gift to us. In gratitude for the gift of life we take care of our bodies.

Conclusion

In this chapter we have proposed a new way of seeing that is more adequate to the task of interpreting the meaning of "God is with us." There has been a back–and-forth between two important considerations. On the one hand, we learn from the Incarnation that God is in dynamic relation with all things. On the other hand, once we know this about God, the Incarnation in Jesus the Christ becomes more coherently conceivable. Five elements have contributed to this new way of seeing.

The first was a proposal to take a fresh look at how divine attributes have traditionally been derived. They have been derived in binary opposition to the attributes of the natural world—which makes a problem of incarnation. The focus is on divine transcendence. We propose working instead from the Incarnation and the insight it brings that "God is with us." God will have not only transcendent attributes but also immanent attributes that are consistent with creative-responsive love. In this way of seeing things, Christians do not have to choose between a low Christology focused on humanity and immanence and a high Christology focused on divinity and transcendence. We may see a transcendent-immanence, an immanent-transcendence.

The second step was to propose that God's relation to the world is internal (allowing God to be affected by what happens in world process) rather than just external (God affecting world process but not being affected by it). God suffers when God's beloved creation suffers. This offers a more coherent and religiously viable understanding of "God is love."

Next we replaced the traditional absolute divide between Creator and created with a wider concept of "creativity" in which both God and the world share. God leads the creative advance, but creatures also have capacity for creativity. We are created co-creators. This recognizes the agency and freedom of beings and therefore the prospect of moral responsibility.

The fourth element was an embrace of process panentheism. We affirm that God is in the world and the world is in God, but God is more than the world. We rejected pantheism (that collapses the world into God) on the one hand, and pancosmism (that collapses God into the world) on the other. The world's presence in God and God's presence in the world are the deeper reality that the Incarnation makes visible.

Lastly, we showed the advantages of a "philosophy of organism" for articulating the intrinsic value and vital interconnectedness of all things. Among other advantages, this shift makes incarnation ("being present in another being") more conceivable.

In this chapter we have proposed that the Incarnation necessarily changes the way we think about God. For example, instead of thinking of God as primarily transcendent, the divine immanence comes to a fuller realization through the lens of incarnation. Obvious as this may seem, there are some long-standing assumptions about the nature of God and the nature of reality that have gotten in the way of seeing the deeper implications of the Incarnation for a fuller understanding of the nature of God. For this reason, instead of opening up to a fresh vision of the nature of God, the tradition has often held tightly to prevalent presuppositions about God that cloud over the fresh vision that the Incarnation offers. These presuppositions also have the effect of problematizing incarnation as such.

Here we have drawn upon insights of process-relational theology. These insights directly challenge some of these long-standing and intractable presuppositions about God, thereby making it possible to really see the deeper implications of the Incarnation for who God is and how God may be "with us." Embracing these new insights has a double effect. On the one hand, when the cloud of these problematic presuppositions is cleared away, incarnation can shine through in a way that truly transforms our doctrine of God. At the same time, the resulting fresh vision of God makes incarnation more coherently conceivable—no longer a contradiction or an impossibility.

We review the insights drawn from process-relational theology here briefly and show their connection with incarnation.

Process-relational theology challenged the presupposition that God and the world are in binary opposition, with God manifesting only attributes of transcendence and the world manifesting only attributes of immanence. In the Incarnation, what we see is better understood as a transcendent-immanence or an immanent-transcendence. God is both/and, not either/or.

The tradition has sometimes presupposed that while God can affect the world, the world cannot affect God (divine impassibility). God's relation to the world is "external" to God and not "internal" to God. The process proposal that this relation is internal to God and God is affected by what happens in the world is decisive for incarnation. What we see in the Incarnation is that God is with us in such a way that God is affected—divine self-giving, suffering love is manifest in the Incarnation—in Jesus' life and ministry and certainly in his death on the cross.

The tradition has articulated an infinite qualitative distinction between Creator and created. Yet in the Incarnation, the divine Word becomes flesh—a divine incorporation (so to speak) of created reality. Looking through the lens of incarnation the absolute divide does not seem to apply. Process approaches that do not presuppose an absolute divide between Creator and created can more readily interpret what we see in the Incarnation. Process approaches speak instead of a "creativity" that both God and the world share. It is God who leads the creative advance, but creatures also have a capacity for creativity and the agency, freedom, and moral responsibility that go with it.

In classical theism, there is a consistent emphasis on the separation between God and the world. Process panentheism challenges this presupposition, holding instead that God is in the world and the world is in God—even though God is more than the world. The Incarnation is surely the paradigmatic instantiation that reveals God's true relation to the world as being in all things.

Process thought articulates a "philosophy of organism," a perspective that sees all things in their interconnection and intrinsic value. The world is to be seen as a communion of subjects. This is in contrast to common dualistic ways of thinking that separate spirit and matter, allowing that some things may be regarded as mere material objects. The divine embrace of materiality as such in the Incarnation challenges the devaluation of material existence that we see in prevalent presuppositions of dualism of spirit and matter. The philosophy of organism also has the advantage of greater capacity to convey interconnectedness. With this in place we can better understand how something can be "in" something else. In the Incarnation what we see is God "in" Christ.

Seeing God through the lens of incarnation changes how we think about God. The Incarnation of God in Jesus the Christ reflects back on *what kind of God* this is. In him, divine reality of being "in, with, and for" the world becomes transparent. We have concluded that the Incarnation decisively reshapes our understanding of God. Now we turn to consider how it changes the way we think about human beings—both who we are and what we are called to do.

Chapter 3

How Does Incarnation Change the Way We Think about What It Is to Be Human?

Part 1: Who Are We?

One classic text reflecting on the place and the calling of the human being within the wider creation is Psalm 8:3–6:

> When I look at your heavens, the work of your fingers,
>   the moon and the stars that you have established;
> what are human beings that you are mindful of them,
>   mortals that you care for them?
> Yet you have made them a little lower than God,
>   and crowned them with glory and honor.
> You have given them dominion over the works of your hands;
>   you have put all things under their feet.

This text beautifully reflects human nature in its dual aspects—our humble place and our extraordinary capacities. It has been said that we are "creatures with roots and wings," "grounded yet unbounded." We are creatures in the image of God, and we are creatures of the Earth as well—at home in the cosmos.

This vision of who we are has profound implications for human vocation. Learning who we are teaches us what we are called to do. Seeing ourselves as being created in the image of God has implications for our relation to the wider company of beings. It implies a calling to love the world as God loves it and thus to extend care and blessing that mirrors God's care and blessing. Seeing ourselves as being at home in the cosmos helps us to know our place as a member of a much larger community of beings and perhaps develop a more down-to-earth self-understanding.

We are embodied and embedded in the wider natural world. Anthropocentric habits of thought are undercut. These are implications of the divine creative activity that forms us in God's own image and situates us within the wider cosmos as part of—and not separate from or over and above—the natural world.

Divine incarnation pervades the natural world. God is in the world, and the world is in God. This reality is manifest paradigmatically in the Word made flesh. Incarnation also has implications for our self-understanding and our understanding of our relation to all else. That God is, in a sense, "embodied in all things" imbues all things with a dignity and intrinsic value. Matter matters. Bodies matter. With this incarnational orientation, neither the earth nor any of its creatures can be treated in a cavalier manner. Ecological responsibility is implied. Human beings and human bodies should also be treated with respect and care. Human bodies should not be objectified, commodified, or harmed either. Social responsibility is implied. Such an incarnational orientation necessarily changes our self-understanding and our understanding of the wider world of nature. Ecological responsibility and social responsibility can be grounded in incarnation. This incarnational orientation also has practical ethical outworkings. Understanding ourselves as embodied, we see that *bodies matter*. Implications for social responsibility necessarily follow. Understanding ourselves as embedded in the material world, we come to know that *matter matters*. Implications for ecological responsibility necessarily follow.

In the Image of God

Several prominent themes arise as we explore what being "in the image of God" means in connection with incarnation. Some of the problems laid out in chapters 1 and 2 are helpfully addressed by this understanding. For example, the claim that all human beings are *already* in the image of God may ease the seeming contradiction of divine incarnation in human form in Jesus of Nazareth. We can imagine an intensification and perfection of the image that is already present (though not fully realized) in human beings. Further, the absolute divide between Creator and created that was highlighted as problematic seems to be bridged when we see the image of God in human beings. Since we are in the image of one who is creative, we should exercise creativity, too. Lastly, this understanding of human being urges us onward in the reconsideration of binary oppositions between attributes assigned to God and attributes assigned to the world.

If human beings are created in the image of God, a next logical question is what kind of God is the human being to image or reflect? The response to this question can give essential content to who we are and what we are called to do. In chapter 1, our discussion of Trinitarian theology proposed that God is a "Being-in-Relation." If so, then to be in God's image must also entail Being-in-Relation. In chapter 2, we worked from the fundamental affirmation that "God is love" and sought to reimagine some traditional ways of thinking and talking about God that did not seem consistent with this affirmation. If God is a God of love, we show forth the divine image best by being loving.

Essential to our understanding of the Incarnation is the affirmation that in Jesus the Christ, we see what it is to be truly human. While we are "in" the image of God, it is said that he "is" the image of God. A biblical passage that illustrates this way of thinking is 2 Corinthians 3:18–4:6. Selected verses are noted here:

> And all of us, with unveiled faces, seeing the glory of the Lord as though reflected in a mirror, are being transformed into the same image from one degree of glory to another; for this comes from the Lord, the Spirit. . . . Seeing the light of the gospel of the glory of Christ, *who is the image of God* . . . For it is the God who said, "Let light shine out of darkness," who has shone in our hearts to give the light of the knowledge of the glory of God in the face of Jesus Christ. (emphasis added)

In Jesus' life and ministry, in his relation to God and to others, we see a true reflection, the veritable image of God. "For in him all the fullness of God was pleased to dwell" (Col. 1:19).

If we see in Jesus the Christ a true reflection or the veritable image of God, this is not an exception to the condition of his being human. Rather he manifests a *full realization* of what it is to be "truly human." In him we see an intensification and perfecting of what is divinely intended for all human beings. His is a life lived in loving relation to God and to all others and is aligned with the divine intention. He is the exemplar par excellence of how to be human.

The text from 2 Corinthians quoted earlier expresses a hope that we may be transformed into the same image. Irenaeus put it this way: "He became as we are that we might become as he is."[1] We do not reflect God's image to the same degree that we see in the Incarnate One. We never fully manifest it. And yet, as Calvin proposed, there is day by day, more and more of our growing into union with Christ.[2] As we are drawn into union with Christ we are conformed to God's image manifest in him. "For in him the whole fullness of deity dwells bodily, and you have come to fullness in him" (Col. 2:9–10).

From this vantage point we might argue that being in the image of God is not simply a *given* that is constitutive of human being but is rather a *gift* and a calling. In the history of Christian thought, some have understood "image" along the lines of a stamp (like an image indelibly stamped on a coin). Qualities, such as rationality, are stamped upon the human being and are thought to be constitutive of human being as such. Others have understood "image" in more dynamic, relational terms as we are commending here. In this light, "image" may be more like a reflection in a mirror. A mirror only gives a true reflection of an image when turned toward it, in right relation with it. In a similar way, the human being who is turned toward God (*coram deo*) can offer a true reflection. The image of a mirror is in fact used in 2 Corinthians 3:18 quoted above: "all of us, with unveiled faces, seeing the glory of the Lord as though reflected in a mirror, are being transformed into the same image from one degree of glory to another."

To reiterate, being in the image of God entails Being-in-Relation. If "God is love," we reflect God's image best in loving relation to God and all else. This way of thinking reconceives the *imago Dei* in the light of the Incarnation. It challenges some of our habits of thought that have taken *imago Dei* primarily as a signal that human beings are set apart from the rest of creation and given the right to rule over all the rest. We see this

---

1. Irenaeus, *Against Heresies*, vol. 5 preface, in *Ante-Nicene Fathers*, ed. Philip Schaff (1885; repr., Grand Rapids, Eerdmans, 2001, 1:526). In a similar approach, Athanasius uses the exchange formula, "For he became human that we might become divine" (*De Inc.* 54) Athanasius of Alexandria, *De Incarnatione* 54, in *Athanasius Contra Gentes and De Incarnatione*, ed. and trans. Robert Thomson (Oxford: Clarendon, 1971), 118.

2. "I confess that we are deprived of this utterly incomparable good until Christ is made ours. Therefore, that joining of Head and members, that indwelling of Christ in our hearts—in short, that mystical union—are accorded by us the highest degree of importance, so that Christ, having been made ours, makes us sharers with him in the gifts with which he has been endowed. We do not, therefore, contemplate him outside ourselves from afar in order that his righteousness may be imputed to us but because we put on Christ and are engrafted into his body—in short, because he deigns to make us one with him. For this reason, we glory that we have fellowship of righteousness with him" John Calvin, *Institutes of the Christian Religion* 3.11.10; ed. John T. McNeill, trans. Ford Lewis Battles, LCC (Philadelphia: Westminster Press, 1960), 736–37.

especially in the history of interpretation of some key biblical texts, such as Psalm 8 when it speaks of our being "a little lower than God" and having "dominion" over the works of God's hands. Similar problems that have arisen with interpretations of Genesis 1:26–28 should be drawn into conversation at this point as well:

> Then God said, "Let us make humankind in our image, according to our likeness; and let them have dominion over the fish of the sea, and over the birds of the air, and over the cattle, and over all the wild animals of the earth, and over every creeping thing that creeps upon the earth."
>
> So God created humankind in his image,
>> in the image of God he created them;
>> male and female he created them.
>
> God blessed them, and God said to them, "Be fruitful and multiply, and fill the earth and subdue it; and have dominion over the fish of the sea and over the birds of the air and over every living thing that moves upon the earth."

In both of these texts, the theological fixation has often been on "dominion," and this has taken interpretation in a thoroughly anthropocentric direction, distorting our *relation* with the rest of the natural world. The human is treated as if we are separate from and over and above all else. The questions most interesting to interpreters seem to be, How does the *imago Dei* make us different from the rest of the natural world? How does it set us above and apart from all else? The agenda behind these questions is one of establishing human exceptionalism, superiority, and "right to rule." We are in charge. Whatever else there is, is there for us. We can do whatever we want with it.

Even the environmental movement sometimes unwittingly falls into this predominant picture of human beings' relation to the natural world. Invoking protection for "our natural resources" is problematic. It instrumentalizes the rest of the world of nature. We are enjoined to preserve our natural resources so that we will be able to *go on using* them indefinitely. Instead of claiming the intrinsic value of the natural world we focus on its value *to us*. Is it really all about us? An anthropocentric orientation implicitly grants license for unbridled exploitation of nature.

Would it be possible for us to affirm the human being as created in the image of God and not go down the road of anthropocentrism, separationism, and exploitation? The recognition of human "dominion" over nature and our "godlike" powers could be interpreted in two very different ways. It could be—and has been—taken as a license to exploit. Unfortunately, this seems to be the commonplace interpretation. An alternative is possible. What if we would instead underscore the heightened responsibility that attends the extraordinary powers human beings possess? That would surely reorient our relation to nature. What if our interpretation of the image of God in human beings underscored that we are "beings-in-relation" to the whole creation—not separate from or above it all? What if we underscored our calling to be like God as a calling to love the world as God so loves it?

The present reality is that our "godlike" powers have gone unchecked by concern for the fate of the Earth, our home. Humanity's impact on the Earth is now so profound that Earth scientists have declared a new geological epoch—the Anthropocene.[3] Scientists mark the beginning of this new era with the dawn of the nuclear age, when radioactive elements were dispersed across the planet by nuclear bomb tests. The previous epoch, the Holocene, was a period of approximately twelve thousand years of stable climate since the last ice age during which all human civilization developed and flourished. However, the increasing levels of carbon dioxide emissions since the mid-1900s have led to sweeping changes for the planet. Sea levels rise, the oceans acidify, we have a global mass extinction of species, and the land is ravaged by deforestation and desertification. These changes mark the end of the stable Holocene geological era. Earth's future will be largely determined by the impact of human beings. What will be our impact? How will we use our godlike powers?

If we are "created in the image of God" and our powers are "godlike," a critical question is evoked: *what is God like?* We have presented here a vision of God as a God of love, a Being-in-Relation, as known in the Incarnation. To elaborate further, God is good, and all that God creates is good. In the Genesis 1 creation story, everything that is created is affirmed as "good." This is true even before human beings come on the scene. It is all already good. God blesses the creation and invites its flourishing (Gen. 1:28). If human beings are created in God's image and we would offer a true reflection, then we will use our "godlike" powers for good—to bless the creation and ensure its flourishing. To do that is to offer a true reflection of the God in whose image we are created.

3. Martin Rees, *Our Final Hour* (New York: Basic Books, 2003).

Lifting up our heightened powers as a calling to heightened responsibility is an important step. The calling to model the use of our Godlike powers on a thoughtful vision of what God is *like* completely reorients the meaning of human dominion. Ted Hiebert puts the difference succinctly: "You are in charge, so do the right thing."[4] Human powers are to be acknowledged, taken up, and used for good. Denying or abdicating power does not help any more than abusing power does. Power can be used to repair the damage we have done. Contrary to the commonplace interpretation of what dominion entails, some streams of wisdom in our religious heritage in Judaism have always read the matter rather differently. These sources articulate the calling of the human being to "repair of the world" (Hebrew: תיקון עולם [*tyqwn 'wlm*]). This is a word we need to hear in the wake of the current eco-crises. We can repair and we can take care to ensure that we do no more harm. We can bless the earth and its creatures, promoting the flourishing of all creation.

Another stream of wisdom is available to us in the Yahwist writer's creation account in Genesis 2. This second creation story has a different orientation than the Priestly writer's account in Genesis 1 and offers some new insights. For the Priestly writer there is a heavy emphasis on the human being as "Godlike" in relation to nature, a divine representative ruling over all else. The Yahwist account, on the other hand, speaks from an agrarian context where the human being is more clearly part of and dependent upon the processes of nature. The sense of connection to the earth is clearer there, as we see in Genesis 2:7: "Then the LORD God formed man from the dust of the ground, and breathed into his nostrils the breath of life; and the man became a living being."

Perhaps we would be helped by keeping a better balance between these two visions from Genesis 1 and Genesis 2 of who the human being is in relation to the natural world. John Calvin already saw the differences between these two accounts and urged that readers should keep these two together lest the former become for us an ".occasion of pride."[5] Would that we had followed Calvin's good advice.

The Yahwist account can balance the Priestly account helpfully. There is a wordplay in the Hebrew text that does not come through in

4. Theodore Hiebert, "Biblical Foundations: Recovering Creation," unpublished lecture, Environmental Leadership and Ministry course, McCormick Theological Seminary, May 22, 2017.

5. John Calvin, *Commentaries on the First Book of Moses Called Genesis*, vol. 1 (Grand Rapids: Eerdmans, 1948), 111.

the English translations. God makes a human being (Hebrew: אָדָם ['dm]) from the dust of the ground (Hebrew: אֲדָמָה ['dmh]).

Texts transliterate 'dm to make it a name "Adam," but then they *translate* 'dmh as "dust of the *ground*." The Hebrew word play is completely lost. Perhaps we would get the writer's intent better if both terms were translated so that we have mention of "Dusty" who was made "from the dust of the ground." This is definitely a down-to-earth picture of the human being. The earthiness is underscored and we are—just as in all good science fiction—Earthlings. Another possibility suggested is to say we are "humans" formed from the "humus."

Ted Hiebert, biblical scholar who translated Genesis for the Common English Bible, points out here that the Hebrew word usually translated as "dust" (Hebrew: עָפָר ['pr]) is better translated as "topsoil," the fertile soil. What is usually translated as "of the ground" is better translated as "from the arable soil." For the Yahwist writer, who speaks from an agrarian context, this difference would be important. It would convey a greater dignity on the "stuff" of which human beings are made. We are not just "dust in the wind"; we are made from the valuable, fertile topsoil that is essential for life. Hiebert suggests that "taken seriously, a more accurate translation of 'dm from 'dmh would be 'farmer' from 'farmland.'" The vocation of the human being is to cultivate and serve the earth.[6]

In summation, the Incarnation offers profound illumination regarding what it is for the human being to be created in the image of God. The God in whose image we are created is a Being-in-Relation, a God of love, a God who is good, a God who creates and blesses creation, inviting it to flourish. We reflect God's image best when we mirror this way of being. Biblical texts point to Jesus of Nazareth as the one in whom "all the fullness of God was pleased to dwell" (Col. 1:19). It is said of him that he "is the image of God" (2 Cor. 4:4). While we manifest the image of God in partial or even distorted ways, he manifests it truly. In his life's example, we see divine loving relation made manifest in the flesh. He is the exemplar for us of how to be truly human. "He became as we are that we might become as he is."[7]

The legacy of the Priestly writer is a vision of the human being as created in the image of God. Some interpretations have taken this understanding to emphasize the human being's status over and above all else

---

6. Theodore Hiebert, "The Human Vocation," in *Christianity and Ecology: Seeking the Well-Being of Earth and Humans*, ed. Dieter Hessel and Rosemary Radford Ruether (Cambridge, MA: Harvard University Press, 2000), 139.

7. Irenaeus, *Against Heresies*.

and right to rule over and exploit. In place of this interpretation, we suggested that the *imago Dei* is a calling to heightened responsibility for care that goes with heightened human capacities. The human being should be a true reflection (image) of a God who is a Being-in-Relation, loving, creative, and blessing and promoting the flourishing of the whole creation.

The legacy of the Yahwist writer helped challenge the exaggerated differentiation of the human being from the wider natural world by offering a more down-to-earth picture of the human being, connected to and dependent upon the natural world. We should remember that we are of the earth. Scientific visions of the human being connect well to this way of thinking. It is said that we are made of stardust. We come from the same starry stuff of which all that we know of the cosmos is made. When we look at the Eagle Nebulae, sometimes referred to as a "star nursery," we see interspersed among the stardust bright lights—as new stars are born. Solar systems may one day circle round them, and life, like (or different from) our own, may emerge.

At Home in the Cosmos

If we take to heart the insights of the Yahwist writer we may see more clearly that the human being is at home in the cosmos. From a scientific standpoint this self-understanding is reinforced. We have come to be—like all other life-forms—within the long process of evolution from simpler life-forms. We are composed of the same stuff that makes up the rest of the universe. In God's marvelous unfolding of the cosmos, we are all connected to a common origin. What comes to be has emerged from what went before. We emerge from "preceding natural processes that include cosmic events (the appearance of physical elements in the galactic furnaces) as well as biochemical events (the emergence of life), genetic and neurobiological events."[8] There is an unbroken continuity with the rest of nature. Habits of thought that lift the human being out of the natural world as if we are separate from it or over and above it give a false report on reality. With all other beings we are part of the rich, diverse, complex, and evolving web of life that has been emerging over the eons on this planet. What made everything—from butterflies to belugas—made us, too. Philip Hefner has noted that nature's process is a kind of *bricolage*. Nature works from what is at hand to make new things,

8. Philip Hefner, "The Created Co-Creator as Symbol," unpublished lecture, Advanced Seminar in Religion and Science, Lutheran School of Theology at Chicago, Spring 2002.

reconfiguring them into what is genuinely novel and unique. The unfolding universe moves from simple forms to more complex forms through amalgamation and symbiosis. The human being is just such a bricolage. The human brain carries remnants of our ancestral brains, distinguishable even now as reptilian, mammalian, and human.

We are genetically connected; the history of evolution is in us. This was expressed eloquently in an address by Václav Havel when he said, "We are mysteriously connected to the entire universe; we are mirrored in it, just as the entire evolution of the universe is mirrored in us."[9] Remembering that profound connection, remembering that we are from the Earth, must decisively reframe our understanding of who we are as human beings. Our connection with the natural world comes to light more clearly than our separation from it.

How does understanding this profound connection to the rest of the natural world reflect back on our identity as created "in the image of God"? Perhaps there is a sense in which the whole creation may be said to reflect God's image. John Calvin believed the whole creation is the "theatre of God's glory."[10] It is not the case that the creation is merely the backdrop for the divine-human drama; rather the whole creation is in the play. The human being has an important, maybe even a leading role, but we are not the whole show. Again, our anthropocentrism is checked. Reformed theology builds upon Calvin's insight and draws important conclusions. It affirms that the *whole creation* is a locus of divine revelation. Everywhere we turn our eyes, God is revealed—even if we are too blind to see what is everywhere apparent. Further, the *whole creation* is the locus of God's providential care—lilies of the field and sparrows that fall—all are in God's care. Even our eschatological hope is for the *whole creation*. The consummation anticipated is a "new creation," the restoration of all things. This vision assumes a wider divine embrace enfolding more than just human beings.

What if we thought of the whole world of nature as in some sense reflecting God's glory—each being according to its own measure, by being exactly what it is? The Psalms are full of references to nature's praise of God.[11] A few examples would be Psalms 19, 66, 96, 98, and 104.

9. Václav Havel, Address at the Liberty Medal Ceremony, Philadelphia, July 4, 1994, https://constitutioncenter.org/liberty-medal/recipients/vaclav-havel.

10. John Calvin, *Joannis Calvini opera quae supersunt*, eds. Edouard Cunitz, Johann-Wilhelm Baum, and Eduard Wilhelm Eugen Reuss (Braunschweig: C.A. Schwetschke, 1863), (CO) 8.294. See also Calvin, *Institutes* 1.5.1–2; 1.5.8–10; 1.6.2–4; 1.14.20.

11. See especially Richard Bauckham, "Joining Creation's Praise of God," *Ecotheology* 7 (2002): 45–59; and Terence E. Fretheim, "Nature's Praise of God in the Psalms," *Ex Auditu* 3 (1987): 16–30.

Nature's praise of God is eloquent and exuberant. Barth writes of how "even the smallest creatures" respond in praise to the divine glory. He observes,

> They do it along with us or without us. They do it also against us to shame us and instruct us. They do it because they cannot help doing it. . . . Thus, when man accepts his destiny in Jesus Christ . . . he is only like a late-comer slipping shamefacedly into creation's choir in heaven and Earth, which has never ceased its praise, but merely suffered and sighed, as it still does, that in inconceivable folly and ingratitude its living centre man does not hear its voice, its response, its echoing of the divine glory, or rather hears it in a completely perverted way, and refuses to co-operate in the jubilation which surrounds him.[12]

There is a striking legend emerging from Greek Orthodox spirituality about an elder on Mount Athos distracted in his prayer by the chorus of frogs from a nearby marsh. He sends a disciple to tell them to be quiet until the monks have finished the Midnight Office. When the disciple transmits the message the frogs reply, "We have already said the Midnight Office and are in the mode of Matins; can *you* not wait until *we've* finished?"

The whole creation praises God and reflects God's glory. Humans do this in our own human way. For us the key to reflecting God's glory is christological. We look to the one who "*is* the image of God." Regarding the whole creation reflecting the glory of God, Jonathan Edwards says, "The beams of glory come from God, are something of God and refunded back again to their original. So that the whole is of God and in God and to God and God is the beginning, and the middle and the end."[13] God is all in all.

There are within Christian theology alternative visions of incarnation that take the whole creation into account as relevant for the incarnation. "Deep incarnation," as put forward by Niels Gregersen, connects incarnation with evolutionary processes and the whole history of the cosmos and not just with human beings alone. He proposes that divine

---

12. Karl Barth, *Church Dogmatics*, II/1, *The Doctrine of God*, trans. Geoffrey W. Bromiley (Edinburgh: T. & T. Clark, 1957), 648.

13. Jonathan Edwards, "The End for Which God Created the World," in *God's Passion for His Glory*, ed. John Piper (Wheaton, IL: Crossway Books, 1998), 76.

incarnation "reaches into the depths of material existence."[14] In this way, "the eternal Logos embraces the uniqueness of the human but also the continuity of humanity with other animals, and with the natural world at large." The choice of the Greek term for "flesh" (Greek: σάρξ [*sarx*]) in John 1:14 ("the Word became flesh and dwelt among us") conveys a much broader concept than "the word became human" might have done. *Sarx* is the Greek term that would be used to translate the Hebrew term for "all flesh" (Hebrew: כל-בשׂר [*kl - bśr*]). Of course, to take on flesh is to take on its whole history and thus the full reality of the material world. The cosmic Christology mentioned in chapter 1, for example, is one such vision. It sees *all things* as made, held together, and reconciled to God in the divine Logos who is incarnate in Jesus of Nazareth (Col. 1:15–20).

Similarly, Niels Gregersen's work on deep incarnation insists that the Incarnation in Jesus the Christ is an embrace of the whole of cosmic and evolutionary history. When the Word becomes "flesh" (*sarx*), that term that implies the full reality of the material world. (The text does not say the Word became "human.") For contemporary readers, this would include everything "from quarks to atoms to molecules, in their combinations and transformations throughout chemical and biological evolution."[15]

In this section we have offered multiple instances of the divine investment and incarnation including the whole of creation. This orientation changes the way we understand what it is to be human. We can no longer see ourselves in isolation from the rest of the natural world or as God's sole concern. This vision also changes the way we think about God. We see God in relation to all things, and not just in relation to human beings. As we often say of the Incarnation, its wider embrace of the natural world has far-reaching implications. We learn who God is from this embrace of creation in incarnation. "If this is God, then thus is God."[16] It would seem that the divine embrace in incarnation is wider than we imagined.

A key implication that Gregersen draws out is that because the incarnation is a coming-into-flesh of God's eternal Logos, in and through the process of incarnation, "God the creator and the world of flesh are conjoined in such depth that God links up with all vulnerable creatures, with sparrows in their flight as well as in their fall."[17] Thus the suffering

---

14. Niels Gregersen, "Deep Incarnation: Why Evolutionary Continuity Matters in Christology," *Toronto Journal of Theology* 26, no. 2 (2010): 174–81.

15. Gregersen, "Deep Incarnation," 177.

16. Niels Gregersen, ed., *Incarnation and the Depth of Reality* (Minneapolis: Fortress, 2013).

17. Niels Gregersen, ed., *Incarnation: On the Scope and Depth of Christology* (Minneapolis: Fortress, 2015), 17.

in the natural world is also God's suffering and must be understood from this vantage point, no longer from an anthropocentric point of view. The divine capacity to suffer with creation that was argued in chapter 2 is further amplified in this vision of deep incarnation.

The divine embrace of material existence may cause us to view our own relation with material existence differently. It becomes all the more clear that "matter matters" to God. In the divine embrace of material reality, a dignity is conferred. For process-panentheism this is not an extraordinary exception to God's ongoing relation with the world, but rather a definitive expression of it. (If this is God, then thus is God.) "The God in whom the world already exists"[18] becomes manifest in this person, Jesus of Nazareth. "The Word which was before *incognito*, implicit, and hidden now becomes known, explicit, and revealed."[19] The Incarnation is a decisive revelation of what is already the case about God's nature and God's relation with all things. We see here a chief exemplification of that relation. Because of what God has done in and through Jesus of Nazareth, he becomes a place where the light shines through (as noted in chapter 2). Repeating Allan Galloway's insight, "Once we have encountered God in Christ we must encounter God in all things."[20]

Sacramental language serves well in this connection, as it provides another window (alongside incarnation) into this deeper reality—that God is "in, with, and under" all that is. Sacraments are often spoken of as both signs and instruments. They are signs in the sense of showing forth or revealing divine presence and gracious action. They are instruments in the sense of accomplishing God's purposes of grace. Our experience that common elements such as bread and wine can do this is, in itself, a revelation of the sacred potentiality in material reality. In Greek Orthodox theology sacraments are said to be an "actualization of the potentiality of matter to become fully transparent to the purpose of God."[21] In the sacraments, aspects of the cosmos are "returned or redeemed to their essential significance and purpose. It is a foretaste of the redemption of the whole cosmos and a revelation of the genuine nature of creation."[22]

---

18. Philip Clayton and Arthur Peacocke, eds., *In Whom We Live and Move and Have Our Being: Panentheistic Reflections on God's Presence in a Scientific World* (Grand Rapids: Eerdmans, 2004), 154.

19. Clayton and Peacocke, *In Whom We Live and Move and Have Our Being*, 154.

20. Allan Galloway, *The Cosmic Christ* (New York: Harper Brothers, 1951), 250.

21. Christopher Knight, "Theistic Naturalism and the Word Made Flesh," in *In Whom We Live and Move and Have Our Being: Panentheistic Reflections on God's Presence in a Scientific World*, ed. Philip Clayton and Arthur Peacocke (Grand Rapids: Eerdmans, 2004), 55.

22. Knight, "Theistic Naturalism and the Word Made Flesh," 55.

Our understanding of material elements as such is transformed. If God is present in all things, it is not wrong to think of all we consume sacramentally. No absolute boundary exists between what is common and what is sacred. We can no longer regard anything as simply "profane." When we eat we connect with the wide community of life. Every bite contains life—from the sun, the rain, the earth, and even the whole history of the cosmos that brings this food to this point. We taste the cosmos.

Sacramental theology underscores the broader, deeper implications of incarnation. The Eucharist is still distinctive. Among other things, it is a memorial meal, a place where we remember that God is with us—in the elements, in the presence of Christ, in the people gathered at the table, and outward to the widest scope of all things. What is "broken" in our lives and our relations is *re-membered.* Gratitude overflows, and the Prayer of Great Thanksgiving follows naturally. What was implicit has become explicit at this table.

Both incarnation and sacrament have the impact of conveying "real presence." They are places of transparency, windows into the deeper reality of God in all things. In *Paths from Science towards God*, Peacocke readily connects incarnation and sacrament: "Jesus identified the mode of his incarnation and reconciliation of God and humanity ('his body and his blood') with the very stuff of the universe when he took the bread, blessed, broke, and gave it to his disciples." Taken seriously, sacramental thinking entails a revaluation of material reality. Nature cannot be treated in a cavalier manner if it is a location of divine presence. We pursue the implications of this point in chapter 6.

As we continue to reconceive the human being "at home in the cosmos," two major shifts follow from the deeper implications of incarnation. We see the human being as "embodied" and "embedded." To see ourselves as embodied means overcoming habits of body-soul dualism that see our souls as our true selves and our bodies as "the prison house of the soul." To see ourselves as "embedded" means overcoming habits of thinking of human beings as separate from and over and above the rest of the natural world. The next step is to consider what it means to be embodied and embedded and hint at what might be the ethical implications of this shift in self-understanding.

Human Beings: Embodied

Having reconsidered how we are at home in the cosmos, we now turn to think about the embodied human being—the sense that the cosmos is at home in us. The dualistic framework that has been so persuasive has taught us to think of our own material reality, our embodiment as something outside our true selves. Body-soul dualism persists and needs to be reconsidered for five reasons we will elaborate. Dualism is a false report on human experience.

- Dualistic thinking has a lethal downside in its social consequences.
- Dualism is problematic theologically.
- Dualism is problematic biblically.
- Science discredits body-soul dualism and demonstrates the unity of the human being.

We are challenged here to resist body-soul dualism. When we think about ourselves as embodied beings rather than souls, we may begin to treat bodies differently. Bodies matter.

It has been common in Western classical tradition to think of the human being as having a body and a soul. It is as if our true selves are spirits and we just inhabit bodies that are somehow separate from who we essentially are. This dualistic framework for understanding is problematic for a number of reasons. First, dualism is a false report on human experience. As Whitehead pointed out, "No one ever says, 'Here I am, and I have brought my body with me.'"[23] It is time to reclaim the integrity of the whole person—our embodied selves.

Dualistic thinking has a lethal downside in its social consequences. A long history of body-soul dualism has been both pervasive and destructive. Cultures that are body denying or body hating do not treat bodies well. The dualism of body and soul is a graded differentiation. Soul is more important than body. This particular dualism is inextricably linked to a larger framework of hierarchical dualisms that includes other assumed binary oppositions: soul/body, male/female, culture/nature, mind/matter, light/darkness, good/evil, God/world. In each pair, the first is the more highly valued and meant to rule over the second. In this system of hierarchical dualisms the soul is what matters. Bodies are devalued, objectified, and may even be commodified.

Mary Grey has been an outspoken critic of these dualisms as having disastrous consequences not only for bodies but also for the planet. She insists that the sheer weight of this Western tradition of a God transcendent to the world, a God outside and above the whole dimension of

---

23. Alfred North Whitehead, *Modes of Thought* (New York: Free Press, 1938), 114.

bodyliness, can hardly be overemphasized. This way of thinking undergirds the teaching that the true home of the Christian is beyond this physical world, with the implication that the Earth is ultimately expendable.[24]

The lethal downside of these hierarchical dualisms is especially apparent in how they play out in terms of gender. Women are associated with the presumed "inferior element" in each binary opposition: body, nature, matter, darkness, evil, worldliness. The secondary status of women has been long ingrained. The violence against women that is prevalent in our culture may in part be linked to this interlocking set of graded differentiations.

Maintaining the male-female binary is problematic in yet another way. It does not acknowledge that gender and human sexuality are much more complex and multilayered than this way of speaking allows. It supports a reductionist reading of gender identity and consigns any gender-nonconforming persons to a category of deviancy. This kind of thinking promotes prejudice and practices of discrimination, exclusion, and violence against LGBTQIA+ persons. The social world we have constructed based upon this system of gender binaries is destructive to both human community and the wider community of creation. Dismantling this framework may be the best way forward. Perhaps conscientious efforts in addressing body-soul dualism may—like tugging at the loose yarn in a knitted garment—help us to unravel this construction.

Dualism is problematic theologically. It is somewhat baffling that Christian tradition took this dualistic turn given the world-affirming, body-affirming elements that are central to it. The creation story affirms that God creates embodied, living beings and calls them good. The account of the Incarnation proclaims that God embraces fleshly existence. In sacramental theology, baptism and Eucharist demonstrate how ordinary bodily experiences such as washing and eating may become symbols of and even vehicles for God's grace. In Christian eschatology, the earth is not evacuated but made new, and we do not claim immortality of the soul, but "resurrection of the *body*."

This dualistic turn is surprising in yet another way. In early Christian tradition, gnostic dualism was effectively countered and rejected. Gnostic philosophy held that matter was brought into being by an evil power and that matter is ever in conflict with spirit, which is good and emanates from God. The Christian claim that God is the source of all that is, is a

24. Mary Grey, *Sacred Longings: The Ecological Spirit and Global Culture* (Philadelphia: Fortress, 2004), 124.

direct counter to the gnostic claim. God creates the material world, and it is good. This is the direct implication of the doctrine of creation out of nothing (*ex nihilo*).[25] Whatever there is, is from God. It is not created by some other power, and it is not evil. It is as if we have forgotten the earlier wisdom of laying aside the gnostic option.

The biblical stories around the creation of human beings offer us a more holistic picture. It is instructive to look closely at the accounts of the creation of the human being in Genesis 2. There is no differentiation of body and soul. The human being is created as a "living being" (Hebrew: נפשׁ חיה [*npš ḥyh*]). Ted Hiebert has pointed out that "receiving the breath of life does not grant the first human being a soul or spiritual character different from the animals, since this breath is the physical breath of all animate life (cf. Gen. 7:22). The human being and the animals alike are called 'living beings.'"[26] He notes that English translators of the King James Version imposed a dualism by translating the same two words *npš ḥyh* which mean "living being" differently when they applied to animals than when they applied to human beings. For animals they used "living creature"; for human beings they used "living soul."[27]

Contemporary science tends to discredit body-soul dualism and to demonstrate the unity of the human being. Current neuroscience bears out this more holistic and unified picture. As neuroscience begins to reveal the mechanisms underlying personality, love, morality, and spirituality, the idea of a soul distinct from the body seems less and less plausible. Brain imaging indicates that all of these traits have physical correlates in brain function. Furthermore, pharmacological influences on these traits, as well as the effects of localized stimulation or damage, demonstrate that the brain processes in question are not mere correlates but are the physical bases of these central aspects of our personhood.[28]

It would seem that more holistic ways of thinking about the human being are commended from scientific discoveries as well as from the biblical, theological, and ethical considerations noted above. Chapter 4 takes

25. This is still the case whether one assumes that *ex nihilo* refers to creation out of "no-thing" or creation out of "nothing." The first is a cosmos out of chaos way of seeing creation. God gives measure, form, and order to the chaos that was there when God began creating. There is the potential for being, but it is contingent being (meontic non-being). The second envisions creation out of absolute nothingness (oukontic non-being).

26. Hiebert, "Human Vocation," 139.

27. Hiebert, "Human Vocation," 136.

28. Nancey Murphy and Martha J. Farah, "Neuroscience and the Soul," *Science* 323, no. 5918 (February 27, 2009): 1168.

up the discussion of ethical implications and surveys the differences it could make if we understood our embodied nature and believed that bodies matter.

Human Beings: Embedded

Incarnational thinking invites us to see all things in God and God in all things. God's "real presence" in all that is helps us to see the whole material world differently. Instead of seeing ourselves as subjects in a world full of objects, we may see ourselves in continuity with the wider world, which—like us—is also invested with divine presence and reflecting God's glory. We may then overcome our habit of thinking about human beings as if we were separate from the rest of nature and over and above it all. This has led to a callous disregard for the rest of the natural world and brought us to the brink of ecological disaster. Our anthropocentrism is helpfully corrected by the realization of our embeddedness in the natural world.

Things we are learning from the sciences today are a great help to us in making this needed shift. We are learning that

- Our place in the larger scheme of things is a more humble place than we have realized.
- Continuity, connection, and cooperation are present between us and the rest of nature.
- We are more like our nearest genetic kin than we had heretofore imagined.

We take each of these insights in turn.

Our place in the larger system is much more humble than we have considered to date. We are, in fact, latecomers, fragile beings with a precarious existence, rather small in the great scheme of things, and maybe not alone. The evidence of science reveals that many species have come and gone before our appearance. In the 13.78-billion-year history of the cosmos, we human beings basically just showed up. This becomes clear when the history of the cosmos is mapped onto a yearlong calendar with the big bang happening January 1. The Milky Way forms in March. The sun and our solar system do not appear until August. The first cell forms in September and multicellular life in November. We would see the first vertebrate December 17, dinosaurs appear on December 24, and the first mammals on December 25. Human beings—the first humans that walk upright (*Homo erectus*)—come late in the night (around ten-thirty) on December 31. From there it is still a bit of a progression to modern-day humans (*Homo sapiens*).

Given our late arrival on the scene and the myriad creatures that came and went before us, we are moved to know our place somewhat differently than we typically imagine it. We find ourselves asking, If we are the main point of it all, what was God up to all that time with all those other creatures? Was cosmic meaning on hold until we showed up? How unlikely that seems. Might it be that God's project is a bit larger than human beings—the cosmic latecomers?

Not only are we a very recent species, we are also very fragile. Stephen Jay Gould notes that complex life-forms like ourselves are really at a disadvantage in terms of survival. Our very complexity makes us easy prey to the mass extinctions that periodically plague the planet.[29] Some other species are less vulnerable. According to fossil evidence, cockroaches have been around for three hundred million years, surviving the extinction that killed the dinosaurs. Sharks have been around four hundred million years, surviving all five of the global mass extinctions.

What do we make of the fact that among the forty million species of living things, fully one-quarter are beetle variants? That would be ten million beetle variants. In terms of sheer biomass, though, the real winners on the planet are subterranean bacteria. Even if we do not destroy ourselves through ecological irresponsibility or nuclear annihilation, and even if we survive until the sun finishes its life cycle—how can it all have been about us with our late appearance and precarious existence?

Not only are we fragile latecomers, we are infinitesimally small in the great scheme of things. Physicist Joel Primack has taken a big-picture look at what is out there in the cosmos. This is what he sees: 71.4 percent dark energy, 24 percent dark matter, and 4.6 percent atoms (4 percent not visible and 0.6 percent visible). Within that category, we are included in the .001 percent of visible things heavier than helium. In many respects, we are almost not there. We may well ask with the Psalmist, what are mortals that God is mindful of them (Ps. 8)?

A last note in coming to know our place is the realization that we may not be alone in the universe. What if there is life and even intelligent life out there beyond planet Earth? Daily we discover new exoplanets. There are planetary systems around nearby stars, and some of those planets are in what is called the "Goldilocks zone" (not "too hot"

29. Stephen Jay Gould, *Full House* (New York: Harmony Books, 1996), 2.

and not "too cold" to have liquid water). We begin to wonder whether there might not be myriad other planets with myriad other life-forms. There is a vast cosmos out there. As the theologian in the science fiction film *Contact* pointed out, "If we are all there is, . . . there is a whole lot of wasted space out there."[30]

We come to know our place as more humble than we had imagined when we see that we are latecomers, fragile beings with a precarious existence, rather small in the great scheme of things, and maybe not alone. The whole history of exploration and science has been in some sense a process of a disturbing decentering. We learned that the Earth is not flat and that Europe is not the center. There is no center, no "right side up" from space. It turns out to be totally a matter of perspective, which can be unsettling. With Copernicus we discover that the Earth is not the center of the solar system, just the "third rock from the sun." We are further decentered when we see that our sun is not the center of the galaxy and our galaxy is not the center of the universe. The larger the view we take, the smaller we seem to be. This progressive decentering is disconcerting and calls us to deeper humility.

Knowing our place as a humble place does not require the conclusion that this makes us less important to God. The God who is in, with, and under all of this has an infinite capacity for knowing and loving all of creation and exercising personal and particular care. The writer of the Gospel of Matthew evokes a vision of God as one who numbers the hairs on our heads (10:30) and cares about lilies of the field (6:28) and sparrows that fall (10:29). The implication is rather how very great God is and how very marvelous is God's handiwork. From the greatest to the least, the glory of God is shown forth. "The heavens are telling the glory of God" (Ps. 19:1). Human beings are "fearfully and wonderfully made"—"a little less than God." Created in the image of God we are called to reflect God's glory. We do this best when we love as God loves and reflect God's personal and particular care for the whole of creation—a creation where we are very much at home.

There is a continuity between us and the rest of nature. In fact we are learning that connection is the way of nature. Many remarkable instances illustrate this. Scientists now suspect that the great redwoods may be joined at the roots. All the smaller redwoods seem to share a common root system with the larger ones nearby. Underground the root system

---

30. *Contact* is a 1997 film adaptation of Carl Sagan's 1985 novel by the same name.

is fused into a web, and water and nutrients are shared to such an extent that they may be thought of as a single organism.[31]

There are surprising instances of symbiosis and partnership in nature. We come to see that cooperation (and not just competition) is the way of nature. For example, the hermit crab and the anemone—for all their differences—are vitally connected. The anemone attaches itself to the shell that shelters the hermit crab. This provides its partner with camouflage, and then stray bits of the crab's food nourish the anemone.[32] The common lichen that we see appear to be one single plant, but in fact it is a symbiotic partnership between algae (an autotroph) and fungus (a heterotroph).

Even more extraordinary instances of symbiosis exist. Termites, for example, have a symbiont that lives in their digestive system and aids them in digesting wood. Termites cannot live without this other life-form living within them. There is still more to the story. This protozoan is itself host to three other symbionts.[33] Life within life within life.

As human beings we think of ourselves as individuals. Yet a whole community of life-forms lives on us and in us. The multicellular creatures that live on our skin are more in number than there are human beings on the face of the Earth. Bacteria living within us are about one thousand trillion. Some of them, like the bacteria that aid digestion, are absolutely necessary for our well-being. We are, each one of us, a community of life-forms.

Continuity, connection, cooperation, community—these things characterize the natural world, and we are part of that world. Our true relation to nature is obscured by the language we commonly use. We say we are dependent upon nature. It would be more accurate to say, "We are nature." We are nature through and through. We are at home in the cosmos, and it is at home in us.

Another thing we are learning from science is that we are more like our nearest genetic kin than we heretofore imagined. The areas we have traditionally pointed to as the things that separate us from the other primates—genetics, language, culture, and morality—turn out to be differences of degree.

Genetically, we share 98.4 percent of the same genetic material with our closest relatives, the chimpanzees. We are closer to chimpanzees than they are to gorillas and orangutans. The genes tell the story. But what

31. Richard Preston, "Climbing the Redwoods," *New Yorker*, February 14 and 21, 2005, 220.
32. Lynn Margulis, "Symbiosis and Evolution," *Scientific American* 225, no. 2 (August 1971): 48–61.
33. Margulis, "Symbiosis and Evolution," 50.

about language? Chimpanzees are morphologically different from us and not structured to phonate as we are, but they are capable of learning sign language. Apparently, they are linguistic beings. There are interesting studies here. When researchers first successfully taught chimpanzees sign language, people said they were just making the signs to get the rewards from the researchers. The next round of experiments removed all rewards and removed researchers from sight, using one-way mirrors for observations. They watched the chimps using the signs to communicate with one another. Remarkably, when the next generation was born they taught the sign language to their offspring. Also of some interest was the signing behavior. The offspring signed much more to their peers than to their mothers.

Some evidence also confirms that the higher primates have something like distinctive cultures in a rudimentary sense. For example, the seven regions of Africa have seven different primate populations. These seven primate groupings seem to have not only the expected similarities in behavior but also practices that are distinctive to that primate "culture." These practices are transmitted generation to generation.

Most interesting, perhaps, have been the studies on morality undertaken by Franz de Waal, who heads up the research at the Yerkes Institute of Primate Studies. A commonly held assumption is that the selfish and aggressive tendencies we see in human beings are a remnant of our "animal ancestry" that human beings overcome, keep in check, or cover over with a veneer of (human) morality. The institute has documented a very different picture of these (other) higher primates with whom we share a common ancestry. The research reveals patterns that look very familiar to us: alienation, forgiveness, reconciliation, and peace-making behaviors. Something like a rudimentary morality is clearly there. DeWaal documents evidence of empathy and reciprocity, which are the pillars of morality. In one experiment it became clear that they share our capacity to recognize when an injustice is done—even when it is done to another—and they respond with outrage.[34]

Conclusion

When incarnation is the lens through which we look, we see a very different picture of the human being. Through explorations of biblical,

---

34. Franz de Waal, "Moral Behavior in Animals," TedXPeachtree, November 2011, http://www.ted.com/talks/frans_de_waal_do_animals_have_morals#t-779334.

theological, scientific, and practical considerations we have delved more deeply into what it means to be created in the image of God and at home in the cosmos. We have suggested that to be at home in the cosmos is not counter to our being in the image of God—since God is in, with, and under all that is. Given who we are, what are we called to do? The human vocation, created in the image of God as we are, is to reflect God's creativity and care in our relations with one another and with the wider community of nature. We are at home in the cosmos, and it is at home in us. This situation of embodiment and embeddedness has ethical implications to which we turn in the next chapter.

Chapter 4

How Does Incarnation Change the Way We Think about What It Is to Be Human?

Part 2: What Are We Called to Do?

In the preceding chapters, we have urged that a clearer connection is needed between two visions of the human being. One vision sees the human being as created "in the image of God" and emphasizes human distinctiveness and heightened capacities. The second vision sees the human "at home in the cosmos," a creature of the earth embodied and embedded in the natural world. When these two visions are well connected we discern the human vocation as a calling to use heightened capacities responsibly and to serve the flourishing of all. Philip Hefner has suggested a metaphor that helps us make this connection: the human being as a created co-creator. We are created (at home in the cosmos with all else that is created) and we are divinely gifted to be co-creators, joining in with God's ongoing creative work. The metaphor is particularly fruitful as we move from asking, "Who are we?" to asking, "What are we called to do?" The concept of created co-creator illumines both the nature and vocation of the human being. After exploring this metaphor in conversation with insights of my own, we turn to the practical outworking of this vision in incarnational ethics.

Created to Be Co-Creators

Hefner's approach to what it means to be "in the image of God" is a creative joining of the two alternative understandings of what "image" means. As noted earlier, an image could be seen as either an image stamped on something or an image reflected in a mirror. On the one hand, attributes such as freedom and rationality are just part of how we are created. They are stamped upon our being. On the other hand, in our role as co-creators,

71

there is a more dynamic potentiality—in what we may become and do. The *imago Dei*, then, is not only a gift that goes with being human but also a calling that has to be lived into. Its full realization depends upon our action, just as offering a true image requires a mirror to be in right relation with that which it might reflect. Turning toward God sets right our relations with ourselves, one another, and the whole community of nature. In this state we can rightly "image" the God who is our Creator. With this more dynamic aspect comes the implied risk that human beings may "turn away" and become "estranged from their own normative nature."[1]

In our earlier critique of traditional theological treatments of what it means to be *imago Dei*, we observed that the explorations often go in the direction of asking, How does this make us different from the rest of the natural world? How does it set us above and apart from all else? The agenda behind the question seems to be establishing human superiority and therefore the right to rule over and use all else as we please. We are the spiritual beings in a material world; we are subjects in a world of objects. This way of thinking implies that whatever else exists here is for *us*. This path of interpretation of the *imago Dei* has had disastrous results.

Hefner asks an entirely different question. He inquires into the *imago Dei* to discover what the human being *has to offer* the larger creation. The motivations of the question and the outcomes of the answer are decidedly different. This approach does not legitimate anthropocentrism and separation from the rest of the natural world. Heightened capacities present an obligation for the human being. They assist in our caring and responsible engagement with the wider world of nature.

At this juncture we should ask, what are the heightened capacities of the human being? One helpful resource for reflecting on this question is Wentzel van Huyssteen's work *Alone in the World? Human Uniqueness in Science and Theology*. His research sought to determine if "there is a way that the heart of the Christian tradition of the *imago Dei* can be reconceived and revised through interdisciplinary dialogue with current scientific . . . views on human uniqueness."[2] From his research he proposed several human distinctives: greater cognitive fluidity, embodied imagination (self-transcendence), symbolic propensities, and advanced moral consciousness. We do not delve here into whether this list is comprehensive or whether

---

1. Philip Hefner, "The Created Co-Creator as Symbol," unpublished lecture, Advanced Seminar in Religion and Science, Lutheran School of Theology at Chicago, Spring 2002.

2. Wentzel van Huyssteen, *Alone in the World?: Human Uniqueness in Science and Theology* (Grand Rapids: Eerdmans, 2012), 307.

other living beings might also possess these attributes to some degree. For purposes of this conversation we grant that the human being holds these attributes to a higher degree. This is enough to provide some content to Hefner's assumption that the human being has heightened capacities, from which, he argues, we have heightened responsibility for creativity and care.

Lifting up our heightened powers as a calling to heightened responsibility, as Hefner does, reorients the matter of human powers and "dominion." Human powers are to be acknowledged, taken up, and used for good. Denying or abdicating power does not help any more than abusing power does. Power can be used to repair the damage we have done. Despite the commonplace interpretation of what dominion entails, some streams of wisdom in our religious heritage in Judaism read the matter very differently. Hefner points us to the affirmation in Judaism that human beings are created for the "repair of the world" (Hebrew: תיקון עולם [*tyqwn ʿwlm*]).[3] This is a word we need to hear in the wake of the current eco-crises. We can turn our energies toward repairing the damage, ensuring that we do no further harm, and promote the well-being of the whole creation.

Created: At Home in the Cosmos

In his use of the symbol "created co-creator" Hefner acknowledges an essential aspect of human reality. We are "created." In Christian tradition we affirm that we are created by God. In the discussion that follows, I suggest that God creates in and through natural creative processes rather than by external intervention from the outside, overriding natural processes. A panentheist vision informs this understanding of how God acts in the world. Though God transcends the world, God is also immanent in it. God is in the world, and the world is in God. The world lives and moves and has its being in God. Divine presence and activity are thus already internal to world process. Further, I propose that, as free beings, we participate to some degree in self-creation.

As we saw in chapter 3, if we take to heart the insights of the Yahwist writer's creation story in Genesis 2, we discern that the human being that God creates comes from the Earth and is called to care for it. "The LORD God took the man and put him in the garden of Eden to till it and

3. Philip Hefner, "Created to Be a Creator," in *Created to Be Creators: Human Becoming in an Age of Science, Technology, and Faith*, ed. Mladen Turk and Jason Roberts (Lanham, MD: Lexington Books, forthcoming), 25.

keep it" (Gen. 2:15). Interestingly, the word translated "till" (Hebrew: עבד ['bd]) is often translated as "serve."[4] Might we adjust ourselves to serving the needs of the creation rather than the other way around?

Human beings are at one and the same time created by God and created from the earth—through the ordinary processes of how things come to be. Hefner brings scientific perspectives on this into the conversation. There is a sense in which we come to be who we are because of environment and culture, but also because of our genetic inheritance.

Physically and chemically we reveal our ancestry in the galaxies and stars in which the elements of our planet and our bodies originated. We are creatures of stardust. . . . Biologically we declare our kinship with all life-forms that emerged in the primal soup, or the primal steam vents, or whatever originary conditions are depicted in the various theories of life's origins. In recent years we have been reminded of how much of our DNA we share with chimpanzees, or even earthworms.[5]

Hefner is very clear: "Whatever else we are, we are nature. . . . We are not separate from nature, we are part of it. We are not separate from the animals; we are a certain kind of animal."[6]

We are also created by our relations with others and our wider culture. The human being, unlike many other creatures, is born utterly dependent and will die if not closely attended by others who will care for it.[7] We are in a very real sense co-constituted by our social relations and our wider culture.

Co-Creators: In the Image of God

Given the reality of our utter dependency and our having been created by God through the ordinary processes of nature (which includes our cultural shaping), we clearly do not simply "make ourselves" all by ourselves. However, there is a sense in which we are to some extent self-made. In fact, the whole of the natural world is in some sense engaged in

---

4. In Genesis 2:15 the term translated "till" can equally legitimately be translated as "serve" (Hebrew: עבד ['bd]). The same word is used when speaking of the service of a servant to a master, or of people who serve another nation. In Exodus 4:23 it refers to the service of Israel to God in its life of worship. This is possibility pointed out in Ted Hiebert's chapter "The Human Vocation," in *Christianity and Ecology: Seeking the Well-Being of Earth and Humans*, ed. Dieter Hessel and Rosemary Radford Ruether (Cambridge, MA: Harvard University Press, 2000), 140.

5. Hefner, "Created to Be a Creator," forthcoming.

6. Hefner, "Created to Be a Creator," forthcoming.

7. Hefner, "Created to Be a Creator," forthcoming.

this *autopoesis* (self-making). Interestingly, in the creation story of Genesis 1, God invites the earth to "put forth vegetation" and the seas to "bring forth swarms of living creatures." Augustine's discussion of creation assumes that ongoing creativity is something God has built into the creation. He introduces the idea of "seminal reasons" (Latin: *rationes seminales*; Greek: λόγοι σπερματικοὶ [*logoi spermatikoi*]). These seminal reasons are implanted. They are like seeds that will come to fruition in the continuing creation (*creatio continua*). This view provides a way for Augustine to fully affirm that God is the creator of all that is, even though new things are continually coming into being as creation unfolds over time. This way of thinking about creation is prominent in other Christian theologians—Tertullian, Gregory of Nyssa, Bonaventura, and others. What we observe is a world in process, continually changing, even self-organizing in its creative processes. Is it not a more accomplished Creator that creates creative beings?

The use of the term *co-creator* does not claim equality with God. Hefner is very clear that the "co" here is signifying shared creativity. This view is congruent with what was argued in chapter 2 from a process-relational perspective. There we challenged the common habit of assuming an absolute divide between "Creator" and "created." We urged recognition that creativity is not something God monopolizes but something God shares with creation. There is an interweaving of the work of creative agents who are not necessarily equivalent or interchangeable: God, human beings (individually and together), and the rest of nature.[8]

The human being is particularly equipped for co-creative work given our exercise of enhanced rationality and freedom. We are not reducible to the result of our genetic and cultural inheritance and our social shaping. We have our own part to play in "becoming human." We have a self-transcending power that allows us to imagine possibilities for what we may become and how we shall act in the world. We can imagine alternatives to our present conditions. We can even imagine a better state of affairs more conducive to the flourishing of all living beings and the Earth itself. With such a capacity to imagine there is the attendant responsibility to act, to work to make it so. We also have an ever-present obligation to pay attention to the effects of our actions. As Hefner points out, we cannot really say, "The operation was a success but the patient died."[9]

---

8. Hefner, "Created to Be a Creator," forthcoming.
9. Hefner, "Created to Be a Creator," forthcoming.

There are some confounding ambiguities in having this gift of co-creating. For example, what happens when we turn our co-creating capacities toward human enhancement? The risks and possibilities inherent in our calling as co-creators are nowhere more apparent than when we consider new technologies of human enhancement on the horizon. Increasing knowledge of our world and our bodies has allowed us to cure and even to "improve upon" our bodies. We can "intervene in our own evolution."[10] Recent advances in technology mean that we can enhance nearly every aspect of our humanity. Athletic performance, cognitive capacity, moral reasoning, and longevity are all being improved upon with technologies of human enhancement as human beings want to be stronger, smarter, better, and younger.[11] Some see aging and even death itself as simply engineering challenges to one day overcome. Short of this, we do have remarkable prospects for curing disease and enhancing our lives. The ambiguities run deep, however, and along with these prospects come perplexities. How will we ensure responsible use? There are strong differences of opinion on particular technologies and how or whether they should be used. Germline intervention, for example, alters the genome of an individual in such a way that the trait is hereditable. Is that a good idea? A different set of questions clusters around access to advanced and expensive technological enhancement. How will we ensure equal access? If we cannot, only those already rich and privileged will be "enhanced." The current social and economic stratifications will only be exacerbated. As Hefner rightly observes, we are continuing to evolve and becoming "new beings who cannot be contained by older ideas of who we are. . . . We are undergoing transformations whose end we cannot see, we are caught up in a process of discovery."[12] Hefner's illustration is apt: it is as if we are driving a car along the highway at seventy miles an hour with a map in one hand, to find the destination, and a service manual in the other, trying to diagnose and repair defects in the car at the same time.[13]

To find our way, we need a sustained conversation of ethical discernment informed by the best science of our day. The questions of responsible use of the technologies of human enhancement are already before us. Should everything that can be done actually *be* done? The questions

10. Hefner, "Created to Be a Creator," forthcoming.

11. For a fuller treatment of these advances and the issues they raise, see Ron Cole-Turner, ed., *Transhumanism and Transcendence: Christian Hope in an Age of Technological Enhancement* (Washington, DC: Georgetown University Press, 2011).

12. Hefner, "Created to Be a Creator," forthcoming.

13. Hefner, "Created to Be a Creator," forthcoming.

of equitable access to these technologies are also before us. How can we ensure that everyone will benefit from the use of these technologies? An important step for the human community will be collaboration and the formation of a community of moral discourse that can guide our thinking on these questions. The conversation needs to be broadly participatory. These questions and others pertaining to how humans function in their vocation as created co-creators invite ethical reflection. It is fitting that, as we continue exploring the meaning of incarnation, we ask whether there might be an implied ethic in incarnational theology. The following section starts to address that question.

Incarnational Ethics

We have laid the groundwork here concerning who we are and what we are called to do. Earlier we affirmed that we are "created in the image of God" and that this entails being created for love (since God is love) and as beings-in-relation (since God is Being-in-Relation). We have affirmed that we are "at home in the cosmos," embodied and embedded. Recognizing that we have heightened capacities for rationality and freedom we are charged with heightened responsibility for care and creativity. This includes valuing and blessing the creation, promoting the flourishing of all. If this is who we are and what we are called to do, why are we not better at it?

The Human Problematic

To grapple with this question, I would like to bring some of my own reflections into conversation with particular insights from several theologians (Augustine, Reinhold Niebuhr, Thomas Merton, Philip Hefner, and Wendy Farley). Granting the foregoing description of human beings—who we are and what we are called to do—the truth of the matter is that we do not live up to this description. Many thoughtful responses have been offered through the centuries concerning why this is the case.

One option comes from Augustine. We are created in the image of God, created in love and for love. We are also granted freedom and in our freedom we turn away from God. As Augustine observed, we "are curved in on ourselves" (*incuvatus in se*).[14] We live in isolation and

---

14. Augustine, *The City of God*, in *Nicene and Post-Nicene Fathers of the Christian Church Series*, vol. 2, ed. Philip Schaff (Edinburgh: T. & T. Clark), 12.6, p. 522. Here Augustine explains the misery of the human condition as being grounded in our turning away from God. Human beings "have forsaken Him who supremely is and turned to themselves."

alienation rather than in relation and in love. We live selfish and self-absorbed lives.

Niebuhr locates the condition of the possibility for this "turning inward" in our situation of finitude. We are ever God's good creation, and we never cease to belong to God. However, we are finite (mortal and vulnerable) and we know that we are finite. We inevitably seek to secure ourselves any way we can. Much that is destructive and self-destructive follows from this desperate self-securing behavior. Our turning in on ourselves in self-securing behavior is "inevitable but not necessary."[15] The human being who is turned toward God (*coram deo*)[16] is "secure" even in the state of finitude and vulnerability. We are secured in God and delivered from our desperate self-securing behavior. When we turn away from God, who is our source and our end, and turn in on ourselves we become alienated from our authentic being. Hefner puts it this way: "The crisis of our creativity grows out of our estrangement from our normative nature."[17]

This alienation is a fundamental disorientation that affects the whole human being (our rationality, our freedom, our capacity for relation). The much misunderstood Reformed doctrine of total depravity is, in essence, a way of saying that the totality of our being is affected. We cannot say, for example, that we are misled by our sensuality, but our reason is intact. Our reason is not spared; we use it to rationalize despicable things done in furthering self-interest. Our freedom is not spared; we may be free to make choices (*arbitrio*) but we make them with a will (*voluntas*) that is in bondage to our condition of being turned in on ourselves.[18] Our relationality is not spared—all other relations are in disarray as a result of our disorientation from the foundational relation with God. The problem is a deep fault and not a minor flaw. The wound is not superficial and easily remediable; it goes to the very heart of our being. This is a "sickness unto death."[19]

Most of the problems that plague us and our social world come down to this disorientation from our authentic being as created in the image

15. Reinhold Niebuhr, *Nature and Destiny of Man*, 2 vols. (New York: Scribner and Sons, 1941), 1:242.

16. George Stroup, *Before God* (Grand Rapids: Eerdmans, 2004).

17. Hefner, "Created to Be a Creator," forthcoming.

18. Augustine, *On the Free Choice of the Will*, trans. Thomas Williams (Indianapolis: Hackett, 1993).

19. Søren Kierkegaard, *The Sickness unto Death: A Christian Psychological Exposition for Upbuilding and Awakening*, Kierkegaard's Writings 19, ed. and trans. Howard Hong and Edna Hong (Princeton, NJ: Princeton University Press, 1980).

of God. The traditional personalized picture of the seven deadly sins (pride, greed, lust, envy, gluttony, sloth, and wrath) could be seen in this light. Pride, greed, and envy are issues of selfishness and self-absorption. Lust and gluttony connect with immoderate consumption, addiction, and inordinate desire for subordinate goods. Subordinate goods may be good in themselves but they are capable of perversion or overburdening when undue importance is attached to them.[20] Sloth is seen in the laziness of not exercising the agency we have and using it for good as we should, in abdication of responsibilities, and in settling for less than our best—not becoming all we are meant to be.[21]

Social-political-economic systems have this disorientation and failure of relation at their base as well. The problems growing out of this funda-mental disorientation are myriad: consumerism, materialism, imperialism, white supremacy, xenophobia, racism, sexism, classism, heteronormativity, ableism, casteism, and other isms. Fear, rejection, exclusion, and oppres-sion of the other—whomever the designated other might be—is a failure of relation.

Thomas Merton observes that this failure in relation is in part a func-tion of our clinging to the illusion of the separate self. This is an empty notion—holding on to it we only come face-to-face with nothingness. This empty self is always insufficient, disgruntled, and even malicious. It is prone to falsity and infidelity, for it has not kept faith with its true self. Without God and others we are empty. We struggle to maintain equa-nimity by distracting ourselves and various forms of escape, but we do this "over the face of a thinly veiled abyss of disorientated nothingness."[22]

A realization of how our rationality and freedom are compromised may help to deliver us from inordinate optimism. Wendy Farley, in *Tragic Vision and Divine Compassion*,[23] gives a thoughtful account of the distortions of our freedom and rationality. Among the distortions she names are the harshness of our anxiety around our vulnerability, a restless longing in us that is never fulfilled and is even sometimes self-conflictual, and the reality that all our choices are made with limited information and without a full picture of the consequences. Much here works against us.

20. Edward Farley, *Good and Evil: Interpreting a Human Condition* (Minneapolis: Fortress, 1990), 134.
21. See also Karl Barth, *Church Dogmatics*, IV/2, *The Doctrine of Reconciliation*, ed. G. W. Bro-miley and T. F. Torrance (Edinburgh: T. & T. Clark, 1967), sec. 65.
22. Thomas Merton, *Contemplative Prayer* (New York: Random House, 1969), 78.
23. Wendy Farley, *Tragic Vision and Divine Compassion* (Louisville, KY: Westminster/John Knox Press, 1990).

With respect to the evils humans unleash in the world, we are not entirely free. We are born into a social world in which systems and structures of injustice are already in place. We are socialized into white supremacy, for example, in a way that forms (and malforms) us. We are initially victims of a social world that we did not create. Augustine's doctrine of original sin gets at this reality of being born into something that distorts our way of thinking, being, and doing—something we did not personally create. This is our situation even if we do not embrace a literal reading of the story of an original human couple who fall and pass sin along to their descendants. The situation is tragic. Nevertheless, we are not entirely innocent. We do our part to continue and extend these systems and structures of injustice. We are, at one and the same time, innocent victims and responsible agents. Both tragedy and guilt attend our human situation.

The effect of these several insights into our situation gives us a more realistic picture of the human problematic. The optimism of the modern progressivist view is called into question. Surely it was severely chastened by the realities of the twentieth century—the Holocaust and two world wars. The testimony of history does not bear out the view that every day in every way we are getting better and better.

Hefner agrees that we cannot be overly "optimistic" about a progressivist ascent toward "reason, peace, and prosperity." Neither, he says, should we be "cynical" about the human prospect—as if the human being is wicked through and through.[24] We are always God's good creation and we belong to God, whose grace does not give up on us. We do well to let realism correct our optimism and let hope correct our cynicism.

It has been said that what human beings most want is identity, belonging, and purpose.[25] In our disorientation these all elude us, for we have lost our true humanity. Our identity is inauthentic; we are alienated from communities of belonging; we have no purpose outside meeting our own selfish needs. Despair follows disorientation.

To become our true selves again requires *metanoia*—turning around, turning toward God and neighbors from whom we have become estranged. This is at the same time a turning toward our true selves, reflecting the image of God in us as created by love for love. Instead of

---

24. Hefner, "Created to Be a Creator," forthcoming.
25. Arno Michaelis, *My Life After Hate* (Milwaukee, WI: Authentic Presence Publications, 2010).

being turned in on ourselves we will be turned inside-out—toward God, neighbors, and the Earth, our home. We will serve the common good. In this way, we become our "true" selves—*truly human* in the way that Jesus the Christ was truly human. Merton puts the matter starkly: until we become "truly human" in this way, our lives cannot be lived as an "imitation of Christ" but only as an "impersonation."[26] In that turning toward God we will find our authentic identity, our belonging in beloved community, and a purposeful direction for our lives. We are beings-in-relation, created for love, who are called to co-creating with God a world where all can flourish.

How do we live out this authentic identity of the human being, living with a sense of belonging in beloved community and having a purposeful direction for our lives? We have sought to glean insights about who we are and what we are called to do from biblical, theological, and scientific resources. These sources help us to know our place. Knowing our place—embodied and embedded—nurtures our sensibilities about bodies as such and about the wider community of nature in which we are embedded. This points us toward ethical obligations toward ourselves, one another, and the Earth, our home. As we consider our situation of being *embodied* and *embedded* some current and urgent issues lie before us. While many issues could be addressed, only two are treated in what follows. These two are illustrative of the practical outworking of our vocation as human beings and the shape an incarnational ethic might take.

Bodies Matter

The divine embodiment in incarnation is surely an embrace of embodiment, which invites us to think differently about bodies. Coupled with acknowledgment of the image of God present in all of us, there is significant theological grounding to support insistence upon human rights, dignity, and equality. In the previous chapter we took note of the corrective potential of incarnational thinking for some problematic practices related to bodies. Where body and soul are cast in a hierarchical, dualistic framework, bodies can be devalued, objectified, and commodified. Many "bodies" are vulnerable and violated, suffering from the harsh realities of embedded racism or race trauma, domestic violence, rape, hate crimes against sexual minorities, human trafficking, mass incarceration,

---

26. Merton, *Contemplative Prayer*, 47.

disability discrimination, refusal of asylum, and other dehumanizing circumstances. In this chapter we take a closer look at two of these circumstances by way of example: disability discrimination and racism and race trauma. Here we see devaluation, disempowerment, and discrimination based upon one's particular "embodied" existence. Delving deeply into such complex and pressing issues in this brief treatment is not possible. Nevertheless, each can be shown to be a place where the implications of incarnation, if taken seriously, could make a significant difference.

God, who brought the whole material world into being and who comes to us in the flesh, embraces embodiment. An incarnational ethic evokes reverence and respect for bodies. Bodies matter. That we are all created in the image of God has long stood as an argument for equality, dignity, and respect for all human beings. Even secular thinkers in our context hold the common belief in human rights, dignity, and equality, which likely has its foundation in the influence of religious traditions that explicitly affirm that we are created in the image of God.[27]

While we may affirm that *every*body matters, there is much more to be said. Some bodies are more vulnerable than others. A theology is only as good as its address to the situation of the most vulnerable. Liberation theologians of all stripes insist that God is on the side of the oppressed—that their wounds are God's wounds. When Latin American liberation theologians first talked about God's preferential option for the poor,[28] they met with resistance from those who insisted, "Surely God is impartial." When the Black Lives Matter movement arose, it also met resistance. Many insisted on countering, "All Lives Matter." The relevant consideration is whose life is *vulnerable*. In Scripture, the eighth-century prophets are very clear—the God who loves us all takes the part of the most vulnerable: the poor, the widow, the orphan, the stranger, the prisoner, the captive. This is regularly reiterated in the prophets and is prominent in the teachings of Jesus. Jesus' ministry took place particularly among "the least, the last, the lost, and the little ones."[29]

---

27. Hefner, "Created to Be a Creator," forthcoming.

28. God's "preferential option for the poor" was first fully articulated by Fr. Gustavo Gutiérrez, OP, in his landmark work *A Theology of Liberation* (1971). Gutiérrez asserts that this principle is rooted in both the Old and New Testaments, particularly in the prophets and the teachings of Jesus. Gutiérrez claimed that a preferential concern for the physical and spiritual welfare of the poor is an essential element of the gospel.

29. Anna Case-Winters, "The New Community," in *Matthew* (Louisville, KY: Westminster John Knox Press, 2015), 220–23.

An incarnational ethic insists that bodies matter and that bodies under threat require advocacy and action on our part. Further, we have an obligation to create a social world that ensures the rights, dignity, and equality due to all human beings. We have affirmed that "God is love" and that we who are in the image of God are created for love. As we love our neighbors and seek their welfare, we necessarily involve ourselves in work for justice. We are not changing the topic when we move from "love" to "justice." As Cornel West pointed out, "Justice is what love looks like when it goes out in public."[30] As we turn to consider the ways in which people are made vulnerable by particulars of their embodiment, the need to enact justice/love will become clear.

Incarnational Ethics and Disability

People who are not "able-bodied" are often devalued, disrespected, marginalized, and excluded. Substantial new work in disability theology grapples with this problem. Central to the discussion are themes we have been exploring: embodiment, what it means to be human, and what it means to be created in the image of God.

John Swinton has observed that most influential theologians have been able-bodied and assumed an able-bodied hermeneutic for deciphering human experience and developing images of God. Modes of misrepresentation arise here and distort the way we represent and respond to disability.[31] Ability is the "norm," and disability is perceived as abnormal and not reflecting the image of God. Some interpret disability as a product of sin or some other distortion of the natural order. People are excluded and marginalized by this interpretation. In a religious model that construes this as a result of sin or disruption of the natural order, people may be subjected to "healing" rituals and prayers that they may no longer be as they are. In a medical model their situation is taken to be a personal tragedy that needs correction by medical or rehabilitative measures to bring them as close to "normal" as they can get.

Theologies of disability are informed by disability studies, an interdisciplinary effort examining "how people with disabilities are portrayed

30. Cornel West, *Brother West: Living and Loving Out Loud, a Memoir* (Carlsbad, CA: Smiley Books, 2010), 232.

31. John Swinton, "Who Is the God We Worship? Theologies of Disability; Challenges and New Possibilities," *International Journal of Practical Theology* 14, no. 2 (2010): 277. This article is a very helpful overview of the theologies of disability.

and treated within society."[32] For both disability studies and theologies of disability, it has been important to have persons with disabilities as participants and leaders in the conversation. Insights from disability studies have completely reframed the discussion by insisting that while there may be physical or mental impairments, disability "is as much a social issue as it is a biological or psychological one. Disability is . . . a product of negative beliefs, values, assumptions, policies and practices."[33] As the Union of the Physically Impaired Against Segregation asserts, "It is society which disables physically impaired people."[34] Being in a wheelchair, for example, is only a disability if the built environment prevents you from access and involvement. This social model of disability points to the need for social change and political action for justice and inclusion for persons with physical impairments. In the context of the United States, a civil rights model is appropriated alongside the social model. Persons with impairments are thought of as an oppressed minority group needing political and legal redress of their oppression and exclusion. The Americans with Disabilities Act of 1990 represents this kind of redress.

Theologies of disability offer a full range of insights that illumine this challenge and can inform how we understand and respond to persons with physical or mental impairments. The dynamic between our understanding of who God is and what it means to be in the image of God is particularly prominent in these theologies.

Theologian Burton Cooper has pointed out that our way of thinking about who God is is part of the difficulty. For example, we think of divine power by analogy with our own powers, but extend it to be without limits. "We can do some things, God can do anything."[35] Maximal "ability" provides us with an image of God. Thus, our very theology contains ableism and risks thinking that those who are disabled are somehow not in the image of God. We can observe a similar outcome in our thinking about God having unlimited knowledge. We know some things; God knows everything. For the cognitively impaired this again is an exclusion from being in the image of God. The theological preoccupation with omnipotence and omniscience is deeply problematic here. We may want to ask whether we have even rightly understood the nature of God's

32. Swinton, "Who Is the God We Worship?," 278.
33. Swinton, "Who Is the God We Worship?," 278.
34. UPIAS, "Fundamental Principles of Disability," Union of the Physically Impaired Against Segregation, London, 1976, 3.
35. Burton Cooper, "The Disabled God," *Theology Today* 49, no. 2 (1992): 173.

knowledge and power.[36] What if "God is love" were taken as the orienting center rather than the frequent focus on God being all-knowing and all-powerful (omniscient and omnipotent). How might that change the interpretation and response to disability?

How we think about the image of God in the human being may also be pertinent here—particularly when the disabilities affect one's rationality and freedom, which are often taken to be the veritable image of God stamped indelibly on the human being and therefore definitive of the human being as such. For those who are in some way cognitively impaired, rationality and freedom do not apply in the same way. If this is our understanding of what is constitutive of human being, then some will leap to the conclusion that such persons are somehow less than human. Pursuant to our discussion of *imago Dei*, perhaps it would be helpful to think of the more dynamic quality of "relationality" as what is central to the image of God in human beings. Whatever one's embodied circumstance or abilities, one is still in relation to God and others.

Helpful proposals are coming out of disability theology, most of them rethinking who God is with a view to reframing what it means to be human in the image of God. One of the most fruitful proposals comes from Nancy Eiesland's *The Disabled God*.[37] She offers a strong critique of the ways theology has aided in the exclusion of persons with disabilities.

Unhelpful associations of disability with sin, concepts of virtuous suffering, negative and segregationist views on disability and charity, oppressive readings of the healing miracles, and bias against disabled persons receiving ordination have led many disabled persons to view the church as "a city on a hill"—physically inaccessible and socially inhospitable.[38]

Eiesland commends a thoroughgoing resymbolization of the tradition, especially regarding how we think about God. Much else follows from that. She resymbolizes God as "disabled." Her direction is very much in keeping with the incarnational thinking already presented here and shows its profound implications for theology and practice. By virtue of coming to us *in the flesh* God shares in God's very being the experience of disability. God becomes one of us, vulnerable to the limits and frailties and pain and death to which flesh is heir. This is more than divine sympathy from the outside; it is "God with us" from the inside. If

36. Anna Case-Winters, *God's Power: Traditional Understandings and Contemporary Challenges* (Louisville, KY: Westminster/John Knox Press, 1990).

37. Nancy Eiesland, *The Disabled God: Toward a Liberatory Theology of Disability* (Nashville: Abingdon, 1994).

38. Eiesland, *Disabled God*, 20.

God is, in this way, "disabled," then disability is not a barrier to being in the image of God. It does not make one any less human and it cannot be allowed to be a barrier to the fullest possible participation in church and society. In this way we see the practical outworking of the implications of incarnation.[39]

Incarnational Ethics and Racism

A lively new initiative around incarnational ethics is arising in multiple locations. It engages the very questions we have been discussing concerning what it means to be a human being (embodied) and what being created in the image of God implies. One center for this discussion is the Incarnational Ethics Initiative led by Professor Reggie Williams at McCormick Theological Seminary. As he describes it,

> The central task of the Initiative is recalibrating what it means to be human and Christian in a society and culture that has long embraced and protected the dominant white, wealthy, heteronormative, masculine image of God. The concept of incarnational ethics is aimed at destabilizing this image as the norm and eliminating the barriers maintained by that image that prevent us from recognizing all human life and keep us from being together in true community.[40]

A major area of focus in the work thus far has been on the dynamic of "racialization," which Cornel West defines as "the imaginary process of assigning race, character traits, and human worth according to specific physical features. It is the construction and maintenance of a hierarchy

39. Other fruitful proposals coming out of disability theology are summarized in John Swinton's helpful article noted above. Jennie Weiss Block's *Copious Hosting* (New York: Continuum, 2002) speaks of divine "accessibility" and hospitality in God's "Grace-full" movement toward us in Christ. She underscores how the life and ministry of Jesus were about creating access for people on the margins of his social world. Debbie Creamer's work embraces "limitations" as an unsurprising characteristic of human beings that need not be problematized. Limits that emerge in disabilities are just an instance of the limited condition of all human beings. She also references divine self-limitation in incarnation (Phil. 2:5–11). Tom Reynolds, in *Vulnerable Communion: A Theology of Disability and Hospitality* (Grand Rapids: Brazos Press, 2008) points out that although our culture values autonomy and independence, this is not our reality. We are dependent and vulnerable. In Christ, God embraces vulnerability, which is the core of love.

40. McCormick Theological Seminary, "Initiative for Incarnational Ethics Launched," October 18, 2018, https://mccormick.edu/news/initiative-incarnational-ethics-launched.

of humankind according to an idealized superior human being."[41] He further elaborates that it is the white European body that is taken as the "normative" and idealized.[42] Williams talks about how racializing people circumscribes their reception and their role in society. This practice and its consequences are ongoing in the struggle of Black people for genuine equality and co-humanity. Segments of our society use words like "color-blind" and "postracial" to obscure the reality of the ongoing operation of race in circumscribing the lives of Black people. Williams puts the matter straightforwardly:

> Those terms are nothing more than white supremacist adaptations to changing social dynamics. Race is a grotesque narrative about humanity that works like a virus, unyielding and adapting as it wreaks havoc on the body politic. The notions of post-racial and of color-blindness buttress efforts to refuse acknowledgement of the continuing, powerful presence of race in society.[43]

In terms of "embodied experience," race matters.

Black bodies are routinely under scrutiny, under suspicion, under surveillance. They are subjected to humiliation and degradation in the streets and in the courts. The present reality has a long and shameful history. Recent work on what has come to be known as the "doctrine of discovery" catalogues the many places where a theological rationalization has justified European exploitation of other lands and peoples. Mark Charles and Soong-Chang Rah, in *Unsettling Truths*,[44] have traced this practice to a set of fifteenth-century papal bulls. In these official church edicts, Christian explorers were given the right to claim, settle, convert, and civilize territories they "discovered." This way of thinking has in our day become institutionalized as an implicit national framework that justifies American triumphalism, white supremacy, and ongoing injustices. The result is that the dominant culture idealizes a history of discovery, opportunity, expansion, and equality, while minority communities have been traumatized by exploitation, colonization,

41. Reggie Williams, "Empathetic and Incarnational: A Better Christian Ethic," *Fuller Magazine*, no. 4 (2015), 28 (issue on Reconciling Race).

42. Cornel West, *Prophesy Deliverance: An Afro-American Revolutionary Christianity* (Louisville, KY: Westminster John Knox Press, 2002), 47–65.

43. Williams, "Empathetic and Incarnational," 28.

44. Mark Charles and Soong-Chan Rah, *Unsettling Truths: The Ongoing, Dehumanizing Legacy of the Doctrine of Discovery* (Downers Grove: InterVarsity Press, 2020).

cultural annihilation, slavery, and dehumanization. Healing begins when this deeply entrenched framework with its shameful history gets "unsettled."

This dynamic has been decisive and death-dealing in the treatment of Africans brought to this country in the horror of Middle Passage and chattel slavery.[45] An appalling legacy of oppression and cruelty, it has been said that slavery is America's original sin. The long journey of atonement and restorative justice has hardly begun. Even with the abolition of slavery the control of Black bodies was only transferred from their masters to a racial caste system enforced by Jim Crow laws that maintained segregation in all public spaces. This included schools, ensuring a separate—but not equal—education for Black children. White supremacist ideology aided and abetted this system of segregation and enforced inequality.

> White supremacist ideology is based first and foremost on the degradation of black bodies in order to control them. One of the best ways to instill fear in people is to terrorize them. Yet this fear is best sustained by convincing them that their bodies are ugly, their intellect is inherently underdeveloped, their culture is less civilized, and their future warrants less concern than that of other peoples.[46]

Alongside the ideology of white supremacy were the activities of organized white supremacist hate groups such as the Ku Klux Klan that acted with intent to terrorize Black communities with cross burnings and lynching. "Jim Crow, lynching and educational disenfranchisement functioned as the physical methods that choreographed and circumscribed Black bodies into postures of perfect submission" reminiscent of the Slave Codes under slavery.[47]

Even scientific research programs were pressed into service to support white supremacist ideology. Various methods (cranial measurement, IQ testing, etc.) were employed to justify the existing racial classification

---

45. A chattel slave is an enslaved person who is owned forever and whose children and children's children are automatically enslaved. Chattel slaves are individuals treated as complete property, to be bought and sold. Chattel slavery was supported and made legal by European governments and monarchs.

46. Cornel West, *Race Matters* (Boston: Beacon Press, 1993), 85.

47. Eboni Marshall Turman, *Toward a Womanist Ethic of Incarnation: Black Bodies, the Black Church, and the Council of Chalcedon* (New York: Palgrave Macmillan, 2013), 69.

and stratification.[48] Black bodies were used unethically in medical experimentations such as the Tuskegee Study.[49] In general the subjects of such experiments were treated as "permissible victims"[50] in the advance of science. Countless African American women were involuntarily sterilized. This pseudoscientific work, the experimentation, and the sterilization all served to sanction the dehumanization of Black African bodies. These practices were at one and the same time a result of white supremacy and a reinforcement of it. Blackness and Whiteness, respectively, "represent the negative and positive poles of a dichotomous racialized hierarchy . . . wherein whiteness is recognized as positive, honorable, and virtuous, while blackness is posited as negative, dishonorable, and bestial."[51] There was even a demonization of Black bodies to support the urgency of keeping them under control because they were "literally wild beasts, with uncontrollable sexual passions and criminal natures stamped by heredity which required restraint."[52]

Jim Crow laws were not repealed until 1965. Since then, control of Black bodies has been transferred to the complex and insidious institutional violence of the criminal justice system. Racial profiling and police brutality are common experiences for African Americans. There is an embedded inequality in treatment throughout the system. Although Black citizens are only one-eighth of the population, they represent about one-half of the prison population. Black males in particular have an incarceration rate twenty-five times higher than that of the total population. Race-specific incarceration rates are grossly disproportionate.[53] Although the white, non-Hispanic population outnumbers the Black non-Hispanic population six to one, there are as many Black as white

48. Scientific racism is a pseudoscientific belief that empirical evidence exists to support or justify racism (racial discrimination) and racial inferiority or superiority. It employed physical anthropology, anthropometry, craniometry, and other pseudo-disciplines to create typologies dividing the human race into discrete human races.

49. Turman, *Toward a Womanist Ethic of Incarnation*, 69.

50. Frances Wood, "Take My Yoke upon You: The Role of the Church in the Oppression of African-American Women," in *A Troubling in My Soul*, ed. Emilie Townes (Maryknoll, NY: Orbis Books, 1993), 40.

51. Turman, *Toward a Womanist Ethic of Incarnation*, 1.

52. Turman, *Toward a Womanist Ethic of Incarnation*, 69.

53. Becky Pettit and Bruce Western, "Mass Imprisonment and the Life Course: Race and Class Inequality in U.S. Incarceration," *American Sociological Review* 69, no. 2 (April 1, 2004): 151–69.

inmates on death row. Multiple sets of data confirm the racialization of the criminal "justice" system.[54]

As I write this book we are living in the aftermath of the murder of George Floyd at the hands of a police officer who had him in custody, handcuffed, on the ground, and subdued. The officer knelt on his neck until he was dead. There was no arrest or prosecution of the officer and his accomplices until the public outcry overwhelmed business as usual. Vocal, peaceful protests have been nonstop. Not until after the looting and burning began did those in power begin to propose some reforms on the way to stopping this madness.

This all happened during the COVID-19 pandemic, which further exposed the inequities and vulnerabilities in our racially stratified society. African Americans are dying from COVID-19 in disproportionate numbers. In my context, here in Chicago, the statistics at the writing of this book were that although only 30 percent of the city's population is African American, 70 percent of the deaths from COVID-19 were of African Americans. A greater percentage of Black people have preexisting conditions that are a function of economic inequality and more limited access to health care. Making a bad situation worse, when testing centers first opened, they opened in predominantly white communities.

If bodies matter, it is time to recognize that some bodies are much more vulnerable than others and the situation that creates that inequity requires dismantling. In the work of incarnational ethics, we cannot simply adopt a universal view that sits above embodied existence—the view from nowhere. We need an embodied approach. We need the particularity of the embodied, situated experience of racialization and racism to be in full view. In our teaching for justice at the seminary we are adopting this approach. Reggie Williams puts it well; we need

> to speak to one another about justice, across social locations and cultures, in a way that does not repeat the problem of disembodied universal moral reasoning. We must be able to bring more to the table of fellowship than our differences. Cross-cultural communication requires a healthy universal language that acknowledges our difference in a meaningful way, and allows honest dialogue from real

54. Black youths are much more likely to be detained at each of the three stages of the juvenile justice system: police, court intake, and preliminary hearing detention. They are more likely to be committed to physical regimen–oriented facilities than their white counterparts and more likely to be tried as adults.

people within real communities, rather than the imagined ones of our racialized hierarchical discourse.[55]

Situated, embodied, incarnational approaches are more likely to be effective in teaching and working for change.

Resistance: Challenging White Supremacy

There are multiple efforts to address the problem of white supremacy and systemic racism. One of the most dedicated and effective has been Black Lives Matter. This is an activist movement, originating in the African American community. The Black Lives Matter campaigns against violence and systemic racism toward Black people have used protests, speak-outs, and die-ins in an effort to make people uncomfortable enough to actually address the issue. The Black Lives Matter movement has resisted racial profiling, police brutality toward (and murder of) Black people, and the ongoing racialization that is embedded in the US criminal justice system. Political slogans used during demonstrations have included "Hands up, don't shoot" (a reference to Michael Brown), "I can't breathe" (referring to Eric Garner and George Floyd), "White silence is violence," "No justice, no peace," and "Is my son next?"

Claudia Rankine describes the reality of the daily strain of being Black in America, "knowing that as a black person you can be killed for simply being black: no hands in your pockets, no playing music, no sudden movements, no driving your car, no walking at night . . . no standing your ground, no standing here, no standing there, no talking back, no playing with toy guns, no living while black."[56] In the aftermath of Ahmaud Arbery's murder by a former police officer we must now add, "No jogging while Black." The conditions for Black people in America today call to mind James Baldwin's observation in 1961, "To be a Negro in this country and to be relatively conscious, is to be in a rage almost all the time."[57] Rankine concludes that the condition of Black life is "mourning." The Black Lives Matter movement can be read as an attempt to keep mourning as an open dynamic in our culture because Black lives exist in a state of precariousness. "Black Lives Matter aligns with the dead, continues the mourning and refuses the forgetting in front of all of us."[58] This

---

55. Williams, "Empathic and Incarnational," 28.

56. Claudia Rankine, "The Condition of Black Life Is One of Mourning," *New York Times*, June 22, 2015.

57. James Baldwin, "The Negro in American Culture," *Cross Currents* II, no. 3 (1961): 205.

58. Rankine, "The Condition of Black Life Is One of Mourning."

movement is a rich and complex part of the broader, decades-long US civil rights movement. Black Lives Matter issues a compelling outcry for respect, dignity, and justice in the face of white supremacy and its many manifestations.

Part of the task is to recognize white supremacy and understand its workings in our social world.

> White supremacy is the historical pursuit of the idyllic community, framed by the social imaginary of an idealized humanity that informs politics, legal structures, how goods are distributed and how systems are created, and inspires the historical practice of terrorizing people of color into compliance as assimilated inferiors. Historically, for people of color, the horizontal experience is the experience of white supremacy as a social organizing principle.[59]

It is also important to understand how deeply entrenched white supremacy is. Charles and Rah claim that neither white fragility[60] nor individual racism really accounts for the intractable resistance to dismantling white supremacy. There are depths to this resistance not yet plumbed. Psychologist Rachel MacNair proposes that one factor is "perpetration-induced traumatic stress" (PITS).[61] This is a form of stress experienced by those who are participants in causing trauma. PITS is common among soldiers, executioners, and police officers in roles where it is socially acceptable or even expected for them to cause trauma, including even death. Knowledge of the harm they and their forebears have done keeps

---

59. Williams, "Empathic and Incarnational."

60. Robin DiAngelo, *White Fragility: Why It's So Hard for White People to Talk about Racism* (Boston: Beacon Press, 2918). To summarize, Robin DiAngelo coined the term "white fragility" to describe the disbelieving defensiveness that white people exhibit when their ideas about race and racism are challenged—and particularly when they feel implicated in white supremacy. This is one of the pillars that upholds racism. The social costs for a Black person for what she calls "awakening the sleeping dragon of white fragility" are so high that many Black people do not risk pointing out discrimination when they see it. Along with this fragility there is the expectation of "white solidarity"—white people will forbear from correcting each other's racial missteps to preserve the peace. These dynamics are part of what holds racism in place. The social world is seemingly designed to insulate white people from having to think about their part in racism and to restore equilibrium when this unpleasant subject is brought up and disturbs them. Many liberal white people who are adamantly opposed to racism do little to dismantle it.

61. Rachel MacNair, *Perpetration-induced Traumatic Stress: The Psychological Consequences of Killing* (Westport, CT: Praeger Publishers/Greenwood Publishing Group, 2002).

white people from working to make reparations and seek conciliation.[62] The shame and guilt are too great; acknowledging the harm done would create an unbearable cognitive dissonance for people who think of themselves as good, normal, and moral people. Furthermore, acknowledging complicity in ongoing racism would mean admitting an insurmountable debt.

Eula Biss describes the situation of white debt with the metaphor of people who bought a home on credit and have lived in it so long that they think of it as theirs even though it is nowhere near paid for. White people will say, "We never personally owned slaves and we do not owe a debt." Using a similar metaphor Ta-Nehisi Coates writes of the reality of white Americans as being like people who have "run up a credit-card bill, and, having pledged to charge no more, remain befuddled that the balance does not disappear."[63]

In our time churches and seminaries are beginning to do a thoughtful inventory of the ways in which they have benefited from and continue to collude with white supremacy. As they do this work they are taking a step toward a new reality.

Listening to the "Oppressed of the Oppressed": Womanist Voices
For a deeper analysis of this situation and how incarnational ethics might guide us, we privilege here the voices of womanist thinkers.[64] Their insights are particularly notable for taking into account the wider range of interlocking oppressions. They recognize that social location is complex and multidimensional. We all have overlapping identities and are not reducible to our race, class, or gender. "Womanist theology opposes *all oppression* based on race, sex, class, sexual preference, physical disability, and caste."[65] I draw the work of Delores Williams, Eboni Marshall Turman, and Stephanie Crumpton into the conversation at this point.

Delores Williams is a founding figure of womanism. She was clear and vocal in her critique of Black theology for ignoring issues of gender and her critique of feminist theology for ignoring issues of race. She offered something more holistic that addressed multiple oppressions. She

62. Charles and Rah in *Unsettling Truths* speak of "conciliation" rather than "reconciliation" since this is not going to be a return to a previous state of amicability. That state has never existed.
63. Eula Biss, "White Debt," *New York Times*, December 6, 2015.
64. The phrase "oppressed of the oppressed" comes from Delores S. Williams, *Sisters in the Wilderness: The Challenge of Womanist God-Talk* (Maryknoll, NY: Orbis Books, 1993), 144.
65. Williams, *Sisters in the Wilderness*, xiv.

bears testimony to how ordinary African American women—in the face of race, class, and gender oppressions—are continually "resisting and rising above" and "making a way out of no way."[66] Striving against death-dealing forces that would destroy and subvert their power, they endure whatever they must. They endure so that their children will have a chance for a better life and so that their families and communities can be hold together in the midst of the struggle that is their embodied existence.

Williams takes the story of Hagar as her exemplar. Race, class, and gender are all dynamics of the story as Hagar faces interlocking oppressions. Hagar is an African slave of the biblical patriarch Abraham and his wife Sarah. They "own" her, and her life is circumscribed by their hopes and desires. Her body is not her own, and they force her to be a surrogate for Sarah, who is barren. After Hagar gives birth, Sarah is jealous and physically abusive toward her. When Sarah herself gives birth she orders Hagar and her son Ishmael to be cast out. Hagar has no agency in this and finds herself in the wilderness. God meets her there and makes a way out of no way for Hagar and her son, providing a spring in the desert so that they can survive in this barren place. In words reminiscent of the covenant that God establishes with Abraham, Hagar is promised that her descendants will be too many to count.[67]

Hagar is a prototype for the struggle of African American women, an image of survival and defiance. She faces poverty and slavery; she is a foreigner and an exile; she is a victim of violence and sexual exploitation. These experiences resonate with the embodied experience of many African American women from slavery to the present. There is religious resonance also in Hagar's sojourns in the wilderness and her encounters with God—a kind of prefiguring of the exodus story that becomes a defining story for African American religious self-understanding.

The genius of Williams's work has been to name and address multiple interlocking oppressions and to do so not simply theoretically but from the standpoint of the embodied experience of African American women. This is the situated knowing commended both as a pedagogy and as the best approach in working for change.

Womanist Stephanie Crumpton has researched trauma, particularly race trauma. The womanist pastoral methodology she employs maintains the intersectional nature of race, gender, class, sexuality, ability, and nationality. She sees the effects of race trauma in general but also shows

---

66. Williams, *Sisters in the Wilderness*, xi.
67. Williams, *Sisters in the Wilderness*, 15–33.

how these effects fall disproportionately on Black women (the oppressed of the oppressed). In particular she researches the problem of physical or sexual abuse—what she terms "intimate violence"[68]—through personal narratives of trauma, survival, and healing.

The narratives highlight the ambiguity of involvement in communities of faith. On the one hand, they are a source of comfort and healing and empowerment. On the other hand, churches often reflect the attitudes and stereotypes of their wider context. Particularly problematic are patriarchal structures and leadership paradigms that disempower women. Religious communities "mediate rather than mitigate the misogyny that sanctions intimate and cultural violence."[69] Crumpton names a number of problematic concepts and practices, including several that we have already underscored. Dualistic theologies that make a division and contrast between bodies and souls typically downplay the importance of the body. She comments on "disembodied views of incarnation" that treat Jesus' embodiment as incidental to the divine revelation in him. This misses the chance to "acknowledge the incarnation as an affirmation of the flesh as ontologically 'good.'"[70] This also allows body-denying and death-dealing practices to go unchallenged. Bodies do not matter; souls are what matters. There are also exclusively masculine images of God that are operative in the church and make it hard for women to see themselves as being in God's image. This is compounded by all-male leadership in many churches. Furthermore, in theories of the atonement, theologies that valorize suffering invite one to bear with suffering as Jesus did rather than resisting with all one's might. These theologies that valorize suffering cut the nerve of rebellion. With these theological stumbling blocks in place, here is a double-bind for women in the Black church; it both nourishes and undermines Black women as they confront intimate and cultural violence. New images, theologies, and practices are needed to effectively counter these dualistic, patriarchal, and racist dynamics that create a hostile social terrain for Black people and Black women in particular.

Crumpton has also been working on racialized violence and active resistance to it.[71] She inquires as to how activism can be motivated, supported, and sustained. Activists are overburdened and exhaust themselves and sometimes burn out. They have to navigate direct and vicarious

---

68. Stephanie Crumpton, *A Womanist Pastoral Theology against Intimate and Cultural Violence* (New York: Palgrave Macmillan, 2014), 1.

69. Crumpton, *Womanist Pastoral Theology*, 93

70. Crumpton, *Womanist Pastoral Theology*, 120.

71. Stephanie Crumpton, "Sanctuary: Care in the Movement for Black Life" (forthcoming).

trauma at the same time as white retaliation, as seen in such things as the weaponization of the criminal "justice" system.

How can this hard and painful work be done? How can hope for a different kind of social world be sustained? What is the role of faith communities in this? Churches may be a source of much-needed sanctuary and inspiration for activists if they are committed to social justice and exercise critical consciousness in their theologies and practices of care. This does not always happen. Cultivation of a "messianic martyr mythology" in the church, for example, is deeply problematic for activists, and Crumpton commends more life-affirming and communal models of activism. An emancipatory historiography that recognizes how entire communities engage in resistance holds promise as an alternative. Theological education, shared life in faith communities, and ritual practices are all seen as essential resources. This work will serve as a resource for faith leaders and caring professionals as they seek to support and care for activists for Black life and by extension for activists addressing other injustices.

Eboni Marshall Turman shows a profound understanding of the connection between incarnation and ethics. Tracing the christological controversies leading up to Chalcedon and the shape of the affirmations made at Chalcedon, she then links these essential insights to the embodied existence of the "oppressed of the oppressed." She unapologetically concludes that a womanist incarnational ethics will insist that Christ is *homoousious* (of the same substance) with Black women as to his humanity. This is congruent with what we have already argued. The problem is in not seeing certain bodies as being in the image of God. The failure to do this is a failure to see them as "truly human." "Dehumanizing" allows the web of oppressions that afflict the human community to go unchallenged. If Black women are seen as truly in the image of God, and truly human, their status is unquestionably one of equality and dignity. It has been said that the horrific things that people have done to one another through the centuries require a prior step of "dehumanizing" them—these things could not be done to someone who is seen as genuinely human, in the image of God.

There is a confluence between the politics of God incarnate and the problem of being Black in America. In particular Turman acknowledges the "broken body" of Christ situated with us in our brokenness as the antecedent to our wholeness. She recognizes in the Black church a community that asserts, "There is still hope for the broken body that was born at the interstices of abolition and enslavement."[72]

---

72. Turman, *Toward a Womanist Ethic of Incarnation*, 172.

An ethical consideration that Turman draws out very effectively is the brokenness of the church's practice as it perpetuates injustice even as it means to escape it. This is seen in a pigmentocracy that internalizes the inferiority of Blackness that has been drilled into the Black psyche by white supremacy. She is naming the colonization of the mind that happens when the very racism one resists takes root in one's own consciousness. Perpetuation of injustice is also seen in the gender differential in the Black church and the exclusion and oppression of sexual minorities in the church. Womanists oppose all systems of oppression, and Turman calls the church to be true to its commitment to justice for *every*body.

Turman embraces the deep insights of incarnational theology. In our "brokenness we claim that God is not only *with* us in terms of God's presence in history on the side of the oppressed; but more, that God is *in* us, namely, that God is in the flesh of the oppressed of the oppressed." She further reflects that "'God in us' presumes an already 'there-ness' of God and thereby compels the church to recognize injustice against any *body*, most especially those bodies that defy normativity, as injustice against God."[73]

Conclusion

An incarnational ethic insists that bodies matter. Bodies, whatever their differences, are to be given respect and dignity and humanity. Systems and structures that compromise this are to be resisted and dismantled. The commitment to the care of bodies is rooted in the recognition that all are made in the image of God, made by love and for love. The divine embrace of embodiment is apparent—in creation; in the divine presence in, with, and under all that is; and in the incarnation. Bodies matter. Yet daily there are bodies that are disrespected, discriminated against, and dehumanized. There are bodies that are not accepted and welcomed to accessible spaces because of their disabilities. There are bodies across the gender spectrum that are treated as "abnormal." There are bodies that are commodified and trafficked. There are bodies that are beaten and raped. There are bodies that are incarcerated. The bodies of these vulnerable persons are at risk in our culture. The system must be dismantled and new ways of being human together found.

Jesus' preaching of the kingdom of God proclaims dramatic reversals—where the last shall be first and the first last. "The least are the

73. Turman, *Toward a Womanist Ethic of Incarnation*, 172.

greatest, the 'little ones' come first, and the lost get found."[74] The "new community" that Jesus ushered in is to be a different kind of community reflecting his dramatic reversal. Ada María Isasi-Díaz renames what is referenced here as the "kingdom of God" as the "kin-dom" of God; it is not so much oriented to kings as it is to community.[75] What is needed is a full realization of the "beloved community" that Martin Luther King envisioned.[76]

74. Case-Winters, "New Community," 220–23.

75. Ada María Isasi-Díaz, *Mujerista Theology* (Maryknoll, NY: Orbis Books, 1996).

76. Martin Luther King Jr., *Stride toward Freedom* (San Francisco: Harper and Row, 1958), 102. The vision of the "beloved community" articulated here holds promise as a contemporary image of what the church is called to be and what—at its best—it may offer to the wider society. King said of the nonviolent resistance in the civil rights movement, "The end is reconciliation, the end is redemption, the end is the creation of the Beloved Community." In a context of fragmentation and alienation, the church can be a force for community. In a place where difference leads to conflict, the church can be a sanctuary, a sacred space where issues can be deliberated in a community of moral discernment. In a context of violence and oppression, the church can be a community of peacemakers and justice seekers, a place of both forgiveness and accountability (Matt. 18:15–35).

Chapter 5

How Does Incarnation Change the Way We Think about the Christ Event?

L ooking through the lens of incarnation fundamentally reshapes how we think about Jesus and about God's saving work in him. Much Christian interpretation of God's saving work centers around the cross. In our day, some problematic distortions have arisen that challenge us to reexamine how we think about the meaning of the cross. Such a reexamination is aided by locating the cross under the wider horizon of the incarnation and the whole of the Christ event. In doing so, we also find a deeper, richer perspective on the multiple ways in which God's work in Jesus the Christ is salvific for us. I illustrate by taking a closer look at four aspects of the Christ event: birth, life and ministry, death, and resurrection. Each of these aspects could be a book unto itself; in this brief treatment I narrow the scope to attend particularly to how incarnation shapes our understanding of each. I drill down further by special attention to the Gospel of Matthew as a scriptural resource. Diverse theological voices from across the centuries are drawn illustratively, and multiple metaphors for how God's saving work is manifest in the Christ event are offered along the way.

Challenges from Our Context concerning God's Saving Work

In our day, a fresh exploration that takes the whole of the Christ event into account is particularly needed. Some popular interpretations of the meaning of the cross have arisen that are deeply problematic theologically and require a thoughtful response. After a brief look at those interpretations, I widen the scope to consider more than the cross and to frame the cross within the fullness of the Christ event. I hope that this approach illumines our thinking and challenges recent problematic readings.

When we think of God's saving work on our behalf, the cross is of great import theologically. It is the symbol without parallel in Christian tradition. A wider vision of the fullness of the Christ event may help us to reclaim the cross from misunderstandings. Joanne Carlson Brown and Rebecca Parker charge that "Christianity is an abusive theology that glorifies suffering."[1] Substitutionary atonement, they say, looks a lot like "divine child abuse . . . God the Father demanding and carrying out the suffering and death of his own son so that God can forgive our sins." This challenge needs an answer.

Womanist theologian Delores Williams, in her book *Sisters in the Wilderness*, points out that interpreting God's saving work in Christ primarily through the images of substitution and sacrificial suffering does not play itself out as "good news" for people accustomed to having roles of surrogacy and sacrifice and suffering forced upon them. This was the situation for Black women especially under the conditions of slavery as their labor and their bodies provided surrogate services for white men and women. A vision of Jesus as a surrogate for us in God's economy of salvation is destructive. It sacralizes surrogacy. Williams objects that it is not by his sacrificial or substitutionary death that Jesus saves but by his life's example—"a vision of abundant relational life."[2] She also questions the habit of seeing salvific outcomes linked to Jesus' violent death. JoAnne Terrell sharpens this critique—"permitting injury or disadvantage to someone for the sake of someone else does not have divine sanction"—and betrays God's intention for right relations.[3] This merits a thoughtful response as well.

What theological responses are available to us for addressing these challenges? If preaching about the cross has been heard as a glorification of sacrifice and suffering, then the meaning of the cross has been misrepresented or misunderstood. Perhaps it would be good to begin again at the beginning. Second Corinthians 5:19 (KJV) expresses God's saving work in this way: "God was in Christ, reconciling the world unto himself." This story does not seem to be about God punishing someone or requiring that someone pay or needing for someone to suffer in order to love and forgive us.

1. Joanne Carlson Brown and Rebecca Parker, in *Christianity, Patriarchy, and Abuse: A Feminist Critique*, ed. Joanne Carlson Brown and Rebecca Parker (New York: Pilgrim Press, 1989), 26.

2. Delores Williams, "Black Women's Surrogacy Experience and the Christian Notion of Redemption," in *After Patriarchy: Feminist Transformations of the World Religions*, ed. Paula Cooley et al. (Maryknoll, NY: Orbis Books, 1991), 1–14.

3. JoAnne Terrell, *Power in the Blood? The Cross in the African American Experience* (Eugene, OR: Wipf and Stock, 1998), 124.

If we lean into incarnational theology when thinking about the cross, then the cross is viewed very differently. Looking at the cross through this lens, it can be seen as a primary mode of "God with us." The cross turns out to be a story of God's own suffering. God was in Christ, and God's incarnation in him means that God knows suffering from within. We see God's presence and solidarity with us in our sin and suffering. God in Christ becomes one with us and *one of us* in a way that offers healing and emancipatory hope.

We are also helped by framing the cross within the wider Christ event, each element of which is an aspect or instantiation of incarnation manifesting its deep and multiple meanings. The cross is best understood not in isolation but in the context of the entire Christ event.

Recentering Jesus' Birth in the Incarnation

For the Gospel of Matthew, the redemptive meaning of the birth of the Messiah is apparent. Matthew draws upon the prophetic text from Isaiah (7:14) to interpret the meaning of Jesus' birth: "'and they shall name him Emmanuel,' which means, 'God is with us'" (1:23). The fundamental meaning of the incarnation is that God chooses to be, and really is, *with us*. Theologically this has been explored in the doctrine of the Incarnation and especially in our contemplation of the sense in which Jesus the Christ is truly God and truly human. In the Incarnation we see "true God" in divine self-giving. In the Incarnation we also see "true human being," as being in union with God. The incarnate One is at one and the same time a manifestation of divine love and a demonstration of the divine intention for human beings.

God's Saving Work: The Word Became Flesh

Incarnation is the wonder of the Word made flesh. There is a sense in which the incarnation all by itself is sufficient. Although this line of thought is not prominent in Western Christian classical tradition, it has significant adherents through Christian history. It can be traced from the Gospel of John through Irenaeus (second century), Gregory of Nyssa (335–395), Gregory of Nazianzus (329–390), Bonaventure (1221–1274), and Friedrich Schleiermacher (1768–1835), and is highlighted by several more contemporary theologians. Greek Orthodox understandings of salvation make this the center point. For Greek Orthodox theology, incarnation is even more central than the cross as the locus of God's

saving work in Christ. Though there is more to the Christ event than the
Incarnation, in this understanding it is by "assuming our flesh" that God
heals us. As Gregory of Nazianzus said, "That which he has not assumed
he has not healed, but that which is united to his Godhead is also saved."[4]
If you ask Greek Orthodox Christians, "How are we saved?" they will
answer that it is by God becoming one with us in Christ.

Irenaeus is an interesting instance of this perspective. He offers an
alternative to Augustine's particular reading of salvation history. Irenaeus
sees our perfection as being at our end rather than at our beginning.
He pictures human beings as created immature (in God's likeness) and
intended to grow toward fullness of being in God's image. Sin is a mark of
immaturity and ignorance (rather than rebellion), and it summons forth
God's compassion (rather than punishment). God is like a parent who has
compassion upon seeing a beloved child stumble as they learn to walk. In
the incarnation God comes in the flesh to show us how to become what
we are meant to be. Jesus is understood to be the "pioneer and perfecter
of our faith" (Heb. 12:2).

Irenaeus is intrigued by Jesus' passage through all the stages of human
life and proposes that as he "recapitulates" our lives, he is redeeming as
he goes. Because he experienced and brought to perfection all the stages
of human life he is able to redeem all of human experience. With each
step, another aspect of our life is taken up into the divine life.[5]

This way of thinking made it very important that the *fullness* of human
personhood should be assumed by the divine Logos. In the fourth- and
fifth-centuries' controversy over how one person could be both divine
and human, there were two schools of thought: the Alexandrian school
emphasized the unity of the person, and the Antiochene school emphasized the integrity of the two persons. Apollinaris in Alexandrian enthu-
siasm proposed that the problem could be solved in this way: the divine
Logos simply took over the functions of the mind/soul in the person of
Jesus. In this way Jesus had a divine mind/soul enlivening and directing
a human body. Gregory of Nazianzus, who was in the Antiochene camp
emphasizing the integrity of the *two persons*, countered this proposal
energetically. He insisted that the human mind is absolutely essential to

---

4. Gregory of Nazianzus, "Letter 101 (To Cledonius against Apollinaris)," in *Christology of
the Later Fathers*, ed. Edward R. Hardy (Philadelphia: Westminster Press, 1954), 218.

5. This theological reflection is connected with the Adam-Christ contrast Paul sets forth in
Rom. 5:18: "Therefore just as one man's trespass led to condemnation for all, so one man's act
of righteousness leads to justification and life for all."

human personhood. If the Logos did not assume a human mind, then the mind is not healed.

Those who emphasize incarnation as the means of salvation say, "He became as we are, that we might become as he is."[6] This divine embrace of our lives in the Incarnation accomplishes our salvation. Incarnation is enough.

From this standpoint, the Incarnation is not simply the necessary pre-condition of the crucifixion—an emergency measure on God's part due to a human fall into sin. It lies, rather, in the primordial creative intent of God. The goal of the whole creation is union with God. What is manifest in Jesus of Nazareth is intended for all. There is a sense in which the work of Christ is redemptive precisely *because* the union with God—which is intended for all—is manifest in him. At the heart of created reality there is an openness to the God who "unfolds" and "enfolds" all things (Nicholas of Cusa). The whole of creation is enfolded (*complicatio*) in its divine source and is unfolded (*explicatio*) in space and time.[7] This union with the divine is both our origin and our destiny.

The vision of God offered in the birth of the Messiah is a vision of God's "real presence" in this world that God loves. The work of creation and the work of redemption are joined. In both there is the wonder that Matthew expresses in 1:23—God is with us.

God's Saving Work: Theosis

Denis Edwards pursues union with God (*theosis*) as a way of thinking about how the Incarnation is salvific and notes that many great theologians of the past and present hold with this view. In particular he mentions Maximus the Confessor (580–662) in the East and Duns Scotus (1266–1308) in the West. The creation is a work of love that has at its center divine self-giving in Word and Spirit. Athanasius held that the whole natural world exists only because it partakes of the Word in the Spirit, and it would "relapse into nonexistence" if it did not.[8]

---

6. Irenaeus, *Against Heresies*, vol. 5 preface, in *Ante-Nicene Fathers*, ed. Philip Schaff (1885; repr., Grand Rapids, Eerdmans, 2001).

7. Nicholas of Cusa, *On Learned Ignorance: A Translation and Appraisal of De Docta Ignorantia*, trans. J. Hopkins, 2nd ed. (Minneapolis: Banning, 1985), 2.3.

8. Denis Edwards, "Incarnation and the Natural World: Explorations in the Tradition of Athanasius," in *Incarnation: On the Scope and Depth of Christology*, ed. Niels Gregersen (Minneapolis: Fortress, 2015), 159–60.

This is a very strong affirmation of the world's permeation with the Word and Spirit of God. In this sense God is already "incarnate" in the world. For Athanasius the Word is "present in all things and extends his power everywhere" and "gives life and protection to everything, everywhere, to each individually and to all together."[9] The Spirit activates everything. Athanasius offers a Trinitarian formula: "The Father creates and renews all things through the Son and in the Holy Spirit."[10]

For Athanasius incarnation in all things from the beginning of creation is very much congruent with his affirmation that union with God is the goal of creation. He presents this fully in his work *On the Incarnation*. There he uses the exchange formula, "For he became human that we might become divine" (54).[11] Other terms he associates with *theosis* include sanctification, illumination, and vivification. In his view the whole creation will share in this transformation and glorification.

Edwards draws out the implications of this thoroughly incarnational theology. One implication is that God is "forever matter, forever flesh."[12] As Edwards summarizes, "The Christian claim is not that we find God by going to the transcendent spiritual world beyond, but that God has come to us in the flesh—and it is as creatures of flesh that we are transformed in Christ. . . . God gives God's very self to creation in the Word made flesh and in the Spirit poured out."[13]

Karl Rahner in the Roman Catholic Church and Thomas Torrance in the Reformed tradition both gravitate to this deeper reflection on incarnation, seeing it as a better way of understanding how God was in Christ reconciling the world than the more prominent Western understanding of sacrificial or substitutionary atonement. Torrance notes the broad sweep of this approach: "The incarnation was not just a transient episode in the interaction of God with the world, but has taken place once-for-all in a way that reaches backward through time and forward through time from the end to the beginning and from the beginning to the end."[14] Incarnation is central to God's intentions and actions from creation to new creation.

9. Athanasius of Alexandria, *Contra Gentes* 41, in *Athanasius Contra Gentes and De Incarnatione*, ed. and trans. Robert Thomson (Oxford: Clarendon, 1971), 113–15.

10. Edwards, "Incarnation and the Natural World," 162.

11. Edwards, "Incarnation and the Natural World," 163.

12. Edwards, "Incarnation and the Natural World," 168.

13. Edwards, "Incarnation and the Natural World," 169–70.

14. Thomas Torrance, *The Christian Doctrine of God: One Being Three Persons* (Edinburgh: T. & T. Clark, 1996), 214.

Recentering Jesus' Life and Ministry in the Incarnation

A closer look at the embodied Jesus is an important step to take. The particulars of his appearance do not matter in terms of God's salvific work in him. However, in our time there are reasons why we might want to take a closer look. Some observe that our vision of the embodied Jesus has been "white-washed." In my context, for example, it is a blond-haired, blue-eyed, white-skinned man whose serene portrait hangs in many a church fellowship hall—and in our imaginations. In chapter 4, we discussed the idealization of the white, male, European body and how it may reflect and play into the dynamics of white supremacy. When we remember that Jesus was a Palestinian Jewish man living in Galilee in the first century it challenges that portrait. He would probably have been dark-haired, dark-eyed, with skin "dark brown and suntanned,"[15] according to biblical scholar James Charlesworth. Somehow we have failed to represent the brown-skinned Palestinian Jewish man living in Galilee.

We also tend to forget his precarious beginning. He was conceived by an unwed teenage girl and born in a stable. Jesus begins his life fleeing with his family of refugees under the threat of death in Herod's slaughter of the innocents throughout the region. His family sought asylum in Egypt and lived there in exile as immigrants for some time. All his life and ministry were conducted in an occupied country oppressed by imperial powers.

Instead of this genuinely embodied portrait of Jesus we get a disembodied, fabricated version that has been silenced, sanitized, sabotaged, and sanctified. A popular depiction in Christian iconography is "Christ the almighty" (Greek: Χριστός Παντοκράτωρ [*christos pantokratōr*]). It conveys a picture of Jesus that is imperial in character and, by extension, represents God in this way. Rather than coming to understand God *differently* by virtue of God's incarnation in Jesus, the Palestinian Jew (humble and harassed as he was), an imperial overlay displaces this embodied incarnation. We have, as Whitehead quipped, "rendered unto God the things that belong to Caesar."[16] This move indicates a theological preference for an elevated image more like the conquerors and colonizers of

---

15. Interview with James Charlesworth, Princeton biblical scholar and head of the Dead Sea Scrolls Project, as quoted in Christena Cleveland, "Why Jesus' Skin Color Matters," *Christianity Today*, March 2016.

16. Alfred North Whitehead, *Process and Reality* (1929; repr., New York: Macmillan, 1978), 520.

the world than the embodied Jesus.[17] This version becomes the "Jesus of empire" who can be pressed into imperial service, rather than the Jesus who destabilizes systems and structures that benefit the few at the expense of the many.

Making Jesus into a kind of imperial ruler is a strange thing indeed. The Gospel of Matthew is full of anti-imperial messages and is clear that Jesus engages in nonviolent resistance against the empire of his day.[18] The common people were oppressed and dispossessed by Rome and by the elites who colluded with Rome. Many aspects of Matthew's Gospel challenge the imperial arrangements either directly or indirectly. For example, Old Testament citations in Matthew come from Isaiah and invoke the eighth-century BCE situation of oppression by the Assyrian Empire. The texts chosen are ones that imply divine opposition to empire. Another aspect of the narrative of resistance is the extremely negative portrayal of Rome's representatives, Herod and Pilate. Another example concerns taxes. Taxes were a costly enactment of Roman oppression that siphoned off much-needed resources from the people, who cannot safely refuse to pay. Although Jesus instructs Simon to pay the tax, he will pay it with a coin Jesus instructs him to find in the mouth of a fish. This is an interesting twist, given the imperial claim to rule over not only peoples and nations but also the fish and the sea.[19] The story conveys where true sovereignty lies. In Matthew's accounting, Jesus makes clear that sovereignty and allegiance belong to God and not to Rome.

Many of Jesus' teachings have to do with nonviolent resistance in face of the empire's claims. One of the best theological discussions of his approach and one that is timely for us today is that of Howard Thurman in his classic text *Jesus and the Disinherited*. We interact with this work at some length here as it offers an insightful reading of the Gospel accounts of the life and ministry of Jesus as a kind of manual of resistance for the poor and disenfranchised. Thurman asks, "What do the teachings of Jesus have to say to those who stand at a moment in human history with their backs against the wall . . . the poor, the disinherited, the

17. Kwok Pui-lan, *Postcolonial Imagination and Feminist Theology* (Louisville, KY: Westminster John Knox Press, 2005).

18. Warren Carter has extensively studied resistance to the Roman Empire in the Gospel of Matthew. See Warren Carter, *Matthew and Empire: Initial Explorations* (Harrisburg, PA: Trinity Press International, 2001).

19. "Every rare and beautiful thing in the wide ocean—belongs to the imperial treasury" (Warren Carter, *Matthew and the Margins: A Socio-Political and Religious Reading* [Sheffield: Sheffield Academic Press, 2000], 359).

dispossessed?"[20] He believes Jesus' teachings have much more to offer than is usually appropriated. Thurman insists that the real genius of Jesus' teaching, in the authentic flowering of his Jewish religious heritage, is his teaching that we should love God and love our neighbors as ourselves. This teaching has been betrayed by his followers, who have individualized and privatized what they received. Christian faith has been reduced to "loving Jesus in your heart." Thurman says Jesus' religion of incarnation has been *dis-incarnated*—separating body from soul, spirit from matter, God from the world. It has become an otherworldly religion of "pie in the sky by and by." For the present, the faithful are counseled to just "bear the cross" of suffering—be like Jesus.

In my view, this disincarnated reading seems designed to cut the nerve of resistance. Jesus' way was perverted and diverted from its true course as accounted in Luke's Gospel (4:18): to "let the oppressed go free," to "bring good news to the poor," and "release to the captives."

Jesus' teachings, when they are overtaken by the powerful, invite humble submission to authorities (slaves, obey your masters) and keep the focus on heaven. Such a Christianity is no help, as Thurman says, "to those who need profound succor and strength to enable them to live in the present with dignity and creativity."[21]

Thurman is in touch with the "embodied" Jesus in his real-life situation, which very much resembles that of the great masses of our own time. He was a man with his back against the wall. In particular, Thurman makes the connection with the situation of African Americans today—who because of their race are denied full citizenship; the rights, power, and privilege enjoyed by others; and equal protection under the law.

Thurman sees the Jesus movement as, in some sense, a strategy for dealing with oppression.[22] He observes that, faced with his situation, Jesus advocated a very different path from the options prevalent in his community as represented by the Sadducees, Pharisees, and Zealots. The Sadducees were upper-class people, some of whom were high priests. They had economic security from the profits of the temple. They advocated nonresistance, assimilation, and capitulation (going along to get along). They were keeping their status while colluding in their own oppression—and everyone else's. The Pharisees opposed Roman occupation and oppression, but they kept their "resistance" internal, dissimulating and

---

20. Howard Thurman, *Jesus and the Disinherited* (Boston: Beacon Press, 1996), ix.
21. Thurman, *Jesus and the Disinherited*, 1.
22. Thurman, *Jesus and the Disinherited*, 18.

not displaying their hatred, bitterness, fear, and contempt. The Zealots advocated active—even violent—resistance. In contrast to these, Jesus' way was definitely resistance, but not with violence. It was a way forward that was neither acquiescence nor armed conflict. "'Give therefore to the emperor the things that are the emperor's, and to God the things that are God's" (Matt. 22:21). The conclusion is that your allegiance, your agency, and your soul belong to God alone.

Thurman urges a reclaiming of Jesus' essential message of loving God and neighbor even to the extreme of loving your enemies. He warns against giving in to hate, hypocrisy and dissimulation, or fear. "Hatred is destructive to hated and hater alike." Jesus rejected hatred and made the demand—outrageous under the circumstances—that his followers should "Love your enemy; that you may be like your father who is in heaven."[23] To create a different social world, one has to begin by being different. Unless we do, it will always be more of the same. "Do not repay anyone evil for evil" (Rom. 12:17). Someone has to say, "The hostilities stop here."[24]

Thurman admits that dissimulation (deception and hypocrisy) may be a necessary survival strategy at times. Only the victim of race trauma can judge, but it may be soul destroying. A victim may choose a pattern of deception, of acting and speaking in one way while feeling very differently. This duplicity will, over time, have a dis-integrating effect and become a continuous degradation. Thurman quotes Mahatma Gandhi, who wrote in a letter to Muriel Lester, "Speak the Truth without fear and without exception."[25]

Race trauma is fear inducing.[26] The threat is always there, either implicit or explicit. It restricts one's movements and keeps one in check. Victims of race trauma may even internalize the contempt they receive. The mind is "colonized." There is but a small step between being despised and despising oneself. Fear creates a background noise even without any immediate threat. Thurman describes it as being like the abiding terror of the rabbit running from the hounds and knowing it will not ultimately escape. There is no protection: they cannot protect themselves (the power is unequal), and no one else will protect them. People commit to memory the ways of behaving that will keep them safe—for example,

23. Thurman, *Jesus and the Disinherited*, 25.

24. Anna Case-Winters, *Matthew* (Louisville, KY: Westminster John Knox Press, 2015), 101.

25. Thurman, *Jesus and the Disinherited*, 59.

26. See, e.g., ch. 2 in Rick Ufford-Chase, ed., *Faithful Resistance: Gospel Visions for the Church in a Time of Empire* (San Bernardino, CA: n.p., 2016), 51.

a body language of submission or agreeableness.[27] This situation of race trauma is damaging to health, causing actual physical, chemical changes in the body, bloodstream, and muscular reactions. Adrenaline that prepares the body under threat for the fight-or-flight response never shuts off. To "fight" means being met with a disproportionately violent response. "Flight" can be humiliating ("I should have stood up for myself," the victim says). The stress hormone cortisol is continually produced. In this contemporary situation, the calling to "fear not" that recurs in the Gospel of Matthew is a difficult calling, but it is an invitation to resist the soul-destroying power of the situation. "Do not fear those who kill the body but cannot kill the soul" (Matt. 10:28).

The religion of Jesus put the love ethic first. It was the essence of his Jewish religious tradition. Walter Wink summarizes Thurman's insight. There are two options for people with their back against the wall, living under constant threat from the death-dealing powers that oppress and dispossess them. One option is nonresistance (compliance, complicity, collusion). The other is violent resistance. Jesus offers a third way of nonviolent resistance: not cooperating with evil nor resorting to violence—rendering no one evil for evil.[28] If this is so, then Jesus' work of healing, his nonviolent resistance to evil, and his teachings about love of neighbor and love of enemies provide a genuine alternative as a pattern for our own faithful living and a new understanding of God's saving work.

God's Saving Work: Christ the Example

Reconnecting with the embodied Jesus rather than the imperial pantocrator Christ takes us to a different place in our understanding of God's saving work in our midst. The focus is not so much on the cross as on the person, life, and ministry of Jesus. He shows us the way; he is a moral example ("exemplar") of what it looks like to love God and neighbor (even neighbors who are enemies). In not giving in to hate, hypocrisy, or fear in the face of oppression, Jesus shows a different way forward—a third way that is neither acquiescence nor violence. Jesus spends his life

27. Police violence against young Black men on the South Side of Chicago is so frequent and so overboard that a local church, Trinity United Congregational Church, has produced a set of educational resources as well as an instructional video, *Get Home Safely: 10 Rules of Survival*, for anyone stopped by the police.
28. Walter Wink, *The Powers That Be: Theology for a New Millennium* (New York: Doubleday, 1999).

and ministry in the saving work of teaching, healing, and feeding. He proclaims the coming reign of God and calls for repentance and transformation of life that befits those under God's reign. In Matthew he is presented as the authoritative interpreter of the law, and he teaches that its center is love of God and neighbor. He calls his followers to a "higher righteousness" (Greek: δικαιοσύνη [*dikaiosunē*]) reflected in the exercise of justice and mercy for the least, the last, and the lost. In his ministry Jesus demonstrates divine compassion for people at the margins. In his life and ministry, Jesus is the exemplar of God's love and the exemplar who shows us how to live. He is the pioneer and perfecter of our faith (Heb. 12:2).

While "Christ the exemplar" or the moral influence theory of the atonement has not been the predominant understanding of God's saving work, it is definitely featured in Scripture and in theological reflection on the life and ministry of Jesus. Peter Abelard (1079–1142) first articulated this vision, and it is still the understanding held by many. Abelard rejected the ransom theory of the atonement that pictured Jesus' death as a kind of ransom paid to the devil to save sinners. He also rejected the sacrificial/ substitutionary theory of the atonement, in which Jesus is seen as a sacrificial offering for the sin of human beings or a substitute who takes the punishment humans deserve in their place. Against these options Abelard offered an alternative understanding of Jesus as a manifestation of God's love. This demonstration of love has the power to cause the sinner to return to God.

In Abelard's view, the human problematic is not so much human sin and God's wrath. It is rather a problem of our sense of shame for our sin that alienates us from God. It is not that God has turned away from us in anger; rather, we have turned away from God in shame. Jesus comes as the manifestation of God's love and acceptance in spite of our sin. This witness of love and forgiveness empowers us to emerge from our hiding and alienation and turn toward God. Jesus is also the exemplar in the sense of showing us how to live a truly human life—a life lived in love of God and neighbor.

This way of thinking about the human problematic may be more prominent in the biblical witness than is usually recognized. In the story of Adam and Eve in the Garden, for example, when they have eaten the forbidden fruit, they hide from God and hide from one another with coverings of fig leaves (Gen. 3:8). God seeks them out. "'Where are you?'" (Gen. 3:9). This is a classic, deep symbol.

Contemporary feminist theologian Susan Nelson Dunfee proposes that "the sin of hiding" is every bit as much of a problem as the more emphasized sin of pride.[29] This is a problem of self-negation rather than self-assertion, a problem of not becoming all we are meant to be rather than a problem of overreaching. In Dunfee's experience, socialization in a patriarchal society inclines women to the sin of hiding more than the sin of pride that Augustine emphasized. The saving word manifest in the incarnation is the affirmation that one is beloved, accepted, and forgiven. One can come out of hiding. Once we know of God's great love, we are drawn out of guilty hiding and also inspired to live lives marked by the love, acceptance, and forgiveness we ourselves have received.

This is sometimes referred to as a subjectivist theory of the atonement since it is a revelation of what is already the case with God. What changes is not our objective state before God but our subjective disposition toward God. Jesus teaches and exemplifies what it is to be truly human—who we are and what we are called to do. As we grow in grace, our lives come to be, more and more, conformed to his pattern.

God's Saving Work: "The Spirit of the Lord Was upon Him"

Yet another way we can understand how God was in Christ and how our restoration in him comes about is by closer attention to the Spirit's work in incarnation. In much of the discussion of incarnation, the Spirit is sidelined. A more thoroughgoing Trinitarian-relational approach would frame incarnation better. Incarnation is not the work of two persons of the Trinity in isolation from the Spirit. Significant voices in the tradition have elaborated a "Spirit Christology" and interpreted God's saving work in Christ with an emphasis on the Spirit's role. This section sounds some of the depths of a Spirit Christology.

The common neglect of the Spirit in discussion of incarnation is surprising given how central the Spirit is in Jesus' life and ministry. Each Gospel account contributes something distinctive about the Spirit's relation to Jesus. Mark has no birth narrative but begins with the proclamations of John the Baptist. He announces that one is coming who will "baptize you with the Holy Spirit" (Mark 1:8). When the Spirit descends on Jesus like a dove, his identity is revealed. Then "the Spirit immediately drove him out into the wilderness" (Mark 1:12). Matthew includes the birth narratives and contributes that the child conceived in Mary is "from

29. Susan Nelson Dunfee. "The Sin of Hiding: A Feminist Critique of Reinhold Niebuhr's Account of the Sin of Pride," *Soundings: An Interdisciplinary Journal* 65, no. 3 (1982): 316–27, www.jstor.org/stable/41178220.

the Holy Spirit" (1:20). Luke's account is distinctive for its vision of Jesus as "full of the Holy Spirit" (4:1). After the temptation in the wilderness he returns to Galilee "filled with the power of the Spirit" (4:14), and his ministry is inaugurated with the announcement (4:18–19),

> The Spirit of the Lord is upon me,
>   because he has anointed me
>   to bring good news to the poor.
> He has sent me to proclaim release to the captives
>   and recovery of sight to the blind,
>   to let the oppressed go free,
> to proclaim the year of the Lord's favor.

The Gospel of John adds to the picture a more reciprocal relation between Jesus and the Spirit. Jesus is not only the one who has received the Spirit, but one who gives the Spirit. As John the Baptist testifies, "He on whom you see the Spirit descend and remain is the one who baptizes with the Holy Spirit" (John 1:33). He is one who "gives the Spirit without measure" (3:34). In the resurrection appearance to the disciples in the upper room, Jesus "breathed on them and said to them, 'Receive the Holy Spirit'" (20:22). In all these texts—and many others could be mentioned—we see the central role of the Holy Spirit in Jesus' life and ministry.

Ambrose of Milan (339–397) is known for his Spirit Christology. He went so far as to propose that the Spirit is "the author of the incarnation."[30] His argument comes from the Spirit's role as attested in the birth narratives of Matthew and Luke, where Jesus' coming into being is of the Holy Spirit. Ambrose further extends the Spirit's role to the coming into being of all creation. He saw creation as a work of the full Trinity in one undivided act, even as the roles of each may be somewhat different.

When we look at the creation stories, a more universal picture of how the Spirit pervades and is incarnate in all living things takes shape. Old Testament texts illumine the role of the Spirit. The word translated "spirit" (Hebrew: רוח [rwḥ]) means wind, breath, and spirit. It has the same essential meaning content as the Greek term πνεῦμα (*pneuma*). In the Genesis story, in the beginning of creation, "The earth was a formless

---

30. Ambrose of Milan, *On the Holy Spirit*, in Fathers of the Church, Second Series, vol. 44 (Washington, DC: Catholic University of America Press, 1991), 2.5.41, p. 110.

void and darkness covered the face of the deep, while a wind [Spirit, breath] from God swept over the face of the waters" (1:2). In Genesis 2, God forms the first human from the dust of the ground, who, upon receiving the breath of God, becomes a "living being" (v. 7). As Ted Hiebert points out this is the life-giving breath humans share with all creatures, the breath of all animate life (cf. Gen. 7:22). The human being and the animals alike are called "living beings."[31] Theologically the picture of the Spirit as the life-giving breath of God in all things led to the affirmation in the Nicene Creed of the Spirit as "the Lord and Giver of Life." Reformed theologian Abraham Kuyper echoes this affirmation when he speaks of the life-giving work of the Holy Spirit, "and what is this quickening and animating principle but the Holy Spirit?"[32]

In the work of creation, Word and Spirit are both active. Denis Edwards, following Irenaeus, thinks of Word and Spirit as the "two hands" of God. They are "reciprocally related in the one great act of ongoing creation."[33] They work together as closely joined as a word is joined to the breath by which it is spoken. Psalm 33:6 affirms, "By the word of the LORD the heavens were made, / and all their host by the breath of his mouth."

The Spirit continues to breathe life into the creation. Stephen Hawking asks a famous question at the end of his *Brief History of Time*: "What is it that *breathes fire* into the equations and makes a universe for them to describe?"[34] Denis Edwards answers that it is the Spirit, "the Breath of God." "This Spirit continues to breathe life into the exuberant, diverse, interrelated community of living things."[35] This is a divine incarnation already ongoing in divine self-giving. "The grace of the incarnation is intimately connected to God's gracious self-communication to all of creation and humanity."[36] As we have elsewhere argued that the incarnation is no emergency measure due to "the fall," Irenaeus, Duns Scotus, Karl Rahner, and Denis Edwards concur with this view. Incarnation is an

31. Theodore Hiebert, "The Human Vocation," in *Christianity and Ecology: Seeking the Well-Being of Earth and Humans*, ed. Dieter Hessel and Rosemary Radford Ruether (Cambridge, MA: Harvard University Press, 2000), 139.

32. Abraham Kuyper, *The Work of the Holy Spirit* (Grand Rapids: Eerdmans, 1941), 26.

33. Denis Edwards, *Breath of Life: A Theology of the Creator Spirit* (Maryknoll, NY: Orbis Books, 2004), 44.

34. Stephen Hawking, *A Brief History of Time: From the Big Bang to Black Holes* (New York: Bantam, 1988), 174.

35. Edwards, *Breath of Life*, 33.

36. Denis Edwards, *Jesus and the Cosmos* (New York: Paulist Press, 1991), 74.

embodiment of God's love and self-giving to the creation and was always already present in the divine primordial intent.

Spirit Christology is yet another approach that makes it easier to think of God's incarnation in Jesus of Nazareth. God's Spirit is *already* in all things. Why would it not be in him as well? The indwelling of the Spirit is not something that distinguishes us from him, but something that makes him truly one of us. The Spirit that was in him is in us too. Jesus is both truly God and *truly human*. When we think of the stories of Jesus' baptism (Matt. 3:13–17; Mark 1:9–11; Luke 3:21–22), we could see them in this way: Jesus of Nazareth opened his heart fully to God's Spirit in him, and the heavens opened to him. The Spirit descended on him like a dove. He was manifest as the Son of God. By being totally receptive to the Spirit that was in him, Jesus became "human" in the truest sense. His receptivity and openness to the Spirit represented a union with God so profound that in him we can see God—truly God and truly human.

The christological controversies around being "of the same substance" with God (*homoousius*) were aggravated by substance thinking—as if two entirely different, mutually exclusive natures or substances had to occupy the same space. With a Spirit Christology we can more easily think relationally, in terms of the relationship between God and this human being. On the human side of the relationship we can speak of Jesus as a person who was led by the Spirit and transparent to divine purposes. His life did not obstruct or distort divine presence and activity in him. He was indwelt, inspired, and empowered by God's own Spirit. On the divine side, we can speak of God acting decisively in and through the person of Jesus. What was unique about Jesus was his relationship with God, not some superhuman, sinless perfection, nor some kind of supernatural substance added to his humanity. It was a relationship with God—the Spirit of God abiding with him and in him.

In his person Jesus embodies, at one and the same time, a definitive communication of God and a definitive human response to grace. He received the Holy Spirit and became the one in whom God came most fully to dwell. "For in him the whole fullness of deity dwells bodily" (Col. 2:9). The Spirit of the Lord was upon him. It filled and directed him in living a life of love for God and neighbor. One metaphor of the inter-Trinitarian relation that seems to fit this relational vision is the Trinitarian image of God as the Lover, Jesus as the Beloved, and the Spirit as the Love that flows between them. The Spirit is the *viniculum amoris*, the bond of love. The Lover initiates, and the Beloved reciprocates. This same Love may draw us, through the Spirit, into the communion of love that is the inter-Trinitarian relation. Edwards points out that Basil saw the Spirit, "always in the Communion of the Trinity, as dwelling not only in human beings, but also in all the diverse creatures of the universe and so enabling them to exist from the divine Communion as well."[37] Thus the Spirit in all things is drawing all things into communion with one another and into the divine communion of Love.

As beings in whom the Spirit of God is present, human beings like us have the possibility of being "Spirit-filled" in the way that Jesus exemplified. We also may follow in the way of Jesus and be filled with the Spirit. What did it mean for Jesus to be Spirit-filled? The Spirit's anointing led him to preach good news to the poor, release to the captive, and recovery of sight to the blind, and to set at liberty those who are oppressed (Luke 4:18).

Perhaps Jesus' most basic teaching was his life and ministry. He was the Word *Incarnate*. The Word he was and the words he spoke, he embodied. Considering his life and ministry we see what a Spirit-filled life looks like. The Spirit of God anointing us, abiding in us, and reorienting our lives would be a fundamental transformation. This is yet another way of understanding God's saving work in Jesus the Christ. The Spirit that was in Jesus is in us too. If we respond to the Spirit as he did, there is hope and promise of transformation and renewal for us all. In Jesus of Nazareth, what we see is a continuation and intensification of what God's Spirit has been doing all along and will bring to fulfillment when we are fully formed in the image of God. To live a Spirit-filled life is to be truly human.

Recentering Jesus' Death in the Incarnation

The meaning of the cross is clarified and enlarged when recentered in the incarnation. Misleading distortions that have arisen can be corrected. As pointed out at the beginning of the chapter, common readings of the cross that glorify suffering and sacrifice are not helpful and may even harm people who regularly have these roles forced upon them. Glorification of suffering and sacrifice have regularly been used *against* oppressed people to cut the nerve of rebellion. Thurman pointed out how Jesus' religion of incarnation commonly gets *dis-incarnated*, separating body from soul, spirit from matter, God from the world. Christianity becomes

37. Edwards, *Breath of Life*, 44.

an otherworldly religion of "pie in the sky by and by." The faithful are counseled to just "bear the cross" of suffering—be like Jesus. Through the lens of incarnation, keeping "God with us" as our focus allows for a fresh understanding of the meaning of the cross. If the one who is there on the cross is not only truly human but also truly God, we can see there a manifestation of God as one who is in solidarity with the suffering ones. We take several steps in this section with the intent of reclaiming the cross from its common distortions:

- We revisit the cross as depicted and interpreted in the Gospel of Matthew. The interpretation we see there does not lend itself to the distortions we commonly see in popular interpretations.
- We reconsider with critical appreciation two prominent theories of the atonement: sacrificial and substitutionary. Digging a little deeper into their origins may clear away some of the distortions that have accrued to them.
- We reclaim the cross as a site of God's solidarity and resistance in the face of what hurts and destroys.

The cross is perhaps the symbol without parallel for Christians. It is at the forefront of our understanding of God's saving work in Christ. In our day this symbol needs to be reclaimed in ways that correct for its misunderstanding as a glorification of suffering, sacrifice, and surrogacy.

Matthew's Gospel does not elaborate a theory of the atonement in connection with the cross. Crucifixion is primarily presented as a social and political response to the challenges Jesus posed to the principalities and powers of his day. Dorothee Soelle, in her book *Suffering*, has urged that we open our eyes to the suffering that is all around us and realize that, in a sense, people are "crucified" every day.[38] What is distinctive about Jesus is not his crucifixion but the life he lived that led him to the cross. It was a life of love for God and neighbor. Part of the work of following Jesus is to "stop the crucifixions." We remember that Jesus was executed, a victim of crucifixion by the officials of the Roman Empire's occupation. In remembrance we may readily associate his death on the cross with all the other violent deaths in situations of social and political oppression. James Cone made the connection between the cross and the lynchings perpetrated in American history in his book *The*

---

38. Dorothee Soelle, *Suffering* (Minneapolis: Fortress Press, 1984), 232.

Cross and the Lynching Tree.[39] As Elizabeth Johnson points out, "Crosses keep getting set up in history."[40] Liberation theologian Ignacio Ellacuria has spoken of "the crucified peoples of history."[41] When we see the Christ in these victims we are compelled to ask about the context's unjust social and political arrangements. What have we done to put these people on these crosses? What must we do to take them down? It is time to reclaim the cross—not as a glorification of suffering but as a scene of "dangerous remembrance, empowering resistance, and emancipatory hope."[42]

Matthew would not have had on his radar the contemporary problematic interpretations of the cross that we highlighted at the beginning of this chapter—as divine child abuse or as a glorification of suffering. Nevertheless, recovering his account may help us to avoid these pitfalls. Matthew "does not present Jesus' death as something that must happen so that God could be forgiving."[43] Furthermore, God's saving work pervades the whole of the Christ event in Matthew and does not begin only at the point of the passion and crucifixion.

Another thing that is important to observe is the *truly human* portrait of Jesus we have in Matthew's Gospel. This is a presentation of someone who does not know all the details of how this story will turn out and is simply manifesting stoic, courageous endurance. Why would Jesus pray his agonized prayer in the garden of Gethsemane (Matt. 26:36–46)? The Jesus whom the reader meets there actually struggles with his fear of the suffering and death that lie ahead of him. He is not "an actor reciting the lines" of a "divinely scripted drama."[44] Matthew's presentation is not one of an all-knowing, all-powerful being, but of a *truly human* being. This is no docetic Christology of one only "appearing" to be human.

The Gospel of Matthew presents a range of interpretations of who Jesus is and how God's saving work happens in him, but it offers no fully

39. James Cone, *The Cross and the Lynching Tree* (Maryknoll, NY: Orbis, 2018).

40. Elizabeth Johnson, *Ask the Beasts: Darwin and the God of Love* (London: Bloomsbury, 2014), 205.

41. Ignacio Ellacuria, "The Crucified *People*," in *Systematic Theology: Perspectives from Liberation Theology*, ed. Jon Sobrino and Ignacio Ellacuria (Maryknoll, NY: Orbis Books, 1993), 580–603.

42. Joy Ann McDougall, unpublished paper, American Academy of Religion, Boston, Massachusetts, Nov. 20–23, 1999.

43. Eugene Boring, "Matthew," in *New Interpreter's Bible* (Nashville: Abingdon, 1995), 8:87–506, quote at 495.

44. Boring, "Matthew," 495.

developed theory of the atonement. Over time, biblical interpretation and theological reflection led to multiple theories of the atonement, and among them we do find the sacrificial and substitutionary theories that have been challenged as problematic. A good first step in responding is to take a closer look at how these metaphors for understanding God's saving work arise in biblical interpretation and theological reflection. It is helpful to view them in their own right, without the overlay of distortions arising from later developments.

God's Saving Work: A Sacrificial Metaphor

The Epistle to the Hebrews interprets the meaning of the cross through images from the Jewish sacrificial system. Misunderstandings of this model treat it as a kind of transaction through which forgiveness is purchased. However, for the Jewish sacrificial system, this was not the primary understanding of ritual sacrifice. The priest stood as mediator between God and the people, offering sacrifices to atone for sin, but the shedding of blood was understood as an act of expiation, not propitiation. Expiation is a sign of sorrow for sin. Propitiation has more the character of making an offering to appease divine wrath or curry divine favor. While the metaphor in this theory of atonement is sacrificial, it is not transactional in the way some later interpretations took it. Interestingly, the Epistle to the Hebrews where this sacrificial model is most prevalent makes clear that God neither desires nor takes pleasure in sacrifices (Heb. 10:5; 10:8). The articulation of the place of Jesus' sacrifice here is made complex by its double trajectory. His role is that of the "high priest," mediating between God and the people (Heb. 2:17). At one and the same time, he presents himself as a sacrifice; "we have been sanctified through the offering of the body of Jesus Christ once for all" (Heb. 10:10).

It should be recognized in passing that the sacrificial system as such has its own critique within Judaism, given with clarity by eighth-century BCE prophets. Amos presents God as rejecting the sacrificial offerings of the people and calling for justice instead: "But let justice roll down like waters, / and righteousness like an ever-flowing stream" (Amos 5:24). In Hosea's message, God announces, "I desire steadfast love and not sacrifice, / the knowledge of God rather than burnt offerings" (Hos. 6:6). Within Judaism, the direction of the prophets was embraced. For example, the tradition of Yom Kippur, the Day of Atonement, historically included animal sacrifice, but over time it turned entirely toward "internal reconciliation with God and neighbor and becomes explicitly anti-sacrificial."[45]

There remain in the sacrificial metaphor the troubling associations of violence and bloodshed. Unfortunately, Western Christian tradition has often allowed the logic of violence to dominate its reflections on atonement. There has been an accompanying tendency to sanction sacrifice and violence.[46] Violence is, of course, an element in all human communities and is broadly echoed in religious ritual practices that either employ or symbolize it. René Girard offers a keen analysis of this harsh reality and presents insight into reinterpretation of Jesus' "sacrifice."[47] Girard references the "scapegoat mechanism" as a way of dealing with tensions and violence growing in human communities. If a scapegoat can be designated as the presumed cause of the tension, all the violence comes to focus on the scapegoat and the community is once again united—against this common enemy. When this enemy is driven out or destroyed, the illusion of peace and harmony is restored. The community is deluded, however, for this is not an elimination of the threat of violence, but only a matter of visiting violence upon one vulnerable victim.

Girard points out that Jesus' crucifixion is a scapegoat mechanism like the others in human communities; "it is set in motion and develops like the others. Yet its outcome is different from all the others."[48] What is different in Jesus' case is that the scapegoat mechanism is unveiled. The presumption of the mechanism is that the scapegoat is guilty—responsible for what is going wrong in the community. In Jesus' case, by contrast, the victim is utterly innocent. Once this reality is confronted, the mechanism is shown for the farce that it is. In the case of Jesus, the resurrection demonstrates that his life is divinely vindicated. The scapegoat mechanism loses its power now that it is revealed for what it is. In this way, Jesus' sacrifice may be thought of as a "sacrifice to end all sacrifices."[49] The scapegoat mechanism is discredited.

45. Mark Heim, *Saved from Sacrifice: A Theology of the Cross* (Grand Rapids: Eerdmans, 2006), 78.

46. Anthony Bartlett, *Cross Purposes: The Violent Grammar of Christian Atonement* (Harrisburg, PA: Trinity Press International, 2001).

47. René Girard, *The Scapegoat*, trans. Yvonne Freccero (Baltimore: Johns Hopkins University Press, 1986), and *I See Satan Fall Like Lightning* (Maryknoll, NY: Orbis Books, 2001).

48. Girard, *I See Satan Fall Like Lightning*, 148.

49. Heim, *Saved from Sacrifice*, 134.

The Jewish sacrificial system and the Christian appropriation of it are both more complex in their meaning and impact than common depictions convey. Further, as already noted, this is only a metaphor—one among many for understanding God's saving work in Christ.

God's Saving Work: A Juridical Metaphor

The Pauline writings interpret the meaning of the cross through the use of a juridical metaphor, as if there were a courtroom scene in which human beings stand accused as those who have broken the law. Christ is pictured both as our advocate and as the one who takes upon himself the consequences of our crimes. Here the substitution theme arises as a metaphor for understanding God's saving work. Because of its frequent and popular use, the tendency is to forget both the metaphorical character of this image and the limitations of this and every other metaphor for fully conveying how God's saving work occurs. The metaphor is strained when so heavily laden.

Paul's metaphor is later drawn out further by Anselm in his book *Cur Deus Homo?* This title could be rendered, "Why a God Man?" Anselm offers an argument for why the one who saves us *must be* both truly God and truly human. Anselm's presentation is an interesting recasting of the Pauline metaphor. It is redescribed in the feudal setting of Anselm's day (1033–1109). In that context, the seriousness of a crime depended upon the person against whom it was committed. In the hierarchical, feudal social world, stealing a sheep from a serf was less serious and incurred a lesser penalty than stealing from a lord. Anselm reasoned that since our crimes are against God, we incur an infinite penalty. Only an infinite restitution would satisfy the demands of justice, but only God can offer that infinite restitution. At the same time, *the offender* must make restitution, so only a human being will do. The only possible resolution, then, entails action by one who is both *truly God and truly human.* Anselm reasons that nothing less would suffice for God's work of salvation. God walking around giving the appearance of being human (Docetism) will not do. If Jesus is not truly human, then the cross is just play-acting. On the other hand, if he is only human and not truly divine, then the cross does not have saving power. For Anselm this is the logic of the incarnation. The cross is reenvisioned in the light of the incarnation. We should note that nothing appears in Anselm about an angry God demanding that someone must be punished so that God can forgive human beings. The problem is that the moral order of the universe has been disrupted—and it is God, Godself, in the incarnation, who comes to set it right.

Reclaiming the Cross

Moltmann unflinchingly insists that "the Christ event on the cross is a God event"—that what we see here is "the crucified God."[50] This perspective must reframe our whole understanding of the cross. Divine solidarity with us in our sin and suffering is what we see there, God incarnate in Jesus Christ—and him crucified.

From this standpoint, God can no longer be pictured as demanding sacrifice, the great punisher of sin and inflictor of suffering that we see in the contemporary distortions and misrepresentations to which people rightly object. One of the recurring visions of God in the Hebrew Bible is as one who is "merciful and gracious, slow to anger and abounding in steadfast love" (Ps. 103:8). In the Gospel of Matthew, Jesus invites his hearers, "Go and learn with what this means, 'I desire mercy, not sacrifice'" (9:13). The vision of God in Christ, incarnationally embodied and crucified, is a very different picture of God. As Whitehead articulated the vision, this is a "fellow sufferer who understands."[51] The cross is not something God requires in order to love and forgive. It is rather because God loves and forgives that God comes to us in the flesh and enters deeply into our situation of struggle and sin and suffering—our "cruciform" reality with the dissolution and desolation that attend mortal, fragile, vulnerable life. A "crucified God" is a God who is really "*with us*." Joseph Sittler put it this way: "Unless you have a crucified God, you don't have a big enough God."[52]

Viewed in this light, the cross is no glorification of suffering. Instead it is an invitation. If we are "in the image of God," we also should manifest solidarity with the suffering, just as God has done in Jesus the Christ. This is an invitation to take up the cross and follow. We take up the cross, not because we seek to suffer, but because we seek to "stop the crucifixions" of our own context. We need this reclaimed message of the cross. José Pagola, in his book *The Way Opened Up by Jesus: A Commentary on the Gospel of Matthew*, summarizes themes from the theology of Johann Baptist Metz, who urged that we keep alive the dangerous

---

50. Jürgen Moltmann, *The Crucified God* (New York: Harper and Row, 1974), 205.
51. Whitehead, *Process and Reality*, 351.
52. Joseph Sittler, *Grace Notes and Other Fragments* (Minneapolis: Augsburg, 1981), 228.

memory of Jesus Christ and the dangerous memory of suffering. Metz warned that without the cross Christianity becomes a "bourgeois religion" that invents a more "convenient God," one that better fits into our agendas and better serves our interests. "The gospel is not a sedative."[53] Metz's provocative statement only works if we understand—as he does— that the cross calls us to struggle against suffering rather than to justify it or rationalize it.

Recentering Jesus' Resurrection in the Incarnation

When we recenter resurrection in incarnation, multiple considerations come into play. In taking up this topic we explore five questions in particular:

- What changes when we take an incarnational approach to resurrection?
- What do we make of the ambiguities around resurrection?
- What is the place of the resurrection for Christian faith?
- What is the import of the affirmation of resurrection *of the body*?
- How does resurrection function as part of God's saving work in the Christ event?

"Deep Resurrection"

In light of God's incarnation in the "Word made flesh" we have come to see material reality differently—apparently matter matters to God. Niels Gregersen has proposed the concept of "deep incarnation." God's incarnation in Christ reaches into the heart of material, biological, and social existence to the extent that God has conjoined the material conditions of creaturely existence ("all flesh") sharing in and ennobling the fate of all biological life-forms.[54] In this way God is seen to be in profound union with flesh—finite, fragile, and vulnerable as it is. If viewed in the light of deep incarnation, the expectation of resurrection is enlarged beyond the scope of human beings to embrace the whole of creation. In this way, deep incarnation flows into "deep resurrection." Resurrection is the first fruit of the transformation of *all things*, a "new creation," cosmic in scope.

---

53. José Pagola, *The Way Opened Up by Jesus: A Commentary on the Gospel of Matthew* (Miami, FL: Convivium, 2012), 109.

54. Niels Gregersen, "Deep Incarnation: Why Evolutionary Continuity Matters in Christology," *Toronto Journal of Theology* 26, no. 2 (2010): 174–81.

Resurrection of the body and the promise of new creation are inextrica-bly connected. As Ambrose of Milan affirmed, "In Christ's resurrection the earth itself arose."[55] Deep resurrection implies that Jesus' resurrec-tion not only began the anticipated "resurrection of the dead" but also inaugurated the all-inclusive transformation envisioned in the concept of the "new creation" or "a new heaven and a new earth." As this trans-formation comes to fruition, all things are reconciled to God (Greek: ἀποκαταλλάσσω [*apokatallassō*]) as referenced in Colossians 1:20 and all things are reconstituted or restored (Greek: ἀποκατάστασις [*apokatasta-sis*]) as referenced in Acts 3:21.

All things that exist are brought into being by divine love (*creatio ex amore*),[56] all things are upheld in their being by love, and all things will find their fruition in love. Pauline theology makes a connection between divine creative power in the beginning and divine creative power in the end. It is the same loving, creative God who both "gives life to the dead and calls into existence the things that do not exist" (Rom. 4:17). Molt-mann points out that hope for the final fulfillment of all things is "nothing other than faith in the Creator with its eyes turned toward the future."[57] These insights echo those of cosmic Christology, which so seamlessly connects the creation and the consummation of all things: The one in whom all things were created and in whom "the fullness of God was pleased to dwell" is the one in whom all things are reconciled to God (Col. 1:15–20).

Within this larger picture, however, between creation and consumma-tion there is still the very real problem of mortality. Death is universal; all living beings die. Holmes Rolston has pointed out that nature itself is "cruciform."

> Long before humans arrived, the way of nature was already a *via dolorosa*. In that sense, the aura of the cross is cast backwards across the whole global story, and it forever outlines the future. . . . The story is a passion play long before it reaches the Christ. Since the beginning, the myriad creatures have been giving up their lives as

---

55. Ambrose of Milan, *On the Death of Satyrus*, book 2, paragraph 102. A further elaboration can be found at https://www.newadvent.org/fathers/34032.htm: ". . . He had no need to rise for Himself. The universe rose again in Him, the heaven rose again in Him, the earth rose again in Him, for there shall be a new heaven and a new earth. Revelation 21:1."

56. Paul Fiddes, "Creation out of Love," in *The Work of Love: Creation as Kenosis*, ed. John Polkinghorne (Grand Rapids: Eerdmans, 2001).

57. Jürgen Moltmann, *God in Creation* (San Francisco: Harper and Row, 1985), 93.

a ransom for many. In that sense, Jesus is not the exception to the natural order but a chief exemplification of it.[58]

Biologically speaking, new life is continuously coming from death. This is the reality of creaturely existence in both its vulnerable reality and its life-giving potential. The ambiguity of creaturely existence is everywhere apparent. With resurrection in view, however, the eyes of faith see a new reality breaking in. Elizabeth Johnson puts it this way:

> Theologically speaking, without diluting the affliction with facile hope, the language of faith can dare to say that the encompassing mystery enacted in Jesus Christ through the Spirit bears creation forward with an unimaginable promise toward a final fulfillment when "God will be all in all" (1 Cor. 15:28).[59]

Jesus' resurrection represents the first fruits of the hoped-for restoration of all things in deep resurrection. This matter of deep resurrection is taken up again in chapter 6 when we further explore the proposal that "God with us" does not mean just us human beings. In what follows here we focus primarily on what resurrection means for human beings.

The Ambiguities around the Resurrection

The challenge of an embodied or incarnational understanding of resurrection has to do with plausibility. Contemporary theology has confronted the difficulty of affirming the resurrection as a historical event. Some, as a result, have taken the turn of "demythologizing" the resurrection, speaking of it as, for example, the "rising of faith within the early church." While the event of resurrection is surely "mythic" in the sense of being *more than* historical, I do not believe the historical moorings should be laid aside altogether.

There are many considerations. For starters, there is the testimony about the "empty tomb." This, in itself, does not give much to go on. Even the guards and the chief priests know the tomb is empty. Testimony that the tomb was empty has evoked alternative accountings. In Matthew 28:11–15, the guards are paid to spread one of these alternative

---

58. Holmes Rolston, "Cruciform Nature," in *The Work of Love: Creation as Kenosis*, ed. John Polkinghorne (Grand Rapids: Eerdmans, 2001), 60.

59. Johnson, *Ask the Beasts*, 227.

accounts. The guards are to say that while they were asleep in the night, the disciples came and stole the body. Other alternatives are also proposed. Some say that Jesus was not really dead when he was placed in the tomb or that he was resuscitated and walked out. Matthew's notation concerning the great stone (27:60) and the posted guard (27:62–66) seem to rule out this alternative account. Most remarkable is the proposal that it was simply the wrong tomb and Jesus' remains are still there if we could but find the right tomb.

Wolfhart Pannenberg was theologically committed to the historicity of the resurrection. He insisted that one cannot judge what is possible by the constraints of what has already happened in the past. Nothing new can happen under those constraints. If something new in fact happens, it must be judged to be possible. Pannenberg suggested that the best approach in thinking about the resurrection's historicity is to shift attention from the empty tomb to the experience of the risen Christ in the early church. He takes note of the many witnesses and their accountings.

Interestingly, the earliest texts do not hide the ambiguities inherent in the experience of the risen Lord. In the Gospel of Matthew, even when Jesus meets the disciples in Galilee, "some doubted" (28:17). In the shorter ending of Mark, upon finding the tomb empty and hearing the news of resurrection, the women flee from the tomb in terror and amazement and say nothing to anyone (16:8). In the longer ending, Mary Magdalene does tell the disciples the news of resurrection, but the text notes that "they would not believe it" (Mark 16:11). In the Gospel of John, Thomas doubts the news of resurrection. He says, "Unless I see . . . I will not believe" (20:25). The Gospel of Luke reports that the disciples are "disbelieving and still wondering" (24:41).

Among the most compelling evidence of the resurrection has been the transformation in Jesus' followers after his death. In the midst of Jesus' passion, the disciples desert him and flee (Matt. 26:56). However exemplary the life of Jesus had been, and however much faith he had evoked in the disciples, the passion and crucifixion posed a crisis. They abandoned him to it, their hopes in him as Messiah were at an end. It was the end of *him*. He became one more martyr executed by Rome in occupied territory; this was nothing new. "Peculiar to Christianity is the fact that what would normally be the end of the story turned unexpectedly into a new beginning as the community of disciples proclaimed that he was risen from the dead."[60]

60. Johnson, *Ask the Beasts*, 193.

Something took hold of this sorrowing band of deniers and deserters and welded them together, more certain and committed than ever. They went forward in an unprecedented missionary movement. The disciples respond to the crisis of Jesus' death and the death of their hopes in him with strengthened faith and missionary zeal. How can this be? It is a completely inexplicable response—enigmatic apart from the explanation the believers themselves offer.

It is one thing to affirm the resurrection but quite another to claim to know exactly what resurrection *is*. No one captured this on video. The texts we have are remarkably silent on the "moment" of resurrection or its detailed description. The texts seem more intent upon its reality and its meaning than painting a picture of its occurrence.

Believers today are in the position of those who "'have not seen and yet have come to believe'" (John 20:29). Like the early witnesses, even doubting and fearing as we do, many of us encounter the risen Lord along the way. When that happens, perhaps we do not need to see the empty tomb to know the Lord is risen.

The Centrality of the Resurrection

With the ambiguities in full view, the resurrection remains at the very center of Christian faith. In the memorial acclamation the people gathered for Communion attest,

> Christ has died,
> Christ is risen,
> Christ will come again.

The resurrection is the foundation of the church and the focus of its eschatological hope. Although the Eastern church has given more attention to incarnation than resurrection, and the Western church has given more attention to the cross than the resurrection, this secondary status was not the case in the early church. Resurrection was perhaps the central symbol and certainly a primary symbol for God's saving work in Christ. In 1 Corinthians 15:17, Paul insists, "If Christ has not been raised, your faith is futile and you are still in your sins." To say this is to attach redemptive significance to the resurrection and to assume that the cross does not complete God's saving work.

Matthew's accounting of the resurrection treats it as a cataclysmic event of eschatological importance (28:1–10). It is the beginning of the general resurrection anticipated at the end time. It is also anticipated in the Hebrew Scriptures (Isa. 26:19; Dan. 12:2). This hope is grounded in the conviction that God, who is the giver of life, holds the power of life and death (Job 1:21; Deut. 32:39) and that even the dead are not lost to God.

> Where can I go from your spirit?
>   Or where can I flee from your presence?
> If I ascend to heaven, you are there;
>   if I make my bed in Sheol, you are there.
>   (Ps. 139:7–8)

God is God of the living and the dead.

Resurrection as such would not have been a strange concept in Matthew's context, given this understanding of belonging to God in life and in death and the eschatological hope of a general resurrection. However, for the firstborn from the dead to be someone who was rejected by the religious authorities and crucified by the political authorities as a common criminal was completely unexpected. Nevertheless, Jesus' resurrection was understood by the early church as divine validation of his person and work—confirmation that he was indeed the Messiah, in spite of his rejection by the religious authorities and his crucifixion by the political authorities. His resurrection is the first installment on the general resurrection, the inauguration of the age to come.

Resurrection of the Body

An incarnational approach to resurrection underscores the affirmation of resurrection of *the body*. This understanding is in stark contrast to the Greek philosophical belief in the "immortality of the soul." There is a significant difference between these alternatives. The philosophical dualism from Plato forward divides soul from body and presumes that the soul is "an inherently indestructible element of human life which is separable from the mortal, corruptible body that it temporarily inhabits."[61] For Plato, the body is, in fact, the prison-house of the soul. Death sets the soul free from the lifeless corpse at death.

---

61. Daniel Migliore, *Faith Seeking Understanding: An Introduction to Christian Theology*, 2nd ed. (Grand Rapids: Eerdmans, 2004), 243.

In affirming "resurrection of the body," the dualistic understanding of the human being is roundly rejected in favor of a more holistic understanding. God's saving work is not a matter of setting the immortal soul free from its prison-house in the body. The whole self, "dust and breath together," is redeemed and transformed in the resurrection of the body.

This vision is more closely aligned with the Genesis 2:7 account of the creation of the human as a "living being" (Hebrew: נפש חיה [*npš ḥyh*]). A human being is not a material body inhabited by a spiritual soul; embodiment is part of who we essentially are. This perspective rings true to how we actually experience ourselves. As Whitehead observed, no one ever says, "Here I am, and I have brought my body with me."[62] In the resurrection of the body, the whole self receives the gift of life.

Affirmation of resurrection of the body makes a profound difference theologically. "Immortality of the soul" assumes that souls possess immortality as an inherent quality, which is very different from a vision of God bringing new life where there was death. Resurrection of the body is God's doing. It is a gift—not a given.

Accounts of the resurrection participate in the same dynamic of continuity-discontinuity that attends Christian eschatology generally. For example, the hope for a "*new* creation" (discontinuity) is nevertheless still a hope for a *creation* (continuity). This is an example of what Michael Welker and John Polkinghorne have called the "strange logic of eschatology."[63] This kind of continuity-discontinuity that characterizes Christian eschatology generally shows itself particularly in resurrection.

The New Testament accounts depict a human body significantly transformed. There is reference to a "spiritual body" in Pauline writings (1 Cor. 15:44). In the Gospel of Matthew, Jesus' resurrected body walks and talks and travels (28:8–20). Matthew gives the explicit detail of the women who met Jesus on the way taking "hold of his feet" (28:9)—this is a body that has feet. In the Gospel of John, Jesus cooks and eats breakfast (21:9–13), yet he also passes through walls (20:19). His scars are visible (20:24–28) yet he is not always recognizable to those closest to him. In the story of Mary Magdalene at the tomb in John's Gospel, Mary thinks Jesus is the gardener until he calls her by name (20:11–18). In Luke 24, two disciples on the road to Emmaus walk with Jesus all day but do not recognize him

---

62. Alfred North Whitehead, *Modes of Thought* (1938; repr., New York: Free Press, 1968), 114.

63. Michael Welker and John Polkinghorne, introduction to *The End of the World and the Ends of God: Science and Theology on Eschatology*, ed. John Polkinghorne and Michael Welker (Harrisburg, PA: Trinity Press, 2000), 12.

until their eyes are opened in the breaking of the bread (vv. 30–31). He shares a meal of bread and broiled fish (24:42–43) with them.

These accountings are altogether strange. Such a transformation is at least as unimaginable as the full-grown oak would be from examining the acorn from which it began. Affirming the resurrection is one thing. Understanding what it is, is quite another. Faced with these ambiguous images, Daniel Migliore observes, "Even if we cannot adequately conceive of a resurrection body, the symbol stands as a bold and even defiant affirmation of God's total, inclusive, holistic redemption."[64] The central conviction here is well expressed by Jürgen Moltmann: "Death is the boundary of our lives, but not the boundary of God's relationship with us."[65]

Process theology[66] envisions two aspects of an ongoing relationship with God beyond this life. First, there is what might be called "objective immortality" for us in the trajectory of the ongoing *effects* of our lives in the world. Furthermore, our effects in the world are at the same time effects in the divine life. In the process-panentheist vision of the God-world relation, God is continuously experiencing the world and its process *internally*, moment by moment, event by event. Everything we do and are has effects and significance in the divine life. Our joy contributes to God's own joy. Our sorrow is nowhere more felt than in God's own being. Things do not simply "perish," but rather God acts with "tender care that nothing of value be lost." There is also the prospect of "subjective immortality" because, just as we (even now) live our lives "in God," so also we will be "in God" when we die. God is the one in whom "we live and move and have our being" (Acts 17:28). In that sense, we even now participate in God's everlasting life.

The meaning of resurrection, however it is understood, is God's gift of new life in the face of death and all that hurts or destroys us. That meaning has been variously interpreted. We close this section with two contrasting interpretations. Karl Barth proposes that death, as such, is not the primary problem. Mortality is only the "shadowside" of life and is not in itself genuinely evil. Death may even place a "salutary limit to life."[67] Rather, our lives as we live them make a problem of death. "The sting of

64. Migliore, *Faith Seeking Understanding*, 244.

65. Jürgen Moltmann, "Is There Life after Death?," in *The End of the World and the Ends of God: Science and Theology on Eschatology*, ed. John Polkinghorne and Michael Welker (Harrisburg, PA: Trinity Press, 2000), 246.

66. Whitehead, *Process and Reality*, 352ff.

67. Karl Barth, *Church Dogmatics*, III/2, *The Doctrine of Creation*, trans. Geoffrey W. Bromiley (Edinburgh: T. & T. Clark, 1956), 553–72.

death is sin" (1 Cor. 15:56). Eberhard Jüngel, drawing out Barth's view, says that "the shadow cast by death (over human life) is no more than the haunting primordial shadow, now extended and magnified, which our life casts upon our ending."[68]

Miroslav Volf counters this point of view and insists that both sin and death, "transience and transgression," overshadow us in life and death.[69] Transience keeps us ever in a state of disruption. "Our present is not at peace with our past and future. We feel anxiety about what we expect and carry the burden of what we remember, and are thus robbed of an unattenuated joy in the present."[70] We need the assurance that, in the resurrection of the body, death will be destroyed. The resurrection narrative tells of the creative power of divine love "triumphing over the crucifying power of evil and the burying power of death."[71]

God's Saving Work: Setting Free

Many dimensions of meaning convey God's saving work in resurrection. The principalities and powers have done their worst in the crucifixion, and now in the resurrection, their impotence is unveiled. Suffering and death do not have the last word; God has the last word. God is the one who restores the dead to life. Resurrection also signals divine validation of the way Jesus lived. His salvific role as exemplar is confirmed. This is the life that God affirms and intends for human beings.

Two models for understanding God's saving work rely on resurrection as the central symbol. In each, our human predicament is likened to imprisonment or slavery from which we cannot extricate ourselves. Our situation is utterly helpless and hopeless. The power of evil has a death grip on us. In the resurrection we see the sign that God has, in Christ, broken the power of evil in our lives and we are set free from sin, death, and the devil. Our captivity is taken captive; death is done to death. For the *Christus Victor* theory and the ransom theory of the atonement, resurrection is the central symbol. They share the same understanding of the human predicament but make use of different metaphors to illumine how

68. Eberhard Jüngel, *Death: The Riddle and the Mystery*, trans. Iain and Ute Nicol (Philadelphia: Westminster, 1974), 74–75.

69. Miroslav Volf, "Enter into Joy," in *The End of the World and the Ends of God: Science and Theology on Eschatology*, ed. John Polkinghorne and Michael Welker (Harrisburg, PA: Trinity Press, 2000), 274.

70. Volf, "Enter into Joy," 275.

71. Anthony Kelly, *Eschatology and Hope* (Maryknoll, NY: Orbis Books, 2006), 85.

the resurrection breaks the power of evil and sets free those who are held in its bondage.

The *Christus Victor* theory uses military images. God and the devil are pictured as locked in combat over the destiny of humankind. Christ is seen as the warrior of God, who, after having been apparently defeated on the cross, by his death invades the realm of the evil one. In this descent into hell he does battle with sin, death, and the devil. When God raises Jesus from the dead, death is "swallowed up in victory" (1 Cor. 15:54). This represents the liberation of human beings from the power of sin, death, and the devil. In Jesus' resurrection he leads out from captivity all those who had been carried off. Sin and death and the devil are put "under his feet" as God overcomes and becomes "all in all" (1 Cor. 15:25–28).

The ransom theory draws upon the metaphor of financial payment. "Redemption" is itself a financial image. In this model, the human condition is compared to slavery or imprisonment. Jesus gives his life as a "ransom" to redeem the enslaved and imprisoned (Matt. 20:28). Origen articulated this model of the atonement, which was prominent in the early church. It was based on the practice of ransoming of captives of war who had been enslaved. The theory was also connected with Mark 10:45 and 1 Timothy 2:5–6, where Jesus and Paul mention the word "ransom" in the context of God's saving work.

Origen was the first to propose the ransom theory of atonement in its fully developed form. In short, because of their sin, human beings are in bondage, captive to death and the devil. Jesus procures salvation by giving himself up to death. In a "glorious exchange," he is taken captive and sinners are set free from their captivity to death and the devil. However, being free from sin (and being God incarnate), death could not hold him. In Origen's dramatic presentation, God tricks Satan in the exchange. Later thinkers did not necessarily bring a Satan figure into the picture. Athanasius, for example, speaks instead of Jesus eliminating death with his own death, since the power of death cannot hold God—the God of life—captive. Death is done to death. Gustaf Aulén, in his book *Christus Victor*,[72] has suggested that the meaning of the ransom theory should not be taken in terms of a business transaction (with one party receiving payment), but rather as the emancipation of human beings from the bondage of sin and death. The resurrection is the sign that the work is done; the transaction is complete. The slaves and prisoners are free.

72. Gustav Aulén, *Christus Victor* (1931; repr., Eugene, OR: Wipf & Stock, 2003).

Beyond the ransom theory and the *Christus Victor* theory, there is another sense in which resurrection is a "setting free." Resurrection fills Jesus' followers with hope that gives courage to join in God's work of resistance against all that would hurt or destroy. The human problematic is larger than personal sin, as social systems and structures of injustice and oppression also pose a threat to well-being and to life. Marcus Borg refers to a "domination system" and connects these dramatic theories of the atonement with being set free from this destructive system of domination. As he says of the *Christus Victor* theory of the atonement, "The domination system, understood as something much larger than the Roman governor and the temple aristocracy, is responsible for the death of Jesus. . . . The domination system killed Jesus and thereby disclosed its moral bankruptcy and ultimate defeat."[73]

Resurrection hope overcomes all "hopelessness in the face of present trouble, complacent inactivity regarding suffering and injustice, and irresponsible self-concern."[74] In Jesus the Christ, God's reign has come near; now the old order can no longer be tolerated. We are people called to transformed lives befitting the reign of God. We participate in God's work of resistance "with an urgency born of this hope."[75] This entails following in the way of Jesus (Matt. 10:38–39) and risking the consequences of faithful discipleship. We walk by faith and not by sight, hoping for what we have not yet seen. Resurrection reminds us that we serve the God of life who is able to bring life to the places where injustice and violence destroy life.

Conclusion

Here we have recentered aspects of the Christ event in the incarnation and shown the difference this makes. We have also explored multiple illuminating visions and metaphors for understanding how God's saving work is accomplished in Christ. Each one of these has its limits and cannot be applied exclusively or literally. Yet each in its own way shines a ray of light on a reality that is (and remains) a mystery beyond all comprehension. It may be that the misunderstandings of the cross that were shared in the

73. Marcus Borg, *The Heart of Christianity* (San Francisco: Harper, 2003), 95.

74. Kathryn Tanner, "Eschatology without a Future?," in *The End of the World and the Ends of God: Science and Theology on Eschatology*, ed. John Polkinghorne and Michael Welker (Harrisburg, PA: Trinity Press, 2000), 226.

75. "Confession of 1967," *Book of Confessions* (Louisville, KY: Office of the General Assembly, Presbyterian Church (U.S.A.), 1999), 9.55.

beginning of this chapter are a result of taking one moment in the Christ event and one particular metaphor for God's saving work and absolutizing them. If this one moment and this one metaphor are allowed to stand for the whole of the Christ event and its full meaning, there is risk of distortion, as sometimes happens with the cross and the sacrificial/substitutionary theory of the atonement, which have been prominent understandings. Working from a fuller range of the alternative perspectives within the tradition, as we have done here, helps to correct this practice.

Reflecting on the four aspects of the Christ event reconceived incarnationally, I would observe that one thing we see in these moments and metaphors is divine saving work as both solidarity and resistance. Divine solidarity is conveyed in "God with us" standing alongside us in our sin and suffering. Divine resistance is conveyed in "God with us" standing against the powers of death and all that would hurt or destroy us. We tend to associate solidarity with the cross and resistance with resurrection. However, solidarity and resistance both pervade each aspect of the Christ event.

Jesus' birth narrative in Matthew carries the fundamental affirmation of Emmanuel, "God is with us"—the strongest statement of solidarity (1:23). At the same time, the birth narratives make clear that this newborn baby poses a threat to Herod and signals the prospect of an alternative reign over against Roman empirical rule (Matt. 2). Resistance is already in the picture at his birth.

The life and ministry of Jesus demonstrate solidarity with us, especially with those at the margins—the least, the last, and the lost. At the same time Jesus' life and ministry demonstrate resistance by instigating change in the circumstances of people at the margins. A major focus of Jesus' ministry is about bodily well-being. There were many stories of healing: "The good news became ever more concrete when lepers' lesions were closed; a mentally deranged man was restored to his senses; a hemorrhaging woman had her bleeding stopped; a blind man began to see; a bent over woman stood up straight."[76] Many other stories were about feeding people—large crowds on hillsides and sharing meals in intimate gatherings in homes. Much of Jesus' table fellowship was with social outcasts, including prostitutes and tax collectors; he treated outsiders as insiders. Those who were his table companions "knew firsthand his desire to nourish hungry bodies as well as thirsty spirits."[77] Among

76. Johnson, *Ask the Beasts*, 200.
77. Johnson, *Ask the Beasts*, 201.

people in situations of oppression he demonstrates nonviolent resistance to oppressors. He teaches that the ones in need (thirsty, sick, and imprisoned people) matter in God's judgment (Matt. 25). The last are first; the lost are found. Those who were excluded now are included; outsiders become insiders. There is powerful resistance inherent in these dramatic reversals; people's embodied existence already matters to Jesus.

In the cross, the first word is solidarity—Jesus with us in our sin and suffering and our experiences of God-forsakenness. The cross manifests, at the same time, a peculiar kind of resistance. God in Christ on the cross exercises the paradoxical power of suffering love. Matthew conveys the consequential effects of this power using dramatic, apocalyptic symbols. The Earth quakes and rocks are split and the temple curtain is torn from top to bottom (Matt. 27:51–52).

In the resurrection, the first word is resistance—God in Christ overcoming all that hurts and destroys. God defeating death, the last enemy. If the first word about resurrection is resistance, the last word surely returns to solidarity. In Matthew's Gospel, the risen Lord announces, "I am with you always, to the end of the age'" (28:20). This Gospel that begins with Emmanuel, "God is with us" (1:23), ends with "I am with you always" (28:20). Perhaps this is the main thing to say about the meaning of incarnation.

Chapter 6

When We Say "God Is with Us," What Do We Mean by "Us"?

We explore in this chapter three issues arising from current realities and ponder how incarnation connects with these questions. All three are rather directly related to the matter of incarnation and its implications. This chapter asks what we might mean by "us" when we say "God is with us." What is the scope of incarnation? How wide is the divine embrace? The following specific questions are addressed:

- In our contemporary context of religious pluralism, we are pressed to ask, does God with "us" mean only us Christians? Do Christian claims about incarnation lock us into an unavoidable exclusivism? Does the incarnation in Jesus of Nazareth mean that God's self-revelation has happened *only* in him and not in other times and places?
- In the face of the hard realities of our current eco-crisis, does God with "us" mean only us human beings? Is incarnation irreducibly anthropocentric?
- Science daily discovers new exoplanets in what we think of as zones habitable for life. What if we should discover other forms of life out there in the wider cosmos? Does incarnation mean that God is with them too?

Only Us Christians?

Reconsidering Exclusivism from an Incarnational Perspective

In our contemporary context of religious pluralism, we are pressed to ask, Does God with "us" mean only us Christians? Do Christian claims about incarnation lock us into an unavoidable exclusivism? Does the incarnation in Jesus of Nazareth mean that God's self-revelation has happened only in him and not in other times and places? The understanding of incarnation that we have been articulating here allows affirmation of God in Christ with the full wealth of conviction while allowing that God's self-revelation and self-giving is not limited. Such exclusivism may be shown to be problematic in a number of ways.

First, exclusivism is problematic theologically. It treats what happens in Jesus of Nazareth as if it were an exception to God's ordinary way of being and acting. Chapter 2 made a case for panentheism—that all things are in God, and God is in all things. Divine presence and activity in Jesus the Christ are not exceptions to God's ordinary way of being. On the contrary they *decisively exemplify* God's presence and activity everywhere and always. Process thought offers a pointed critique of the theological habit of making divine being and acting an exception to all metaphysical principles. God should rather be thought of as their chief exemplification.

If we understand the incarnation as a decisive exemplification of God's ordinary and ongoing presence and action in the world—rather than as an exception to it—then we may be delivered from exclusivist claims. It becomes possible to affirm God's presence, self-revelation, and action in Jesus the Christ with the full wealth of conviction, without presuming that this is the only locus of divine presence, self-revelation, and action. We may say that in him we see one who is "wholly" divine without claiming that he is "the whole" of the divine. He is "all God" (Latin: *totus*), but not "all of God" (Latin: *totem*). To use a mundane illustration, one might say that although San Francisco Bay is "all ocean," it is not "all of the ocean." Reformed tradition is helpful in making this point as it affirms that the second person of the Trinity, the divine Logos in the Incarnation, was present in the flesh of Jesus of Nazareth and beyond. The Logos did not cease to fill heaven and Earth during Jesus' life; it was not dissolved, nor did it disappear into him. Lutherans disagree and in the seventeenth century referred to this understanding derisively as the *extra calvinisticum* (that Calvinist extra [!]). Nevertheless, it is a view that Reformed folk embrace, and one that helps to frame the position we take here.[1]

This orientation reframes incarnation as an instance of transparency to divine presence and action—not an exception to it. Again, as Arthur Peacocke has observed, "The Word which was before *incognito*, implicit, and hidden, now becomes known, explicit, and revealed."[2] What we see in the incarnation is echoed in the sacrament of Communion. "Jesus identified the mode of his incarnation and reconciliation of God and humanity ('his body and blood') with the very stuff of the universe when he took the bread, blessed, broke, and gave it to his disciples."[3] Joseph Bracken summarizes approvingly the earlier work of Gustave Martelet, who believed that "the far deeper truth about the doctrine of the Real Presence is that not just bread and wine but all of creation, including the world of nature, are collectively becoming the Body of Christ."[4] Bracken views this as a progressive integration into the divine field of activity with the passage of time. Taken seriously, a notion of divine *real presence* in incarnation and reiterated in sacrament must entail a re-valuation of all material reality as open to and indwelt by the divine. The whole creation is transparent to the divine, so Jesus is not an exception in this regard. Instead his life is a maximal manifestation of divine presence and activity.

As pointed out in chapter 2, this approach to incarnation has the potential to resolve the supposed contradiction in affirming that God was "in" Jesus of Nazareth. The world's presence in God and God's presence in the world are already the fundamental reality. Incarnation manifests this reality and brings it into view. What happens in the man, Jesus of Nazareth, is emblematic of what is *already the case* for all creation. We here mention again the insight of Arthur Peacocke, who expressed the meaning of the incarnation in this way:

1. These lines of difference can be traced through Lutheran and Reformed disagreements around the nature of the incarnation and of Christ's presence in the Eucharist. Both hold that God is present everywhere (in the incarnation and in the Eucharist), but the nature of that presence is seen differently. The Reformed hold that "the finite cannot contain the infinite" (Latin: *finitum non capax infiniti*). A point of clarification, though: presence is not the same thing as containment. Lutherans, by contrast, hold that the finite can contain the infinite (*finitim capax infiniti*) and speak of a local physical presence in the elements of the Eucharist.

2. Arthur Peacocke, *Paths from Science towards God: The End of All Our Exploring* (Oxford: One World, 2001), 154.

3. Peacocke, *Paths from Science towards God*, 149.

4. Joseph Bracken, *Christianity and Process Thought: Spirituality for a Changing World* (Philadelphia: Templeton, 2006), 102.

The incarnation can thus be more explicitly and overtly understood as the God *in whom the world already exists* becoming manifest in the trajectory of a human being who is naturally in and of that world. In that person the world now becomes transparent, as it were, to the God in whom it exists: The Word which was before *incognito*, implicit, and hidden, now becomes known, explicit, and revealed. The epic of evolution has reached its apogee and consummation in God-in-a-human-person.[5]

In this sense when we speak of "the Incarnation" we are describing an instance of transparency to a deeper reality. The meaning of the Christian theology of incarnation has not yet been tapped for its deeper significance in conveying God's pervasive presence in world process with all its implications for our valuation of material reality.

In Jesus of Nazareth there is a responsiveness to divine initial aims, such that in him we are able to see what God intends and is doing everywhere and always. We see that God is in, with, and for the world. God's intentions and actions for each and for all become transparent in Jesus the Christ. Here is a place where the light shines through. As Allan Galloway put it, "Once we have encountered God in Christ, we must encounter God in all things."[6]

Understanding the incarnation in this way helps Christians to be genuinely open in interreligious dialogue, to receive as well as to share the good news of God. We can move beyond the presumption of thinking that "God with us" means only us Christians. To say that Christians have come to know God in Jesus the Christ is one thing; it is quite another to claim to know that this is the only place of God's presence, self-revelation, and activity. Humility before Holy Mystery invites us to a fitting reticence concerning the ways of God with other people. Who can circumscribe the scope of divine presence and activity?

This open stance is not simply a function of the contemporary experience of a religiously pluralistic context. Through the centuries, streams of thought in Christian tradition have pointed in this direction. One such stream, by way of example, is the Second Helvetic Confession

5. Arthur Peacocke, "Articulating God's Presence in and to the World Unveiled by the Sciences," in *In Whom We Live and Move and Have Our Being: Panentheistic Reflections on God's Presence in a Scientific World*, ed. Philip Clayton and Arthur Peacocke (Grand Rapids: Eerdmans, 2004), 154.
6. Allan Galloway, *The Cosmic Christ* (New York: Harper Brothers, 1951), 250.

(SHC),[7] a sixteenth-century Reformed confession written by Swiss reformer Heinrich Bullinger. While the confession has some ambiguities, there is also a surprising openness. Bullinger's context did not include today's religious pluralism, but the question he did ask was what about those who are not in the church, or those who, through no fault of their own, never heard the gospel? What about Moses, for example? These questions would have vexed sixteenth-century Christians, and they are not unlike our own. On the one hand, echoing Cyprian, the SHC reiterates a view that "outside the church there is no salvation." On the other hand, there is a recognized difference between the visible and the "invisible" church (5.137), and the latter is "known only to God." Bullinger notes that, in the Hebrew Bible; it is clear that "God had some friends in the world outside the commonwealth of Israel" (5.137). He has a sense that we ourselves cannot draw the boundaries of the church. This sensibility runs deep in Christian theology. Augustine, acknowledging this point, said of the church, "There are many sheep without, and many wolves are within."[8] Any of us who have worked in the church for very long can recognize these sentiments.

On the one hand, the SHC says, "So we teach and believe that this Jesus Christ our Lord is the unique and eternal Savior of the human race, and thus of the whole world" (5.077). On the other hand (and this is a continuation of the same sentence!), "in whom by faith are saved all who before the law, under the law, and under the Gospel were saved, and however many will be saved at the end of the world" (5.077). It would appear that people who never even heard of Moses ("before the law"), much less of Jesus, are included. "God can illuminate whom and where [God] will, even without the external ministry, for that is in [God's] power" (5.007). Therefore, we are cautioned, "We must not judge rashly or prematurely . . . nor undertake to exclude, reject, or cut off those whom the Lord does not want to have excluded" (5.140); we should rather "have a good hope for all" (5.055). The openness we see in this centuries-old text is remarkable for its time and loosens the grip of exclusivism in helpful ways, inspiring a more humble attitude as we engage interreligious relations and cooperation today.

7. *The Constitution of the Presbyterian Church (U.S.A.)*, Part I, *Book of Confessions* (Louisville, KY: Office of the General Assembly, Presbyterian Church (U.S.A.), 2004).

8. Augustine, *John's Gospel*, 10:16, *Nicene and Post-Nicene Fathers*, vol. 7, ed. Philip Schaff (1885; repr., Grand Rapids: Eerdmans, 2001), 235.

Incarnational Ethics: Practical Implications
for Interreligious Relations and Cooperation

If we are committed to incarnational ethics (as outlined in chapter 4), it matters how a theological doctrine affects our life together. We have stressed that one of the implications of incarnation is that bodies matter, and matter (the material world) matters. How a belief system causes one to act in the world must be part of the assessment of the moral adequacy of that belief system. If the outworking does not help us work together for the fullness of life of all and join in a shared struggle for the fate of the Earth, then its moral adequacy is in question. Exclusivism seems to impede rather than further this work together. It hampers our efforts in interreligious understanding and cooperation in common work for the common good. How can such a position be religiously viable?

Exclusivism has often been an obstacle and an offense in interreligious encounters. A case in point is how people of other religions responded to the exclusivist claims of Pope John Paul II in *Crossing the Threshold of Hope*. A representative example is the statement,

> *Christ is absolutely original and absolutely unique.* If He were only a wise man like Socrates, if He were a "prophet" like Muhammad, if He were "enlightened" like Buddha, without any doubt He would not be what He is. He is *the one mediator between God and humanity.*[9]

Buddhist monk and Thich Nhat Hanh countered,

> Of course Christ is unique. But who is not unique? Socrates, Muhammed, the Buddha, you and I are all unique. The idea behind the statement, however, is the notion that Christianity provides the only way of salvation and all other religious traditions are of no use. This attitude excludes dialogue and fosters religious intolerance and discrimination. It does not help.[10]

Thich Nhat Hanh encourages the honest recognition of similarities and differences among religions in a climate of mutual respect. He uses the metaphor of an orange and a mango. It is good that an orange is an orange and a mango is mango. Both may have bad places, but we do not

9. John Paul II, *Crossing the Threshold of Hope* (New York: Knopf, 1994), 42–43.
10. Thich Nhat Hanh, *Living Buddha, Living Christ* (New York: Riverhead Books, 1995), 193.

say that one is not a "true fruit." Looking deeply into the orange and the mango, we see the sunshine, the rain, and the Earth in each of them—even though their manifestations are different. Dialogue is fruitful if both sides are open and believe there are valuable elements in each other's tradition. The process may even help them to rediscover valuable aspects of their own traditions. Nhat Hanh concludes, "this situation calls for more understanding. . . . Understanding and love are values that transcend all dogma."[11]

It is important for religious traditions to be who they are and honest about their differences in interreligious dialogue. The tension any particular doctrine creates may not be, in and of itself, a reason to lay it aside. However, we have made the case already that exclusivism should be reconsidered *on theological grounds*—not just because it gives offense.

Now we turn to consider implications of the incarnation in relation to ethical outworking. If incarnation means that bodies matter, we have to grapple with a long and shameful history of religiously motivated or religiously associated acts of violence. To mention the Crusades, the inquisitions, the witch burnings, and the pogroms is only to make a beginning. In our own day, religious minorities in many locations around the globe are oppressed, persecuted, and victimized by hate crimes. In several locations, oppression is so extreme that religious minorities are forced to flee their homes and homelands for their own safety.

Sentiment about religion today is mixed given these dynamics—and rightly so. A representative of the International Monetary Fund (IMF) shared a troubling story in this connection.[12] She had tried to persuade the IMF ethics committee that it would be good to include a religious leader or two. She received a very negative response. In short, she was told that in fully modern, secular contexts, religion is defunct, and in the places where it still exists it is divisive and dangerous. "Defunct," "divisive," and "dangerous"—the press is not good on religion in our day. Unfortunately, it has reason for negative assessment. The acid comment of Jonathan Swift seems very much to the point: "We have just enough religion to hate . . . but not enough to love one another."[13]

We can do better. The world needs religious folks to do better. What would that look like? For Christians, biblical and theological foundations

---

11. Nhat Hanh, *Living Buddha*, 195.

12. Lois Gehr Livesey, "Ethics and Globalization," McCormick Theological Seminary, unpublished panel presentation, fall 2005.

13. Jonathan Swift, *Thoughts on Various Subjects Moral and Diverting*, in *The Works of Jonathan Swift*, *D.D.* (Edinburgh: Archibald Constable and Co., 1814), 9:431.

invite us into deepened interreligious engagement and cooperation. Fundamental to our understanding is the conviction that God "so loves the world" (not just us Christians). Our discussion in chapter 3 contended that our being created "in the image of God" is most manifest when we give a "true reflection" of God. If God loves the world, then we should too. This would include and not exclude religious others. This conclusion is consonant with the Christian calling, "You shall love your neighbor as yourself" (Matt. 22:39). The religious other is not an exception. We love our neighbor—religion and all.

Another relevant consideration is the Christian calling to share the good news that we have received. That can be an important part of interreligious engagement and cooperation. This sharing happens in a spirit of humility, openness, and mutuality. We should be prepared to receive good news in this exchange. Perhaps the best approach is to enter with a holy curiosity about the religious other, what they believe, and how they live. The sharing may be as much in what we do and how we relate to the other as it is in the words we say. Advice popularly attributed to St. Francis of Assisi urges, "Preach the gospel at all times, and if necessary use words."

We are also prepared to receive good news. This expectation is shaped by key insights we have developed already in relation to incarnation. The claim of panentheism articulated in chapter 2 is that all things are in God and God is in all things. Such a stance signals a breadth and depth of divine presence enfolding all peoples and all things. If this is the case, then God is already present with and working within persons of other faith traditions. Our discussion of cosmic Christology in chapter 1 recognized the divine Logos as the very foundation of the whole creation (Col. 1:15–20). It presents what God does in Christ as an indicator of the divine intent to reconcile all things and to bring *all things* into union with God (*theosis*). Cosmic Christology assumes that the divine intent is cosmic in scope and not limited just to Christians. The Spirit Christology discussed in chapter 4 reminded us that the Spirit that was in Jesus is in us too, that this animating breath of God is fundamental to what it is to be truly human. This breath is not something that only Christians possess.

How wide is the divine embrace? In these discussions it seems wide indeed: God present in all things, intending union with all, and filling all with God's own Spirit. Such a vision of God should lead us to expect divine self-giving and self-revelation to be broad in scope. God is always greater than our best concepts of God. A fitting humility reminds us that our picture is always partial and inadequate to the subject matter. Our holy curiosity might want to know how God has been present and active with people of other faith traditions.

In addition to these theological foundations for interreligious engagement and cooperation there are some very practical benefits. At the very least we may gain a basic religious literacy and increased toleration. Heightened mutual understanding will lead to enhanced respect and capacity for living peaceably alongside one another. Perhaps we could finally put an end to religiously based violence.

Coexistence, however, may be a minimalist expectation. We hope to go beyond toleration to authentic engagement and even cooperation. Religion has the potential for bringing people together. The Latin root of religion is *re-ligare* (to link or bind together). If we can really come together we have a chance to make common cause for the common good. We could, for example, work together on initiatives related to peace, justice, and the integrity of creation. Urgent issues of global proportions need a collective response. They are better addressed in a concerted coalition that conspires to make real and lasting change. We are stronger and more effective working together.

There are also issues particular to the practice of religion in particular contexts that we could also profitably consider and address together if we could move beyond exclusivism to a place of openness, engagement, and interreligious cooperation. For example, in some locations, political practices and legal policies pose a genuine threat to religious liberty. There are also places where a religious majority persecutes religious minorities. Shared efforts to address such policies and practices would be much more effective. The burden of responding should not be borne only by those whose religious liberty is threatened or who face persecution. Exclusivism in such circumstances does not serve to strengthen capacities for mutual support and advocacy.

The relation of religion and politics is another area that is complex and challenging for people of faith. Political agendas regularly coopt religious communities. Political parties can, for example, design a platform that lures in certain religious communities around one issue or another and use their support to gain political advantage. In the US context in recent years, we have seen the religious right manipulated in this way to provide political backing for candidates of doubtful morality and integrity. Sometimes those in authority use religious themes to provoke hostility toward a presumed enemy. An example of this technique was use of the phrase "godless communism" in Cold War rhetoric to fuse religious commitment with hostility toward Russia. Similarly, Ronald

Reagan's "evil empire" speech to the National Association of Evangelicals in 1983 associated the Soviet Union with "evil" and the United States with "good."[14] In times of external conflicts, religious language has been invoked to assure us that violence against an enemy is entirely justified because "God is on our side." Rabbi Jonathan Sacks remarks that "when religion is invoked as a justification for conflict, religious voices must be raised in protest. We must withhold the robe of sanctity when it is used as a cloak for violence and bloodshed."[15] Perhaps if we were in a place of deepened engagement and cooperation across religious traditions there could be a new kind of mutual accountability where we could challenge one another to resist political cooptation. Exclusivist interpretations of Christianity are an impediment to this deepened engagement and cooperation across religious traditions.

It may be time to lay aside exclusivist models of interpreting how God is with us in Christ. There are solid biblical and theological grounds for doing so. There are also practical ethical grounds for doing so. For our part, Christians need to be clearer that when we say, "God is with us," we do not mean just us Christians. This standpoint is a better place from which to move forward in interreligious engagement and cooperation in addressing the challenges of our time and our contexts.

Only Us Humans?

Reconsidering Anthropocentrism from an Incarnational Perspective

In the face of the hard realities of our current eco-crisis, does God with "us" mean only us humans? Is incarnation irreducibly anthropocentric?

We argue here that, viewed from an incarnational perspective, this anthropocentrism need not be the case. In chapter 3, following the theme of deep incarnation introduced by Niels Gregersen, we observed that divine incarnation reaches deep into material existence as such. The incarnation of the divine Logos in the person of Jesus of Nazareth is an embrace—not only of humans but of humans in their continuity with other animals (all flesh) and with the natural world at large.[16] We drew

14. "Reagan Brands Soviet Union 'Evil Empire,' March 8, 1983," Politico, March 8, 2018, https://www.politico.com/story/2018/03/08/this-day-in-politics-march-8-1983-440258.

15. Jonathan Sacks, *The Dignity of Difference* (London: Continuum, 2002), 9.

16. Niels Gregersen, "Deep Incarnation: Why Evolutionary Continuity Matters in Christology," *Toronto Journal of Theology* 26, no. 2 (2010): 174.

conclusions from this understanding of incarnation that bodies matter and that matter matters. Human beings are not the only beings that matter, and when we say, "God is with us," the "us" has an all-encompassing scope. These conclusions have major implications for how we value and relate to the rest of the natural world.

The present eco-crisis makes it imperative that we find ways of living with and within the natural world that are just, participatory, and sustainable. Our primary challenge is theological. Our theological ideas about who God is, how God is related to the world, how the world works, and who we are as human beings shape how we interact with the natural world. Given the results, some of these ideas merit reconsideration. Those engaged in ecojustice work often observe that drawing out statistics on global warming, species extinction, or habitat destruction—the "data of despair"—does not seem to motivate change. The problem is not a matter of information; it is a matter of *orientation*. We need a fundamental reorientation—what Rosemary Radford Ruether called "a conversion to the Earth."[17] Our callous disregard and rapacious ways may be symptoms of not knowing our place within the wider natural world. We may need a more down-to-Earth sense of ourselves.

The steps we take in this chapter build upon our argument that incarnation means that bodies matter and matter matters. If this is the case, then "God with us" includes the whole of the natural world and not just humans. Biblical and theological foundations are laid first with an exploration of the enlarged understanding of incarnation that we find in cosmic Christology (Col. 1:15–20). Next we access some theological resources from Reformed tradition. These sources discern that the whole of the natural world—not just humans—is a locus of divine self-revelation, providence, and new creation. Then we revisit some of the central insights of process-relational theology that helped us toward a better articulation of the meaning of incarnation. These same insights also help us to critique habits of thought that have narrowed our vision of "God with us" to just human beings. In particular, the desacralization (stark separation of God and the world) and objectification of nature are confronted. A final step is an imaginative venture into what it might look like if we embraced a view that God with us means *all* of us.

17. Rosemary Radford Ruether, *Sexism and God-Talk: Toward a Feminist Theology* (Boston: Beacon Press, 1983), 255–56.

146 God Will Be All in All

Corrections from Cosmic Christology

Sometimes the incarnation seems to be all and only about human beings. It is taken to be an emergency measure made necessary by human sinfulness. This way of thinking about incarnation lends fuel to a problematic anthropocentrism: "It's all about us." We risk not seeing that it the *whole creation* that God loves and is making new. This narrow vision of what we mean by "us" when we affirm that God is with us has proven disastrous for our relationship with the rest of the natural world. The ecological crisis is in large part a result of this fundamental orientation. Whatever is here is for us and for our use. We are the subjects; the rest of the world is made of objects for our use. This thinking is a license for ecological irresponsibility and exploitation—and has led us to the brink of disaster.

The incarnational ethics discussed in chapter 4 acknowledges that bodies matter and that matter matters. Regarding human beings, we observed that although *every* body matters, some bodies are more vulnerable than others. Advocacy for the most vulnerable shapes an incarnational ethic. In our time, it is becoming clear that the Earth itself and other living beings are also vulnerable. Ecologically irresponsible human activity has undermined Earth's fragile, life-sustaining systems of homeostasis. Our extensive fossil fuel consumption, for example, is driving the climate change we now see in global warming. The results are already apparent in extreme and erratic weather patterns. The desertification of some areas and flooding of others threaten agricultural production. Wendell Berry has rightly pointed out that there is no such thing as a postagricultural society.[18] Habitat destruction threatens wildlife accelerates extinction of plant and insect species. Oceans are rising and will cause tens of millions of people to become climate refugees. The truth of our situation is that we humans "exploit neighbor and nature and threaten death to the planet entrusted to our care."[19]

In the destruction that we are wreaking, some people are clearly more at risk than others. In his encyclical *Our Common Home*, Pope Francis has reframed the conversation about climate change to a conversation about "climate justice." He observes that those who will suffer most will be vulnerable folk who are not the big consumers of fossil fuels and have

18. Wendell Berry, *The Unsettling of America: Culture and Agriculture* (San Francisco: Sierra Club Books, 1977), 86, 94.
19. "A Brief Statement of Faith," *The Constitution of the Presbyterian Church (U.S.A.)*, Part I, *Book of Confessions* (Louisville, KY: Office of the General Assembly, Presbyterian Church (U.S.A.), 2004), 10.3.

received few material benefits from their use. In ecologically informed circles we often hear that, as creatures of the Earth, "we are all in the same boat." That is not exactly true. Those who are affluent and privileged find themselves on Noah's Ark, while the vast majority are on the *Titanic.*

The disruptions in our social and ecological realities are symptomatic of the deep difficulty we have named in chapter 4 as our being curved in on ourselves.[20] Our world is seriously narrowed and selfishly shallow. Some ways of understanding Christology and incarnation are similarly narrow and shallow. The predominant understanding of the meaning of the Christ event has often seemed limited to the work of human redemption. Even that has been a "disembodied" redemption, limited to saving souls and getting to a better world. A disembodied reading of the purpose of incarnation is certainly counterintuitive; it misses the point altogether. This narrow, shallow approach to the nature and purpose of incarnation has led to an acosmic Christianity that devalues the rest of the natural world.

Fortunately, there are broader, deeper readings of incarnation available in our tradition. Cosmic Christology (or Logos Christology), for example, envisions incarnation as embracing the whole of creation. This long-standing tradition is found in a number of biblical texts.[21] It is also prominent in the writings of notable theologians of the early church (Justin Martyr, Irenaeus, Clement of Alexandria) and the twelfth and thirteenth centuries (Franciscans, Bonaventura, Duns Scotus), and it prevails in Eastern Orthodox theology to this day. In medieval Franciscan theology, for example, the incarnation is no afterthought or emergency measure on God's part to deal with human sin. The incarnation lies in the primordial creative intent of God.

In this interpretation, Christ is related to the whole of creation prior to any role in redeeming humankind. The divine Logos is related to the very structure of the universe. Christ is the Word through whom God created all things, the one who was "in the beginning" (John 1). Cosmic Christology assumes that the entire cosmos is included in the divine purposes; it is not just a context for the outworking of the redemptive drama of human beings. The goal of all creation is its relation in union with God: *theosis.* Christ's work is redemptive precisely because this union,

20. Augustine, *The City of God,* in *Nicene and Post-Nicene Fathers of the Christian Church Series,* vol. 2, ed. Philip Schaff (Edinburgh: T. & T. Clark), 12.6, p. 522. Here Augustine explains the misery of the human condition as being grounded in our turning away from God. Human beings "have forsaken Him who supremely is and turned to themselves."

21. See 1 Cor. 8:6; Eph. 1:23; Col. 1:15–20; Phil. 2:6–11; Heb. 1:1–4; John 1:1–14.

which is intended for all, is manifest in him. "He became as we are, that we might become as he is."[22] The affirmation of Chalcedon expresses who the Christ is understood to be: "truly God, truly human, united in one and the same concrete being." This condition of union with God is the destiny toward which the whole creation is drawn. Salvation, understood in this light, is not exclusively or even primarily about salvation of human beings from their sin. God is making *all things* new. God is bringing to completion what God began in creation. Themes of fulfillment and consummation take center stage. God creates so that a (final) life-giving synthesis of God and world might be realized.

Cosmic Christology enlarges the scope of God's connection with and God's purposes in the natural world. This approach challenges anthropocentrism and the habit of seeing the rest of the natural world as composed of mere objects.

Contributions from Reformed Theology

This direction of enlarging the scope of divine connection with the natural world is reinforced in Reformed theology. Three affirmations in particular underscore this connection between God and the world—not just us humans:

- The whole creation is the "theater of God's glory."[23]
- The whole creation is the locus of divine providential activity.
- The whole creation is the subject of eschatological renewal.

We elaborate upon each of these in turn in view of the theology of John Calvin.

The Whole Creation Is "the Theater of God's Glory"

If Spinoza has been called the "God-intoxicated philosopher," then Calvin surely must be the creation-intoxicated theologian.[24] One has only to read through Book I of the *Institutes* to see evidence of this. Everywhere we turn, we see creation in all its vastness and variety reflecting the glory of God.

22. Irenaeus, *Against Heresies*, vol. 5 preface, in *Ante-Nicene Fathers*, ed. Philip Schaff (1885; repr., Grand Rapids, Eerdmans, 2001), 1:526.

23. John Calvin, *Joannis Calvini opera quae supersunt*, ed. Edouard Cunitz, Johann-Wilhelm Baum, and Eduard Wilhelm Eugen Reuss (Braunschweig: C.A. Schwetschke, 1863), (CO) 8.294.

24. Peter Wyatt, *Jesus Christ and Creation in the Theology of John Calvin* (Allison Park, PA: Pickwick, 1996), 91.

The problem with nature as a source of divine self-revelation is not that it does not show forth God's glory (it does), but we do not see what is right before our eyes. Calvin uses the analogy of "weak vision" to talk about our incapacity. Scripture then functions as corrective lenses or "spectacles. "But with the aid of spectacles [we] will begin to read distinctly; so scripture, gathering up the otherwise confused knowledge of God in our minds having dispersed our dullness, clearly shows us the true God."[25]

> Meanwhile let us not be ashamed to take pious delight in the works of God open and manifest in this most beautiful theater. For, as I have elsewhere said, although it is not the chief evidence for faith, yet it is the first evidence in the order of nature, to be mindful that wherever we cast our eyes, all things they meet are works of God and at the same time to ponder with pious meditation to what end God created them.[26]

As the theater of God's glory, the whole creation is a divine self-revelation. Calvin even goes on to say that God appears to us "robed in the fabric of creation."[27] The invisible God becomes visible through the creation.

The Whole Creation Is the Locus of Divine Providential Activity

Another crucial ingredient in the evidence of God's relation to the natural world is God's providential activity in this sphere. God's providential care is not restricted to human beings. It is all-encompassing in its scope and particular in its exercise. Calvin is fond of quoting Matthew 10:29: "That not even a little sparrow, sold for half a farthing, falls to the ground without the will of the Father."[28] All things in nature and in history are governed by God's personal and particular care.

Calvin works out his doctrine of providence in full awareness of the competing perspectives of his day and is concerned to rule out certain alternative interpretations popular among the Stoics (that things are up to fate) and the Epicureans (that things are left to chance) He endeavors to promote the *personal nature of God's providence*, so he refutes the view that

25. John Calvin, *Institutes of the Christian Religion* 1.6.1, ed. John T. McNeill, trans. Ford Lewis Battles, LCC (Philadelphia: Westminster Press, 1954), 70.

26. Calvin, *Institutes* 1.14.20.

27. John Calvin, *Commentaries*, trans. Joseph Haroutunian, LCC (Philadelphia: Westminster, 1958), on Ps. 104:1.

28. John Calvin, *Concerning the Eternal Predestination of God*, trans. J. K. S. Reid (London: J. Clark, 1961), 163.

nature is somehow left on autopilot to function independently according to natural law. Rather, "natural law" is only a descriptive phrase connoting God's self-consistency in exercising power. God is no spectator deity but is involved in a continual relation of sustenance and governance. If for even one moment God were to withdraw, the world would "immediately perish and dissolve into nothing."[29]

Another of Calvin's concerns was promoting the *particularity of God's care*. This is more than a general ordering; it attends to details. Nothing is left to chance (*fortuna*). God acts in freedom; there is no external necessity (*necessitas*) to which God is subject. So Calvin is steering a path between the *fortuna* of the Epicureans and the *necessitas* of the Stoics. In doing so he is preserving the two truths he finds in Scripture: God is active in nature and history, and God is distinct from them both. If God is not the former, the Epicureans are right. If God is not the latter, the Stoics are right.[30]

The significance of this discussion for the present project is that Calvin is ruling out certain ways of thinking about God's relation to the world—God is not excluded from the processes of nature and history on the one hand, and God is not to be identified with them on the other. Most significant is the understanding that God's providential activity does concern nature—not only humans. As important as the God-human dimensions of divine providence are in Calvin, these need to be set alongside God's relation with the whole of nature and all its particulars.

The Whole Creation Is the Subject of Eschatological Renewal

Another element that illustrates God's relation to the *whole* natural world is the shape of Calvin's eschatological hope. Resurrection of the body and new creation are extended to the natural world in Calvin's thinking. Commenting on Romans 8:18–25, a passage about creation waiting with eager longing and the whole creation groaning in labor pains, Calvin attributes the hope of resurrection and restoration to the *whole creation*. "No part of the universe is untouched by the longing with which everything in this world aspires to the hope of resurrection."[31]

---

29. Calvin, *Commentaries*, Gen. 2:2.
30. P. H. Reardon, "Calvin on Providence: The Development of an Insights," *Scottish Journal of Theology* 28, no. 6 (1975): 517–33.
31. Calvin, *Commentaries*, Rom. 8:20.

When speaking of the final judgment, Calvin reads redemptive purpose into this term. As he says, "Some view the word *judgment* as denoting *reformation*, and others as denoting *condemnation*. I rather agree with the former, who explain it to mean, that *the world* must be restored."[32] Calvin is convinced that there will be a "reformation" or "renovation" of the world, not just of human beings. The "restoration of all things," whatever else it may entail, will be restoration to their original purpose. The whole creation will at last fully reflect the glory of God.

As the theater of God's glory, the locus of God's providential activity, and the object of eschatological renewal, the *whole natural world* is permeated by the divine. This relation of God and the world is not through human beings or for their sake only. Our theological anthropocentrism is severely chastened if not ruled out altogether in this larger view. In its place, a biocentrism would be much preferable.

Process-Relational Insights

Here I try to show how the interaction of Christian theology with the philosophy of Alfred North Whitehead has proven transformative in areas where a reorientation is needed. A reorientation is needed in relation to two habits of thought that are theologically and ecologically problematic: the desacralization of nature and the objectification of nature. Process thought offers a helpful corrective here and points the way forward to a better alternative.

Chapter 2 already addressed the problem of the desacralization of nature in a step-by-step reconsideration of the relation between God and the world. Process-relational insights helped us articulate more coherently a deep relationality between God and the world. The claim was that there is already a veritable presence of God in, with, and under all things. This deep relationality is decisively expressed in the Incarnation of Jesus of Nazareth. Seeing God present in all things leads to a resacralization of the natural world that changes how we relate to the natural world. The ecological consequences are significant.

To recap briefly, process-relational thought offers a new way of seeing:

- Seeing the world in terms of process and relation rather than substance.

---

32. Calvin, *Commentaries*, John 12:31.

- Seeing the attributes of God in terms of "dual transcendence" rather than in binary opposition to the attributes of the world.
- Seeing the relation between God and the world as "internal" to God (affecting God) rather than "external" to God (not affecting God).
- Seeing that both God and the world have the capacity for creativity, though in different measure, rather than making an absolute divide between "Creator" and "created."
- Seeing "all things in God and God in all things," even as we affirm that God is more than the world.
- Seeing the dynamic interconnectedness of all things, "the philosophy of organism."

In chapter 2 we covered all the other insights in the listing above as they pertained to the relation of God and the world. Now we proceed using the first and the last in this line-up of insights, to critique the objectification of nature. It is this habit of objectifying nature that leads us to see the human being as over and above the natural world and even separate from it—anthropocentrism and separatism.

The objectification of the natural world has made exploitation and abuse more thinkable.[33] This is a world of mere *objects*—not subjects. This way of thinking has reinforced anthropocentrism as human beings are cast as the only *subjects* in this world of objects. Elements in Whitehead's system that are particularly helpful toward refuting the objectification of nature include his rejection of substance metaphysics and his introduction of the philosophy of organism. Both of these elements proved significant for our discussion of incarnation, and both will work against the objectification of nature. In the next section we cover how moving from substance metaphysics to process-relational metaphysics restores a sense of the integrity and interconnectedness of nature. In the second section we cover how the "philosophy of organism" helps us to see the world as a community of subjects—not objects.

33. This section of the chapter was first presented at the Tenth International Whitehead Conference held in Claremont, California, in 2015 on "Seizing an Alternative: Toward an Ecological Civilization." Proceedings of the philosophical work group have since been published in a collected volume, including my chapter, "Coming Down to Earth: A Process-Panentheist Reorientation to Nature," in *Conceiving an Alternative: Philosophical Resources for an Ecological Civilization*, ed. David Conner and Demian Wheeler (Claremont, CA: Process Century Press, 2017), 99–113.

Resisting the Objectification of Nature:
Seeing the World Whole

An essential ingredient that process thought brings to the work of ecojustice is a conviction of the *integrity of nature*—that nature is an interconnected whole. This is an essential insight for ecological thinking. As it happens, it is an insight well supported by the science of our day. Quantum mechanics, with its discovery of nonseparability[34] or entanglement at the quantum level, reveals that our assumptions of independence and separation are a false report on reality. Though Whitehead would not have been working with a knowledge of quantum mechanics, he did believe that individuation is an abstraction from the deeper reality—an instance of what Whitehead termed "misplaced concreteness." Theologically, of course, there is a long-standing tradition we are utterly connected in the divine life.

Ecologically, connection is clearly the way of nature. Process thought conspires with science, theology, and ecology to remind us that human beings are part of an interconnected and interdependent web of life. Whitehead puts it boldly: "Every actual entity is present in every other actual entity."[35] This insight was beautifully reflected in Václav Havel's comment, "We are mysteriously connected to the entire universe; we are mirrored in it, just as the entire universe is mirrored in us."[36]

Process thought contests substantialist thinking, which has assumed that the final real things are substances, things that, according to Descartes, "need nothing but themselves to exist." Substantialist thinking tends to yield materialistic, reductionistic, and mechanistic models for understanding the world. These have all proved to be unhelpful for ecological thinking. The problem is in assuming things exist as independent entities (or substances) that are only externally (accidentally, incidentally) related to one another. In a machine, for example, the parts themselves are truly independent; they do not need relations with other parts for their own existence. A machine can be disassembled without damage to

34. This comes from the observation that two particles that are members of the same quantum system continue to influence one another no matter how far they are subsequently separated. Even measuring one affects the other. This happens instantaneously and thus is not thought to be a matter of one "communicating" with the other.

35. Alfred North Whitehead, *Process and Reality* (1929; repr. New York: Macmillan, 1978), 50.

36. Quoted by Larry Rasmussen in *Earth Community: Earth Ethics* (Maryknoll, NY: Orbis Books, 2001), 10.

the parts and then reassembled with the function restored. This is not so with organisms! We are learning that the Earth is more like an organism than a mechanism.

Whitehead's insistence that reality is about process and relation resists substance metaphysics with its mechanistic and materialistic habits of thought. By giving priority to process and developing a relational ontology, Whitehead provides an alternative orientation to reality. All things are understood to be co-constituted by their relations. This insight proved immensely helpful in thinking through the Incarnation and the sense in which being truly divine and truly human—two natures in one person—is a genuine possibility. This framework is also much better for understanding our ecological reality and encourages a much-needed sensibility of interdependence.

With this framework, we may perceive the web of relations. We may begin to ask distinctly relational questions. When any particular course of action is advocated as good, we ask: *Good in relation to what? In relation to whom?* We are pushed to consider the effects of our actions upon all those others to whom we are internally and utterly connected. Pursuing purely selfish interest is revealed to be an irrational habit of thought and action. It is living *as if* one is an autonomous individual and not co-constituted by our relations. This is a good parallel to living life, curved in on ourselves *incurvatus en se*, as Augustine put it. This is disorientation and alienation.

If we are reoriented toward relation we may begin to see things *whole*—in their complex patterns of relationality. A corollary to the habit of seeing things whole is the ethical orientation toward making things whole in the sense of healing. Ecologically we need to heal the damage that has been done and reverse the *dis*-integration of ecosystems and social systems. The work of ecojustice insists that we affirm the integrity of nature and therefore *make the connections*.

In the North-South global conversation, for example, people from the northern hemisphere are accused of not making the connections between ecology and economics. When we insist on preserving the rain forest without acknowledging the economic needs that impinge upon persons living in and near the rain forests, we miss the mark. To think in this way is to *dis-integrate* ecosystems from social and economic systems. It is the extreme economic difficulty of their context that motivates them to turn rain forests into pastures and farmlands. That reality must change to make saving the rain forests possible. Economics has to enter the picture; it is the other half of the *eco*-crisis. Whitehead's relational approach requires interpreting reality in ways that *integrate*. We need to see things whole and to make things whole.

Resisting the Objectification of Nature:
Seeing the World as a Community of Subjects

A second contribution from process-relational thought is Whitehead's philosophy of organism.[37] It will prove effective in reconceiving the natural world, no longer as a world of mere objects but as a community of subjects. Jürgen Moltmann makes the point that theology has contributed to the present ecological crisis through "subjectification of the human being" and "objectification of nature."[38] We declare a human monopoly on spirit. Among other things, anthropocentrism places the human being in a transcendent—even Godlike—relation to nature, thereby lifting the human being out of the natural world as a spiritual creature in a material world. Such a move assigns only instrumental value (not intrinsic value) to the natural world. This permits and may even promote exploitation without regard for the natural world in its own right. Nature becomes, to borrow Frances Wood's phrase, a "permissible victim."[39]

An incarnational ethic grounds the call to preserve and protect the natural world upon its *intrinsic* value, not its value to us. When we seek to motivate care by remarking upon how dependent human beings are on "*our* natural environment" and "*our* natural resources," those are anthropocentric, instrumentalist valuations and motivations. The natural world is not simply an "environment" for us like a house we live in. It is a *household* of beings with whom we should be in caring community. It would be far better for us to come to insist upon the *intrinsic value* of species, ecosystems, the biosphere, and so on, in their own right and not because of their usefulness to us.

37. This section of the chapter was first presented at the Tenth International Whitehead Conference held in Claremont, California, in 2015 on "Seizing an Alternative: Toward an Ecological Civilization." Proceedings of the philosophical work group have since been published in a collected volume, including my chapter, "Coming Down to Earth: A Process-Panentheist Reorientation to Nature," in *Conceiving an Alternative: Philosophical Resources for an Ecological Civilization*, ed. David Conner and Demian Wheeler (Claremont, CA: Process Century Press, 2017), 99–113; used here with permission of Process Century Press.
38. Jürgen Moltmann, *Creating a Just Future* (Philadelphia: Trinity, 1989), 25.
39. Frances Wood, "Take My Yoke upon You: The Role of the Church in the Oppression of African-American Women," in *A Troubling in My Soul*, ed. Emilie Townes (Maryknoll, NY: Orbis Books, 1993), 40.

Whitehead affirms, "Value is inherent in actuality itself."[40] Whitehead's philosophy of organism takes the interesting step of proposing that all entities have both physical and mental poles, in varying degrees. Whitehead is working with a meaning for "mentality" that is not anthropocentrically defined and does not require consciousness or sentience; it is simply the "capacity for experience." Griffin's suggestion of "panexperientialism"[41] conveys the meaning better than "panpsychism," a misleading term sometimes employed. Each actual entity in its own "coming to be" is a subject and has intrinsic value. Process thought allows degrees of intrinsic value relative to capacities for sentience, but this represents a continuity with no absolute divide.

Another interesting consideration that Griffin introduces is *extrinsic value*, that is, something's value beyond its value to itself and its value to others or to the ecosystem—"ecological value."[42] He offers an interesting observation here. If we take into account ecological value, some creatures (like plankton, worms, bacteria, etc.) that may not be capable of the richest experience may in fact have great value in the ecosystems. Human beings, on the other hand, who are capable of the richest experience, may have little ecological value. "In fact, most of the other forms of life would be better off and the ecosystem as a whole would not be threatened, if we did not exist."[43] The Gaia hypothesis goes so far as to suggest that we are like harmful bacteria to the organism that is Earth, and it needs to eliminate us! We are a danger to ourselves and others. We may not want to go this far, but the critique implicit in the Gaia hypothesis is one we need to hear. Moltmann takes this up in good humor and tells a story of two planets meeting in space. One asks, "How are you?" The other says, "I am not at all well. I am ill. I have *Homo sapiens*." The first one says, "I am so very sorry. It is a terrible thing. I had it, too, but take heart—it will pass."[44] The question is whether the planetary sickness will come to an end because we do away with ourselves or because we gain wisdom to care for the planet.

40. Whitehead, *Process and Reality*, 100.

41. David Griffin, *Religion and Scientific Naturalism: Overcoming the Conflicts* (Albany, NY: SUNY Press, 2000), 150.

42. David Griffin, "Whitehead's Deeply Ecological Worldview," in *Worldviews and Ecology: Religion, Philosophy, and the Environment* (Maryknoll, NY: Orbis Books, 1994), 192ff.

43. Griffin, "Whitehead's Deeply Ecological Worldview," 203.

44. Jürgen Moltmann, *The Spirit of Hope: Theology for a World in Peril* (Louisville, KY: Westminster John Knox Press, 2019), 16.

As Whitehead follows through on the insights of his "philosophy of organism" (sometimes termed panexperientialism), the old spiritual-material dichotomy dissolves. There are no pure spirits, and there is no "dead" matter. There are only material beings (sentient and nonsentient) with varying capacities for experience. The important point is that in Whitehead's philosophy of organism, interiority extends all the way down to the submicroscopic. "Wherever there is actuality of any sort, it has a spontaneity and capacity for prehending its environment, albeit in a non-conscious way."[45] "By virtue of their capacities for inwardness or subjec-tivity . . . all deserve respect and care on their own terms and for their own sakes, not simply for their usefulness to human beings."[46] Thomas Berry speaks a warning, a wakeup call, which is a mantra for our time: The uni-verse is composed of subjects to be communed with, not a collection of objects to be used.[47] The human being, in this way of thinking, does not have a monopoly on spirit. John Cobb quips, "Process theology does not commit monopoly!"[48]

Treating the world as a community of subjects in a sense gives a face to nature. Here we will shift to some more contemporary theological and ethical sources to draw out the implications of what Whitehead has proposed in his philosophy. We are helped by the thought-provoking work of Immanuel Levinas and Edward Farley.[49] What they have so use-fully done in their work on interhuman relations, I want to see taken and applied in terms of human relations with the rest of nature.

As Farley puts it, the other is a subject, an "I" that is "not I."[50] The existence of "such an other disputes any claim I have to be the one 'I,' the only perspective, the autonomous actor."[51] The "uninterchangabil-ity" and irreducibility of the other makes clear the alterity (otherness) of the other. The recognition that I am not the only "I" and that I am not the center of the universe has a destabilizing and decentering effect that

45. Jay McDaniel, "Process Thought and the Epic of Evolution Tradition: Complementary Approaches to a Sustainable Future," *Process Studies* 35, no. 1 (Spring/Summer 2006): 78.

46. McDaniel, "Process Thought and the Epic of Evolution Tradition," 70.

47. Thomas Berry, *Evening Thoughts: Reflecting on Erath as Sacred Community* (San Francisco: Sierra Club, 2006), 149,

48. John Cobb and David Ray Griffin, *Process Theology: An Introductory Exposition* (Philadel-phia: Westminster Press, 1976), 104.

49. For a fuller discussion of Farley and Levinas on this subject, see Anna Case-Winters, *Reconstructing a Christian Theology of Nature* (Hampshire, UK: Ashgate, 2007), 97ff.

50. Edward Farley, *Good and Evil* (Minneapolis: Fortress, 1990), 35.

51. Farley, *Good and Evil*, 36.

could reorient our relation to others. For Martin Buber, it was a turning to the other in an "I–Thou" relation as opposed to an "I–it" relation.

Levinas[52] has proposed that when we encounter the "face" of another, we experience a claim, a call to commitment and responsibility. Farley expands this in the direction of *compassionate obligation*, a concept rich with meaning in the human encounter with the rest of nature. Compassionate obligation characterizes the face-to-face encounter because in being together we become for one another "mutual interlocutors." We experience ourselves as vulnerable before the interpretations and actions of the other, and we experience the other as vulnerable to our interpretations and actions. What is disclosed in the encounter is our mutual fragility. A response of compassion is called forth from both. Then, once summoned by the face, we become alert to the objective predicament of the other and our obligation to "join with the other in her or his fragile struggles against whatever threatens and violates."[53] Through the suffering face of the other we are awakened to an ethic of love. The "suffering-with" (of compassion) flows into a "suffering-for" (of obligation). One cannot respond to the face of the other as if it were a mere externality, a thing, or an artifact.[54] This is a subject, an "I."[55] What a difference giving face to nature might make!

Acknowledging the integrity of nature and seeing the world as composed of subjects could have the potential of steering us toward a new understanding of the natural world and the place of the human being in it. The recognition of mutual fragility and the response of compassionate obligation are surely essential to the work of ecojustice.[56] At this stage in

52. Emmanuel Levinas, "Ethics as First Philosophy," in *Levinas Reader*, ed. Sean Hand (Oxford: Blackwell, 1989).

53. Farley, *Good and Evil*, 43.

54. Farley, *Good and Evil*, 42.

55. The face as referenced here need not be a human face. Keller, drawing out insights of Nicholas of Cusa in *De vision Dei*, notes that the human face should not be privileged, for "the icon of God has radically distributed itself across the face of the universe, across the surface of all materialities" (Catherine Keller, *Cloud of the Impossible: Negative Theology and Interplanetary Entanglement* [New York: Columbia University Press, 2015], 109).

56. There are at least some hints of this wider frame into which I am urging the discussion in Farley's own analysis. What he is presenting here is his theological anthropology and the work is directed toward the sphere of the interhuman. Nevertheless, Farley does speak of a "universal face" that is "attested to through and mediated by communities of the face" (in Robert Williams, *Recognition: Fichte and Hegel on the Other* [Albany, NY: SUNY Press, 1992], 292). "In the Christian paradigm of redemption, the transregional face is experienced in connection with the experience of the sacred" (Williams, *Recognition*, 289). It is the presence of the sacred that draws situated peoples to transcend though not to repudiate their self-reference. "It is the sacred manifested through the face that lures regional (familial, national,

our history, we human beings are called to live in ways that are "socially just, ecologically wise and spiritually satisfying, not only for the sake of human life but for the sake of the well-being of the planet."[57]

Imagining an Alternative: God with All of Us, the Convivial Community of Creation

The way we look at the world changes when we think of it as a community of subjects. The world is no longer a collection of objects for our acquisition, use, and exploitation. To borrow a contrast suggested by Marilyn Frye, we may go from looking at the world with an "arrogant eye" to looking at the world with a "loving eye."[58] The loving eye recognizes the subject status of the other in its full complexity and difference. It does not try to reduce or simplify the other to something more manageable or usable. The loving eye is not invasive, coercive, or acquisitive in relation to the other.

Unfortunately our consumerist society cultivates in us the gaze of the arrogant eye—or, more specifically, one might say the "acquisitive eye." It tells us that our vocation is primarily as "consumers" and that our happiness will be found in maximizing our acquisitions. We are captivated by shiny objects, continually wanting more. Acquiring more does not content us, however; rather it raises our expectations of more acquisitions. This pertains not only to physical acquisitions but to capital investments that we hope will ensure our capacity to continue and increase our acquisitions indefinitely. The present arrangements are economically unjust and ecologically unsustainable. Any movement for ecojustice must necessarily attend to both *eco*nomics and *eco*logy.

The global market economy where transnational corporations hold so much power is a system of unrestrained competition and consumerism. There is privatization of public utilities and natural resources, like water, so that profit takes precedence over meeting basic human needs. Unlimited economic growth and accumulation of wealth are unquestioned without attendant social obligation. The gap between rich and poor grows ever wider. The 2020 Credit Suisse Global Wealth report

---

tribal) experiences of the face *toward compassionate obligation to any and all life-forms*" (Farley, *Good and Evil*, 289). I think the connections and applications I am making are at least arguably consistent with Farley's direction here.

57. McDaniel, "Process Thought and the Epic of Evolution Tradition," 80.

58. Marilyn Frye, "In and Out of Harm's Way: Arrogance and Love," in *The Politics of Reality* (Trumansburg: NY: Crossing Press, 1983), 66–72.

makes for stark reading. Released at the end of October, it revealed that the top 1 percent of households globally own 43 percent of all personal wealth, while the bottom 50 percent own only 1 percent. The World Bank defines extreme poverty as people living on $1 or less a day. Around 1.89 billion people, or nearly 36 percent of the world's population, lived in extreme poverty. Nearly half the population in developing countries lived on less than $1.25 a day.[59]

Wealth does not seem to trickle down; it seems rather to trickle up.

There is no "happiness" for the poor of the Earth under the present economic arrangements. Remarkably, it is becoming apparent that there is no happiness in it for the rich either. Psychologists measuring life satisfaction have confirmed the old adage, "Money can't buy happiness." It helps, they say, but only up to the point where basic needs are met and a sense of security established. Beyond that, there is no noticeable increase in life satisfaction. In his book *The Poverty of Affluence*, Paul Wachtel observes that the system "creates more needs than it satisfies and leaves us feeling more deprived than when we had 'less.'"[60] There are in fact studies of "diseases of affluence" now. The invitation to "super-size it" has people overserved and overweight and overworked in trying to have it all. There is a disproportionately high level of depression and suicide among the affluent. The advertising industry creates the illusion that we will be happy if only we can buy more stuff. The standard seems to be, "Whoever dies with the most toys wins." So we strive and stress ourselves to acquire more and more. We succeed and yet we are still unhappy. We conclude that we must not be doing this right—that something is innately wrong with us because we should be happy with all this stuff. It seems that in "getting and spending, we lay waste our powers."[61]

Perhaps it would be better to conclude that something is wrong with this system. Economically it is unjust. In its human toll it destroys the well-being of both rich and poor. We can now add that it is ecologically unsustainable. The affluent seem unwilling to live more simply. Our population is increasing, and the poor of the Earth rightly desire a better life. This scenario is a disaster in the making. The Earth cannot sustain the lifestyle of the affluent. Something has to change. This is most apparent for us in our fossil fuel consumption and its effects on global climate

59. https://www.credit-suisse.com/about-us/en/reports-research/global-wealth-report.html.
60. Paul Wachtel, *The Poverty of Affluence* (New York: Free Press, 1983), 16.
61. William Wordsworth, "The World Is Too Much with Us," https://www.poetryfoundation.org/poems/45564/the-world-is-too-much-with-us.

change. As Sallie McFague has pointed out, "Climate change is not just another social and political issue facing us, rather it sums up the central crisis of the twenty-first century."[62]

The time has come to question the system and the assumptions that drive it. We have not stopped to question, for example, the assumption that the human vocation is acquisition and consumption. We have spoken already of our being created by love and for love. Created in the image of God, we are beings-in-relation called to co-create with God in ways that manifest love of neighbors—including all the neighbors in the wider world of nature.

There is another way to understand God, ourselves, and our calling as members of a "convivial community of creation." I borrow the term "convivial" from Catherine Keller, who spoke of a "just and sustainable conviviality"[63] as desirable for an ecological civilization. "Convivial" has the root meaning of "living together" but also conveys a spirit of taking delight in one another in this community—looking with the loving eye instead of the arrogant or acquisitive eye. This community would be one characterized by solidarity, sufficiency, and sustainability.

Solidarity would require of the humans who are members of this community seeing ourselves as all together in this. We are inextricably joined to one another and to the larger world of nature. Remembering the metaphor of the human being as a created co-creator, we are reminded that we belong to the "created." We cannot see ourselves as separate from and over-and-above the rest of creation. We do not have a license to thoughtlessly exploit the rest. In the human community we would seek just and participatory practices in our economics and politics as we together strive to serve the common good.

Sufficiency would require changed lifestyles—going from "living large" to taking only what we need so that there will be enough for all. We would develop a theology and a lifestyle of "enough." As the Chinese philosopher Lao Tzu observed, "Be content with what you have; rejoice in the way things are. When you realize nothing is lacking, the whole world belongs to you."[64] "To know when you have enough is to be happy." Because we are co-creators we cannot see ourselves in the way that our capitalist market economy sees us—primarily as "consumers."

62. Sallie McFague, "The Universal Christ and Climate Change," in *Oneing: An Alternative Orthodoxy*, ed. Richard Rohr (Albuquerque: Center for Action and Contemplation, 2013), 1–6.
63. Keller, *Cloud of the Impossible*, 52.
64. Lao-Tzu, *The Tao Te Ching*, trans. Stephen Addis and Stanley Lombardo (Indianapolis, IN: Hackett, 1993).

Our calling is to be creators. We bring our best efforts to the shared endeavor of creating a world in which everyone has enough. We would use our enhanced rationality, freedom, and relationality for good, creating with others in ways that serve the well-being of all.

Sustainability invites us to realize that if the Earth does not survive, no one survives. We need to live in ways that promote the flourishing of life and Earth's fragile systems that support life and are themselves beautiful and intrinsically valuable. We would seek to live in such a way that, if we continued to do so, the Earth would thrive and life would flourish. If we take care of the Earth, it will take care of us. If we do not . . . well, management assumes no responsibility. We need to use our constructive imaginations to envision a different kind of world. The challenges of our time are as grave as they are urgent; we are hearing a compelling call to action. We ourselves are a part of (not apart from) the cosmos. In human beings we see the cosmos becoming conscious of itself. The human mind is a remarkable thing.

> If you multiply the neural connections in a single human brain by the number of humans on Earth, you get a number that exceeds the number of stars in the observable Universe. It remains to be seen whether humanity will apply this enormous potential toward preserving and protecting the delicate web of interacting relationships that sustains life on Earth.[65]

At the beginning of this section I expressed the conviction that our problem, at its depth, is theological. We need to develop more coherent and religiously viable understandings of God, the world, and ourselves. Concluding this section, I sought to offer a sketch of an imagined alternative—a new way of being consistent with a new way of seeing. Instead of looking at the world with an acquisitive eye, we may look with a loving eye. We are relational beings, created by and for love. The estrangement and self-centeredness in which we are living are not normative for us; they represent an alienated and inauthentic way of being in the world. When we look with a loving eye we see a different world and can imagine living differently. Incarnation carries with it the profound implication that bodies matter and matter matters.

---

65. Grace Wolf-Chase, "The Interactive Cosmos," in *Interactive World / Interactive God*, ed. Carol Rausch Albright, John R. Albright, and Mladen Turk (Eugene, OR: Cascade Books, 2017), 72.

This is conceived as a world where God is with us, *all of us*, not just human beings. The world is resacralized. We see the world whole in its vital interconnectedness, as a community of subjects that are all intrinsically valuable. Human beings are repositioned as members of this community—recognized as kin to all others here. Instead of being turned in on ourselves we are turned outward in love to God and our neighbors—*all* our neighbors. As we look with a loving eye we know that our true vocation in this community is in creating and caring—not in acquiring and consuming. We seek the flourishing of all and live together in a community marked by solidarity, sufficiency, and sustainability—a convivial community of creation.

Only Us Earthlings?

Astronomers regularly discover new exoplanets in what we think of as zones habitable for life. What if we should find other forms of life out there in the wider cosmos? How do we think about incarnation in relation to other life-forms in other worlds? Is God with them too?

When we look out into the night sky we are filled with wonder at the magnificence of it all and humbled by its vastness. Ted Peters has it right: "Your mind fills to the brim and overflows with awe. Infinity fills your soul."[66] We return for a moment to Psalm 8:3–4:

> When I look at your heavens, the work of your fingers,
>   the moon and the stars that you have established;
> what are human beings that you are mindful of them,
>   mortals that you care for them?

William Brown has observed that "the wonder of it all prompts one . . . to wonder about it all."[67] Our twin impulses to worship and to inquire are joined at the root—in wonder. "Wonder is what unites the psalmist, the sage, and the scientist."[68]

Making the connection between these twin impulses of wonder is the orienting center of astrotheology. Ted Peters offers a helpful definition:

66. Ted Peters, "Introducing Astrotheology," in *Astrotheology: Science and Theology Meet Extraterrestrial Life*, ed. Ted Peters (Eugene, OR: Cascade Books, 2018).

67. William Brown, *The Seven Pillars of Creation: The Bible, Science, and the Ecology of Wonder* (Oxford: Oxford University Press, 2010), 4.

68. Brown, *Seven Pillars of Creation*, 4.

Astrotheology is that branch of theology which provides a critical analysis of the contemporary space sciences combined with an explication of classic doctrines such as creation and Christology for the purpose of constructing a comprehensive and meaningful understanding of our human situation within an astonishingly immense cosmos.[69]

In this section we reflect theologically on the remarkable discoveries of current science concerning potentially habitable planets and what that might mean for how we think about incarnation. We engage primarily with astrobiology, the study of the origin, distribution, and future of life in the wider cosmos. Scientists differ as to their assessment of the likelihood of there being life elsewhere and concerning the prospects of our actually finding it. These are highly speculative questions at this point. As Neil deGrasse Tyson quipped, astrobiology "is one of the few disciplines that attempt to function at least for now in the complete absence of first-hand data."[70] Nevertheless, *what if* there is life out there? What does that mean theologically? A lively discussion is now taking place about what this could mean for incarnation in particular. Is there one incarnation or are there many? From our own discussion, we make a constructive proposal consistent with the understanding of incarnation drawn out in this book.

What If There Are Others out There?

Jennifer Wiseman reminds us that speculation concerning other worlds with other living beings dates back at least as far as Epicurus (around 300 BCE), who said, "There are infinite worlds both like and unlike this world of ours. . . . We must believe that in all worlds there are living creatures."[71]

As of this writing, over four thousand exoplanets (extrasolar planets orbiting other stars than the sun) have been discovered.[72] An exponen-

69. Ted Peters, "The Tasks of Astrotheology," in *Astrotheology: Science and Theology Meet Extraterrestrial Life*, ed. Ted Peters (Eugene, OR: Cascade Books, 2018), 11.

70. Neil deGrasse Tyson, *Space Chronicles: Facing the Ultimate Frontier* (New York: Norton, 2012), 36.

71. Jennifer Wiseman, "Exoplanets and the Search for Life beyond Earth," in *Astrotheology: Science and Theology Meet Extraterrestrial Life*, ed. Ted Peters (Eugene, OR: Cascade Books, 2018), 124.

72. See "The Extrasolar Planets Encyclopaedia," last updated April 27, 2021, http://exoplanet.eu/.

tial growth in discoveries has accompanied the use of new technologies for spotting them. We are able to detect wobbles in some stars as they are affected by the gravitational pull of their planets. With powerful telescopes we are now able to see "transits" when a planet crosses in front of the star that it orbits. Discoveries have been so frequent of late that scientists have concluded that most stars have one or more planets orbiting them.

We know that the number of stars out there is "astronomical" (to borrow a pun from Ted Peters). There are roughly ten million quadrillion (10^{24}) stars in the observable universe.[73] When we realize there are more exoplanets than there are stars, this is an astonishing number. As Peters observes, "Our planet, like a drop of water in the ocean, is swallowed up in an apparently endless sea of immeasurability."[74] Many of these planets, by their distance from the star they orbit, are thought to be in the habitable zone or the Goldilocks zone since they are not too hot and not too cold for there to be liquid water on the surface. A planet with liquid water is a place where life as we know it could be possible. The burgeoning field of astrobiology responds to this possibility.

It remains an open question whether any of these exoplanets have even simple life-forms, much less intelligent life or extraterrestrial intelligence (ETI). What can be offered on this question is, at best, scientifically informed speculation. However, we now know that "the raw ingredients needed for life are common in the universe."[75] This has led to the search for "biosigns" in planetary atmospheres. We come steadily closer to being able to detect such signs if they are there.

This search has been particularly fruitful around faint, low-mass stars (stars that are roughly one-half to one-third the size of our Sun). When planets transit their low-mass host stars, they block out more light than if they transited a Sun-sized star and are therefore easier to detect. Low-mass stars are also just bright enough to backlight a transiting planet's atmosphere (if it exists), but generally not so bright that observations are difficult. This enables the study of the atmosphere's chemical makeup. Finally, the planets in the habitable zones of low-mass stars are much

---

73. Wolf-Chase, "Interactive Cosmos," 58.

74. Peters, "Tasks of Astrotheology," 33.

75. Wolf-Chase, "Interactive Cosmos," 59. See also Grace Wolf-Chase, "New Worlds, New Civilizations? From Science Fiction to Science Fact," *Theology and Science* 16, no. 4 (2018): 415–26, 417. "We now know that complex organic molecules (*polycyclic aromatic hydrocarbons* or *PAHs*) necessary to life as we know it pervade our galaxy."

closer to their host stars than those of Sun-like stars, so they orbit with greater frequency, thus allowing for more observation of transits.

A case in point is the work of a team headed by Jennifer Winters at the Harvard-Smithsonian Center for Astrophysics. The team has discovered an exoplanet (LTT 1445Ab) in a three-star system that circles its host star once every 5.4 days. It is a perfect candidate for examining the composition of the atmosphere using telescopes with spectrographs that can spread out the received light spectrum from an exoplanet, revealing the precise patterns of light frequencies distinctive to particular elements. Different elements that might be present in the atmosphere have distinctive signatures that can be read in the spectra. If researchers find oxygen and methane, these would be biosigns that may point to biological origins.[76] Such a discovery is exciting and could, among other things, provide good candidate exoplanets for the "Search for Extraterrestrial Intelligence (SETI) which uses both radio and optical telescopes to search for artificial signals that might be transmitted by technological civilizations."

Scientists disagree on the likelihood of finding other life-forms in the wider universe. They disagree even more sharply about the prospect of finding intelligent life. There are pessimistic readings and optimistic readings. On the pessimistic side are those who, like Fermi, ask, "Where is everybody?" Given the long history of the cosmos, there has been a great expanse of time in which to evolve and develop technologies for communication and transportation that should fill the skies with noise and space travelers. They should be there, but they are not. This is known as the Fermi paradox.

On the optimistic side are people who look at the sheer numbers of planets in the habitable zone. Frank Drake devised a method of estimating the number of technologically advanced societies "likely" to be in our galaxy and to be advanced enough to potentially communicate with us. This method is known as the Drake equation. Estimates differ, but by all accounts the number is staggering. In answer to Fermi's question, "Where is everybody?," the optimists remind us that it could be we just have not heard from them *yet*. It is only relatively recently in Earth's long history that we have had the means to communicate at a distance. Our exoplanetary neighbors may be in a different place technologically.

---

76. Jennifer Winters et al., "Three Red Suns in the Sky: A Transiting, Terrestrial Planet in a Triple M Dwarf System at 6.9 Parsecs," *Astronomical Journal* 158, no. 4 (September 23, 2019): 152.

Optimists also remind us that the absence of evidence is not the evidence of absence. They remain hopeful.

One optimist is Steven Dick, who holds the chair in astrobiology at the Library of Congress. In his 2013 report to the US House Science, Space, and Technology Committee, he pointed to several significant steps in astrobiology that may be taking us ever closer to the discovery of extraterrestrial life:[77]

- The ever increasing number of exoplanets discovered in what we think of as habitable zones.
- Explorations in our own solar system that have revealed that Mars at one time had enough liquid water to support life and that Titan (one of the moons of Jupiter) is rich with pre-biotic compounds and lakes of methane.
- Further research into life on earth which has revealed life-forms in places and under circumstances we thought could not support life.
- Planned research with the James Webb Space Telescope that will allow us to search more effectively for bio-signs on other planets.

With these steady advances toward discovery of extraterrestrial life, perhaps it is time to get ready.

Is it a problem theologically if other life-forms are discovered? In contrast to scientists who think the discovery of ETI should be problematic for religious people (and it is for some), most systematic theologians who have reflected on the matter are ready to put out the welcome mat. John Haught, John Polkinghorne, and Ted Peters do not find this prospect to be a threat to faith. Peters proposes a "Bible Welcomes Aliens" position. He reminds us, "The Bible tells us to welcome the sojourner, the stranger, the outsider, the foreigner, the other. St. Paul tells us to (Rom 12:13) 'extend hospitality to strangers.' Who could be more other or stranger than a space alien? Our disposition to hospitality should be gracious."[78]

In our explorations we may or may not find life, but we will never be able to answer the question "Are we alone?" with a definitive "yes."[79]

77. Steven Dick, Testimony to the US House Science, Space and Technology Committee, December 4, 2013. https://science.house.gov/news/videos/watch/20131204-dr-steven-dick-testimony.

78. Peters, "Introducing Astrotheology," 18.

79. Wolf-Chase, "New Worlds?," 418.

Given that the building blocks of life are ubiquitous and there are more exoplanets out there than there are stars, we may agree with the SETI researcher in the movie based on Carl Sagan's 1985 book *Contact*: "If we are all there is, there is a whole lot of wasted space out there."[80]

One observation I would add is that we may be narrowing our search for life unnecessarily if we look only at what seems to us habitable zones. When we think about life we generally think of some very basic requirements such as water, oxygen, light, photosynthesis, a reasonable temperature range, and so on. However, some life-forms—extremophiles—do not require these for life. Tardigrades, for example, are able to go without water for decades, yet they remain alive. Many anaerobic multicellular organisms do not require oxygen to live. Some sea creatures live in deep places where light never penetrates and photosynthesis does not occur. Many creatures—worms, fish, shrimp—thrive on chemosynthesis rather than photosynthesis. Remarkably, they live at temperatures hot enough to melt lead and in waters full of what we consider toxic chemicals. Life is hardier and more various than we anticipate. When we look at habitable zones, it seems that we are asking whether we could live there rather than asking if life can be there. Perhaps we can widen the search.

If there are others out there, they may be very simple life-forms, as was the case on Earth for the vast majority of its multibillion-year history of life.[81] If there are intelligent life-forms out there, having close encounters with them is more than a little bit challenging. Issues of distance may be prohibitive. The closest exoplanet in a habitable zone is Proxima Centauri b, and it is 4.2 light-years away. We cannot yet move at warp speeds, so traveling to meet them is problematic. Our best effort so far has been the twin Voyager spacecrafts launched in the late summer of 1977. Remarkably, these remote ambassadors still beam messages back to Earth forty-three years later, with data from their deep space travels. Voyager 1 is, at the writing of this book, about fourteen billion miles from Earth in interstellar space, and Voyager 2 is not far behind. We have a long way to go in interstellar travel before we can meet our near neighbors.

What if these near neighbors have a more advanced technological civilization? Perhaps they will make contact with us. This raises a different set of questions. Would they be benevolent? Or would they be like us? Our track record on Earth has not been good when it comes to more

80. Carl Sagan, *Contact* (New York: Simon and Schuster, 1985).
81. Wiseman, "Exoplanets and the Search for Life beyond Earth," 131.

technologically advanced civilizations interacting with less technologically advanced civilizations. Ask the peoples who had close encounters with "settlers," invaders, colonizers, conquistadors.

Close encounters with aliens are probably not on our near horizon, given the great distances and challenges of communication. However, other prospects closer at hand also pose theological and ethical issues. In the not-too-distant future, we are likely to be able to travel to Mars and establish a human presence there. How do we do that in ways that are responsible? We need a wider conversation about how we interact with Mars (and other worlds) in ways that do not repeat the legacy of colonialism that has been so destructive in our own context. In 2018 the Library of Congress's John W. Kluge Center sponsored a conference to further such a conversation. It was titled "Becoming Interplanetary: What Living on Earth Can Teach Us about Living on Mars."[82] What valuable lessons have we learned that we can apply as we become interplanetary?

How do we curb our habits of thoughtless, extractive, exploitative practices in pursuit of selfish interests at the expense of the flourishing of ecosystems and living beings? We argued in earlier chapters that human beings have heightened gifts of rationality and freedom. For this reason they may also be thought to have a heightened responsibility for creativity and care in relation to the whole natural world. We have also claimed, on the basis of incarnational theology, that bodies matter. Surely this would extend to alien bodies also. Given the difficulty we have had living according to this principle with one another here on Earth, what are the chances we will suddenly realize the urgency of applying this principle in interplanetary explorations? We have argued the value of solidarity, sufficiency, and sustainability as the way forward to a better future. How can we do better at living out these values than we as a species have done so far? Perhaps we need a sustained conversation in a community of moral discourse to discern how we are doing and what needs to change.

It is possible that we should get to a different place as a human community before spreading our influence to other worlds. As of the writing of this book in the spring of 2020, we are in the midst of a pandemic. It has revealed the inequities of our society, the vulnerabilities of people of color. It is also the time of the murder of George Floyd at the hands of police officers who already had him cuffed and subdued. The racism and brutality of our culture is undeniable. Pandemic metaphors suggest themselves. Perhaps we should be under quarantine and not spread the

---

82. https://www.youtube.com/watch?v=g2q2tlojDB4 Accessed 5/20/21.

cultural virus we seem to have. It would be better if we found our way to a healthy social and ecological reality marked by solidarity, sufficiency, and sustainability before we share with interstellar neighbors. The "precautionary principle" applies here.[83] We should not introduce into a new context something that could cause harm there.

How can we collaborate as a human species to establish principles of interaction that might cause our interactions to be a blessing and not a curse upon those with whom we have close encounters? If we are indeed created by and for love, as earlier chapters have claimed, what should that look like in our relations with the new others we may encounter? As Grace Wolf-Chase has wisely counseled, "Considering the possibility of extraterrestrial species motivates us to reevaluate humanity's history as stewards of Earth, and to examine critically human behaviors before migrating to other worlds."[84]

One Incarnation or Many?

The prospect of other worlds with other life-forms has generated quite a conversation around Christology. A point of real controversy concerns what the discovery of ETI would mean for our understanding of God's incarnation in the person of Jesus of Nazareth. In the book *Astrotheology*, several contributors respond to the following proposition: "If multiple societies of extraterrestrial intelligent beings on exoplanets exist, we can predict that God will or already has provided a species-specific incarnation for each planet parallel to God's incarnation in Jesus Christ on Earth."[85]

The contributors respond with either a positive or a negative answer and present their reasoning. Both sides engage the proposition thoughtfully, struggle mightily to avoid the pitfalls of either option, and offer extraordinary insights. Here we only interrogate the question, highlight some of the insights and challenges from the contributors, and then propose a response that is grounded in the insights on incarnation emerging from this book. We contend that "God is with us" does not mean "just us Earthlings" and show how the operative understanding of incarnation

83. The precautionary principle states that the introduction of a new product or process whose ultimate effects are disputed or unknown should be resisted. It has mainly been used to prohibit the importation of genetically modified organisms into food, but it could be more generally applied.

84. Wolf-Chase, "New Worlds?," 423.

85. Ted Peters, "One Incarnation or Many?," in *Astrotheology: Science and Theology Meet Extraterrestrial Life*, ed. Ted Peters (Eugene, OR: Cascade Books, 2018), 271.

makes a world of difference. We have proposed that all things are in God and God is in all things (yet transcending them). We referenced Augustine's metaphor for God as an ocean in which the creation is like a sponge that is fully saturated with the ocean while the ocean is vastly greater. When we view God's incarnation in the cosmos in this way it shifts the discourse on the issues under discussion decisively.

The above proposition of a species-specific incarnation needed for intelligent beings on exoplanets seems to the respondents to have two pitfalls:

> If a theologian answers *yes*, then the critics dub the idea of a planet-hopping Christ *absurd*. If a theologian answers *no*, and affirms that the incarnation of Christ on Earth is efficacious for the entire cosmos, then it appears that a pre-Copernican Earth chauvinism is at work.[86]

Those who answer yes to the proposition do so with a concern that divine self-revelation would meet all our intelligent neighbors in space in ways that they can receive it. It is not enough that incarnation happens on Earth; how will it be known by those at a distance? It must surely be manifest to them on their own terms.

Furthermore, what if there is need for redemption out there, just as there is here? Would we not want to affirm that the gracious, generous, loving God we have come to know in Jesus of Nazareth is at work redeeming whatever needs redeeming in these far-off places? Would God be gracious, generous, and loving to them as well? Robert Russell affirms, "God's grace will redeem and sanctify every species in which reason and moral conscience are kindled."[87] Perhaps we can extend this even further. What if the whole creation—other worlds included—"is in some sense like us "groaning in labor pains," awaiting redemption((Rom. 8:22)? Divine incarnation in all creation is loving and responsive to those with reason and moral conscience—and also in ways that are fitting, loving, and responsive to the whole creation.

The critics of this approach make a point of the incoherence of the idea. For example, the potential number of life-bearing planets and the prospect of a staggering number of necessary incarnations from now until the extinction of life in all worlds is mind-boggling. Some critics

---

86. Peters, "One Incarnation or Many?," 273.

87. Robert John Russell, "Many Incarnations or One?," in *Astrotheology: Science and Theology Meet Extraterrestrial Life*, ed. Ted Peters (Eugene, OR: Cascade Books, 2018), 305.

sharpen the incoherence by imposing the puzzling restriction that divine incarnation(s) can only happen "one at a time."

Another argument against this view centers on personhood. We make much of the *person* of Christ in our Christology ("two natures in one *person*"). But what if the intelligent life-forms we find are not "persons" in the proper sense? How can the appearance of the "person" of Christ be meaningful if they are not persons? This question is easily addressed if we shift from an anthropocentric standpoint to recognize the subject status of all beings, as was argued earlier in the chapter.

These critiques and others that can be made push in the direction of the claim for the one incarnation on Earth being sufficient for the whole cosmos. However, the one-incarnation advocates face the challenge of geocentrism and anthropocentrism. Why would what happens on Earth have decisive significance for the whole cosmos? Why would God be incarnate only here? They answer these questions with attention to several theological themes. First, this problem is just another iteration of the unavoidable "scandal of particularity." The claim made that the divine Logos is incarnate in one particular human being was already challenging. When other worlds enter the picture, the situation is not qualitatively different, only expanded quantitatively. Second, through the *communicatio idiomatum* (communication of the attributes), the ubiquity of God's presence is already communicated to the incarnate One. Wherever God is, the Christ is already there. Third, there could be other acts of self-revelation elsewhere (not just on Earth), but the redeeming work of incarnation, because of its transforming power, need only happen once. Its effects pervade the whole of the cosmos, which is becoming a new creation.

This is a very abbreviated presentation of a complex and thoughtful discussion. With the other responders, I want to avoid the pitfalls they acknowledge. However, I have another alternative to propose based on the understanding of incarnation being argued in this book. Two questions arise: What do we really mean by "incarnation"? What is the purpose of incarnation?

What Do We Mean by "Incarnation"?

Incarnation in my meaning is broader in scope: God is in the world, and the world is in God. Yet God is always more than the world. Returning to the classic metaphor Augustine offers in his *Confessions*,

I visualize you, Lord, surrounding [creation] on all sides and permeating it, but infinite in all directions, as if there was a sea everywhere, and stretching through immense distances, a single sea which had within it a large but finite sponge, and the sponge was in every part filled from the immense sea. This is the way in which I supposed your finite creation to be full of you, infinite as you are, and said: "Here is God and see what God has created. God is good and is most mightily and incomparably superior to these things."[88]

It may be that in the proposition being debated we have been working with a meaning for incarnation that is too small. The planet-hopping-Christ scenario is deeply problematic for a number of reasons. The primary one may be that it assumes that God shows up here and there, now and then; underneath that assumption is the unintended acceptance of the ordinary absence of God. Divine incarnation is being treated as an exception to God's ordinary way of being. What if it is the chief exemplification of God's way of being and God is really, already with us—all of us? We followed this line of reasoning in discussing the Incarnation in Jesus of Nazareth. It is not an exception to God's ordinary presence and activity in world process but a place where we can see that God is already present in the whole creation—active everywhere and always.

Cosmic Christology illumines this way of thinking. The divine Logos is the one in whom all things visible and invisible hold together, the one in whom the fullness of God was pleased to dwell, and the one through whom all things are reconciled to God. There is one comprehensive, cosmos-embracing incarnation (Col. 1:15–20). The whole of the material cosmos is embraced in this vision. All matter matters. Bodies matters. Returning to the theme of deep incarnation, Peters comments,

Incarnation is not limited to putting on a show for rational beings who can watch it. The significance of God becoming flesh stretches to every nook and cranny of the physical universe, including plants and animals who do not actively or consciously share communion with God. God's presence is not restricted to the realm of the mental, the intellectual, the spiritual. It is physical as well. [89]

88. Augustine, *The Confessions*, trans. Henry Chadwick, Oxford World Classics (New York: Oxford University Press, 1998), 7.115.
89. Peters, "One Incarnation or Many?," 293.

From this perspective it is a bit of a puzzle why the presence of other planets and potential life-forms poses such a problem for our Christology and not for our doctrine of creation. We seem to have a bifurcation between creation and Christology when these should be joined, as they are in cosmic Christology. Yet we see the bifurcation in the very different responses evoked by the prospect of other planets and potential life-forms. When working from the doctrine of creation, what we perceive is the divine generosity, even prodigality, in creating many worlds. We marvel at this enlarged sense of the creation and see it as the admirable unfolding of God's wisdom. However, when it comes to Christology, the same prospect becomes disruptive. If we fully embrace a cosmic Christology we can avoid this bifurcation.

It is not necessary to imagine a planet-hopping Christ. It is not necessary to resort to geocentrism either. In the far reaches of the cosmos, including all stars and exoplanets, the one who is the foundation of all things visible and invisible is already there—wherever "there" is. The only question is how the deep reality of God's relation to each and to all becomes manifest to the inhabitants. This can happen in whatever ways are most appropriate to a given life-world.

There is no escape from the scandal of particularity, as divine manifestations always come to us incarnate in particular realities, embodied and embedded in particular contexts. The Word comes to us incarnate—in the flesh. For Christians, Jesus of Nazareth is the place where we have come to know what we believe we know about God. For us he is the window that we see through and the way that we find God. We cannot presume to know what the window is and the way for others to find God.

Perhaps it would help if we could extrapolate a bit from the discussion of the relation between Christianity and other faith traditions. We affirmed that we as Christians find a decisive revelation and manifestation of God in Jesus the Christ. We affirmed that he is truly God, but demurred from claiming that he is all there is to God. We kept a fitting reticence to presuming to know the ways of God with people of other religious traditions. We proposed that people of different religious should engage in dialogue that is open and both mutually illumining and mutually critical. What we have learned of God in our own faith tradition is that God is gracious and merciful, slow to anger, and abounding in steadfast love (Ps. 145:8). We may believe God will be like this with other people as well and not just us Christians. Could we not take a similar anti-exclusivist leap when we think about others in other worlds?

My conclusion is that speaking of one incarnation is more plausible (and neither geocentric nor anthropocentric) if we understand incarnation as all embracing. Looking through the lens of cosmic Christology helps. There is one comprehensive, cosmos-embracing incarnation. In this sense, God is in all and through all; God is already "all in all."

What Is the Purpose of Incarnation?

The debate around incarnation provoked by the prospect of extraterrestrial intelligent life included asking whether the incarnation was for the purpose of God's self-revelation or to fix a broken creation. What if it is neither of these? Both may happen in incarnation, but the purpose of incarnation is the loving union of God with the creation. We highlight thoughts on the two options suggested and then explain another alternative that might be preferable.

The fix-a-broken-creation alternative needs to ask a prior question. Will these others *need* redemption? We can make no conclusions here. The first thing to say is, "We don't know." Are they like us? Maybe, maybe not. Do they live in an Edenic perfection, or do they face the predicament of sin and suffering and evil as we do?

I have already expressed reservations about seeing our human predicament as the result of an ahistorical fall of an original human couple. I nevertheless affirm some of the deeper insights that cluster around the Augustinian discussion of original sin. Our situation is not just a matter of needing to make better moral choices—a moralistic vision that assumes absolute freedom. There is a deeper difficulty. "Sin" is more than sins. We are born into a social world full of brokenness that is not of our doing. We are shaped by that system and its structures. Our situation is tragic. Yet for our part, we continue and extend the brokenness. We are guilty. We are at one and the same time innocent victims and responsible agents. *If* they are like us, presumably they will have evolved over time in a state of finitude and freedom like our own. They may potentially have something like our experience of brokenness that needs healing.

In many ways the scenario that Irenaeus proposed has more to offer than the "fall from Edenic perfection" scenario in Augustine. Irenaeus envisions humans at their origin as created immature and capable of growth. This seems a better fit for an evolving, emerging universe. From what we know about how the cosmos works, emergence is the way things are. Novel structures and processes arise during the process of self-organization in complex systems. Things come to be that are more than the sum of their parts. Brain science is a case in point. It could be said that the brain is nothing but chemical, electrical, and biological processes. Yet from these processes, mind emerges and is different from and not reducible to these building blocks. How can brain become mind? Neuroscientists sometimes say in good humor, "It's a gray area." "Something more" is ever coming to be out of "nothing but."

Human beings have emerged as a life-form over eons, and we continue even now to evolve. We are ever "people on the way." We are not yet what we shall be. We are in a sense becoming human—not yet fully there. Jesus of Nazareth, who lived life in union with God, was "truly human" and shows us how to become human—realizing the image of God in us.

We are growing into the fullness of the likeness of Christ, who is the image of God. Mistakes are likely along the way. We are like toddlers just learning to walk. God supports us in our freedom and compassionately reaches for us when we fall. God in a sense walks alongside us and even sometimes ahead of us, beckoning us forward, luring us onward in the creative advance. Divine mercy and grace are extended to us in our condition as beloved, fragile, and fallible beings—beautiful yet broken. We and the whole creation are suffering through to something higher; we experience the birth pains of the new creation. There is suffering that just goes with becoming, but also unnecessary suffering that we bring upon ourselves and others by our self-centeredness. This suffering needs healing, and healing happens in the incarnation. For Irenaeus, in the incarnation, Jesus' own life process recapitulates our life processes—healing as he goes. "He became as we are that we might become as he is."[90] If the situation of the others is anything like our own, it needs compassion and healing and luring toward the good. Surely God's way of compassion, healing, and luring toward the good will be extended to our neighbors as to us.

The healing of our brokenness (our redemption) happens in incarnation, but this is not the purpose of incarnation. With Duns Scotus I resist thinking of incarnation as an emergency measure made necessary by human sin. Incarnation was in the divine eternal intent for loving union with creation. In Calvin's view and Reformed theology generally, the divine intention for incarnation is supralapsarian (before the fall). Incarnation is a divine necessity coming from the place of love. Redemption is a human necessity given our brokenness (infralapsarian [after the fall]). The estrangement resulting from our being turned in on ourselves is overcome, and loving relations with God and our neighbor are nurtured.

---

90. Irenaeus, *Against Heresies*, preface.

The purpose of the incarnation is not redemption as such but loving union. Nevertheless, loving union is redemptive. Neither is the purpose of incarnation merely divine self-revelation. Like fixing the broken creation, self-revelation happens in the incarnation, but there is more going on in incarnation. The purpose was loving union, not merely self-revelation.

Incarnation is a divine self-giving, and it is transformative. God in union with flesh transforms flesh, healing from within. As Gregory of Nazianzus saw it, "What he did not assume, he did not heal."[91] It is the divine taking on of our flesh that heals us. The estrangement between us and God is bridged from God's side. This is justification—not as a juridical declaration that we are righteous, but justification as an actual "setting right." It entails renewal of life. Something actually changes. More is going on than divine self-revelation. It is not a matter of new information about God but new *in-formation* of human beings *by* God. We are formed anew in union with God. We referenced union with God (*theosis*) as the goal of Christ's work: "He became human that we might become God."[92] This makes an ontological difference—a difference in our very being. Our union with God is transformative; it also reveals who God is, heals what is broken, and reconciles us in our estrangement from God and others. Incarnation, then, is the divine eternal intent for union with creation—not just for us Earthlings, but the whole of the cosmos and any others who are out there. It is one comprehensive incarnation with many places of manifestation.

We should be clear: with respect to other life-forms or ETI, we are speculating and do not know what is out there. We are moving from what we have experienced and believe to what we can hardly imagine. It does make sense, theologically, that the God we have come to know in Jesus the Christ—a God of loving relation who desires union with creation—will not be a different kind of God with the rest of the cosmos. Interestingly, in the oft-quoted verse from John 3:16, "God so loved the world," the word translated "world" is in effect "cosmos" (Greek: κόσμος [*kosmos*]).

We have already known for some time that creation is not limited to planet Earth. Our geocentrism has already been challenged, not only by science but by faith. As Ted Peters puts it, "The immensity of God

91. Gregory of Nazianzus, *Letter 101 (To Cledonius against Apollinaris)*, in *Christology of the Later Fathers*, ed. Edward R. Hardy (Philadelphia: Westminster Press, 1954), 218.

92. Athanasius of Alexandria, *Contra Gentes* 54, in Athanasius, *Contra Gentes and De Incarnatione*, ed. and trans. Robert Thomson (Oxford: Clarendon, 1971), 113–15.

surpasses the immensity of the universe. After all, since Anselm we have thought of God as that than which nothing greater can be conceived. It is God, not Earth, who is the center of reality. And the circumference of reality as well."[93]

If we find other life-forms and even intelligent life on other worlds, our understanding of God's creative work only continues to be enlarged. We learn once again that this is no tribal deity but the God of all things visible and invisible. If others are out there, this is not a problem for incarnation either. We only learn that when we say, "God is with us," the "us" is larger than we previously imagined. Incarnation is larger, and God is greater.

93. Peters, "Tasks of Astrotheology," 45.

Chapter 7

How Can We Say God Is with Us in the Face of So Much Suffering and Evil?

Suffering and evil surround us. We are beginning to experience the erratic weather patterns that accompany climate change. Hurricanes are more fierce and more frequent. Floods in some places and droughts in others have afflicted lands that could previously support agriculture. Fires burn uncontrollably in some areas. Islands and coastlands are seeing waters rise. Almost twenty-five million people are currently displaced from their homes due to weather-related disasters. In our social world, political authoritarianism threatens participatory governance, and nationalism destabilizes global efforts to work together on global problems. Our failed global economic order does not provide well for the vast majority of people. Systemic racism, injustice, and violence are death-dealing realities in our time. In 2020 a pandemic unleashed a new terror on top of these ongoing threats to life. It proved a kind of "apocalypse" (which means revelation or unveiling), showing underlying inequities and disproportionate vulnerability for some as compared to others. How can we say that God is with us in the face of so much suffering and evil?

We first explore insights that Christian tradition brings to this question. Next we ask how the Incarnation might change our vision of what "God is with us" should mean. If we are expecting "God is with us" to mean that God will use all-controlling power to prevent evil and make everything all right, we may have to reconsider. This is not what we actually see in the Incarnation in Jesus of Nazareth. We do not see divine power in him as power in the mode of domination and control. What we see instead is a loving, compassionate responsiveness to sinners and people who are suffering. In his ministry he heals and feeds and teaches, and he calls people to transformed life. On the cross the power of God is the power of vulnerable, suffering love. If we reconsider the meaning of "God is with us" in light of the Incarnation, we are able—even in the face of suffering and evil—to affirm indeed that God is with us.

Questions Arise for Us

As I write this book in the spring and summer of 2020, the world is dealing with the crisis of the coronavirus and the untold human suffering, loss of livelihood, and loss of life that have come in its wake. The coronavirus is an instance of suffering that originates from natural causes. It is what is traditionally called "natural evil" because it comes from a natural occurrence rather than the actions of rational beings (moral evil). The virus is doing what a virus does, without malicious intent. However, there is no clear line of demarcation here because a great deal of the suffering that has resulted has been from poor decisions on the part of "rational" agents in leadership. Further, moral evil is at work in the fact that inequities have left some people more vulnerable than others. The fault lines of economic inequity and systemic racism are laid bare now for all to see.

In the midst of this crisis, people are asking, *Where is God in all of this? Why did God let this happen? Is God punishing us (me)? Why doesn't God do something?* Surely these are the worst of times. The questions these times provoke deserve a considered response. We are not the first persons to ask these hard questions and wonder if God is *really* with us. There have been many instances of horrific suffering from natural and moral evil. We briefly touch upon four to illustrate: the Black Death, the Lisbon earthquake, the 1918 influenza epidemic, and the Holocaust.

What is now called the Black Death, also known as the Pestilence and the Great Mortality, was the most fatal pandemic recorded in human history. The Black Death resulted in the deaths of up to seventy-five million to two hundred million people in Eurasia and North Africa, peaking in Europe from 1347 to 1351.

In 1755 the Lisbon earthquake occurred on the morning of November 1, the Feast of All Saints. The earthquake, combined with subsequent fires and the tsunami that followed in its wake, almost totally destroyed Lisbon and adjoining areas. The death toll in Lisbon alone was ten thousand to thirty thousand people. The earthquake caused fissures up to sixteen feet wide to open up in the city center. Survivors rushed to the open space of the docks for safety but then watched as the sea receded and ran as the ensuing great tsunami engulfed the harbor and downtown area. Candles lit in homes and churches all around the city for All Saints' Day were knocked over, starting a firestorm that burned for hours and asphyxiated many remaining survivors, even as far as one hundred feet from the flames. The event was widely discussed and dwelt upon by European Enlightenment philosophers.

This catastrophe led to extensive reflection from philosophers and theologians around the question of theodicy. "Theodicy" is derived from a joining of two terms: God (Greek: θεός [*theos*]) and justice or righteousness (Greek: δικαιοσύνη [*dikaiosunē*]). The term was coined by Gottfried Leibniz. It signified discussion around the question of whether God's justice could be vindicated, given that God is deemed to be all powerful and yet the world is full of suffering and evil.

The 1918 influenza pandemic was the most severe in recent history. It was caused by an H1N1 virus with genes of avian origin and spread worldwide during 1918 and 1919. About five hundred million people— one-third of the world's population—became infected with this virus. The number of deaths is estimated to have been at least fifty million worldwide. Mortality was high in people younger than five years old, twenty to forty years old, and sixty-five years old and older. The high mortality in otherwise healthy people, including those in their twenties and thirties, was a unique feature of this pandemic. There was no vaccine developed, and efforts worldwide were limited to nonpharmaceutical interventions such as isolation, quarantine, good personal hygiene, use of disinfectants, and limitations of public gatherings, which were applied unevenly.

A catastrophe of an altogether different order was the Holocaust, also known as the Shoah. It was no natural disaster (natural evil), but rather a horror of human construction—a straightforward instance of moral evil. Between 1941 and 1945, across German-occupied Europe, Nazi Germany and its collaborators systematically murdered some six million Jews, around two-thirds of Europe's Jewish population. The murders were carried out in pogroms and mass shootings, by a policy of "extermination" through work in concentration camps, and in gas chambers. These unspeakable acts were carried out by ordinary people in whom fear, prejudice, and hatred had been carefully cultivated. When the horrors of what happened came to light, many pretended not to know what had been going on or claimed to have heard about what was happening but not believed it. Those who were directly involved and could not deny it would say, "I was just following orders." Adolf Eichmann, the chief architect of what was euphemistically called "the final solution," said as he awaited trial for war crimes, "To sum it all up, I must say that I regret nothing." Here we come face-to-face not only with massive suffering but also with horrendous evil.

People who faced these historic natural disasters and human atrocities asked the questions we also ask amid the crises of our own day. Can we really affirm that God is with us in the face of the depth and breadth of suffering and evil we see? This is an ancient and troubling problem for Christian faith because we affirm that the world is created and governed by a God who is wholly good and all powerful. If we were willing to let go of either God's goodness or God's power—or belief in God altogether!—then this problem would resolve itself. Suffering and evil would of course still be present, but we would have no reason to believe the world should be any better than it is.

Responding to the Questions

Through the long centuries of struggling with this perplexing matter, a range of responses have emerged in Christian tradition. There are no easy answers here. It has been said that anyone who has an easy answer to this question simply has not understood the question. Nevertheless, the responses available in Christian tradition offer some ways of approaching these questions meaningfully. The discussion here offers a brief sketch of some prominent traditional responses and then proposes an alternative that is grounded in the vision of incarnation articulated in this book.

Augustine (354–430) explored this issue deeply and set the course for much of the discussion that has followed. It has been said that most of Christian theology is composed of footnotes to Augustine. Before he became a Christian, Augustine was attracted to Manichean dualism, partly because it at least had an answer for the presence of evil in the world. For Manicheans, cosmic dualism explained it all. Two forces are at work in the world: one good and one evil, equally powerful and forever in conflict. When Augustine became a Christian, however, he rejected this view with a vengeance. He insisted that there is only one God and that God is both unqualifiedly good and all powerful. He then developed five arguments (theodicies) to defend God's goodness in the face of the problem of suffering and evil.

First, Augustine affirms that everything that exists must be good, since God made all things. Thus, evil cannot have a "proper" existence. Evil can only be the absence or privation of some good (*privatio boni*). He gives the example of blindness, which is only the absence of sight and not something that exists independently. When disease is healed, Augustine observes, it does not go somewhere else as if it had an independent existence. What we call evil is really only the lack of some good. In a sense it has a parasitic character in relation to some good thing, and it is nothing in and of itself. In this way, Augustine argues that evil has no existence in its own right. God did not create evil.

Another answer Augustine gives lies in what may be called the "principle of plenitude." God's goodness is so superabundantly full that, like a fountain, it overflows into a teeming cascade of every kind of being. The richest and most valuable world is one that includes every possible kind of existence. It would therefore include lower as well as higher beings, ugly things as well as beautiful, things of lesser and greater perfection. When humans complain of our situation—characterized by fragility, fallibility, and mortality—it is as if we aspire to be angels rather than human beings. If we were angels, however, an entire order of being (human beings) would not exist. The world would be a poorer place for the loss of any of the orders of being. The plenitude that God has created makes for a better, richer world. In this way, God's goodness in creating us—fragile, fallible, and mortal though we are—is confirmed.

Augustine offers a third argument, sometimes called the "aesthetic argument." It works from the metaphor of God as an artist and creation as a work of art. There is beauty and harmony in the work as a whole, even if we may not see them from our limited perspective. For example, in a painting, the deep shades of blue may be as necessary as the cheery yellows for the beauty of the whole. In fact, the contrast may contribute to the beauty. Our suffering has its place. Not seeing the "painting" in its entirety, we may not understand. Augustine also uses the aesthetic argument to deal with the problem of transitoriness and death: good things pass away, and so do we. Our reality may be thought of as part of a poem with God as the great poet. In poetry, the beauty of a poem does not lie in one line being sustained forever; it is in the passing of each line as it flows into the next that poetry becomes what it is. If we could see things whole, as God the artist does, we would say that they are altogether beautiful. If we complain that God is not just, it is because we cannot see the work as a whole.

A kind of corollary to this aesthetic view is an appeal to the "teleological resolution." In the end, we will see that the whole is good and beautiful. Another form of teleological resolution shifts metaphors from God as artist to God as judge. In this form we may say that things are not as they should be; suffering and evil are real and largely our own doing. In the end, however, God will judge and set things right. Harmony and balance and justice will be achieved. Evil will be punished, good will be rewarded, and all will be as it should be. This is kind of an all's-well-that-ends-well argument. In the end we will affirm that God is good and just.

Augustine's fifth answer, known as the "free-will defense," is perhaps Augustine's primary response to the theodicy question. It has become the default response for most Christians. Evil and suffering are a result of our misuse of God's good gift of freedom. God is not at fault here; we are. As Augustine says, "The cause of evil is the defection of the will of a being who is mutably good from the Good which is immutable."[1] Suffering is the consequence of (or punishment for) the evil that originates in human willing. It is true that God is responsible for giving us freedom in the first place. But freedom is a good thing, so God is not indictable for granting it to us. By the perverse misuse of freedom we have fallen from the state of grace in which we were created. We ourselves are indictable for the evil and suffering in our world—not God.

In any discussion of theodicy, we regularly hear resonances with these five arguments that Augustine offers. The free-will defense is the one offered most often. In addition to Augustine's approaches, another argument is sometimes put forward. This one comes from Irenaeus. It differs from Augustine's, as a result of Irenaeus's very different understanding of the human predicament. As presented earlier, Augustine sees the human situation as a fall from the original perfection that was there at our beginning. Irenaeus rather sees our perfection as something toward which we are growing. We are immature at our beginning (like children) and meant to grow in grace toward the perfection that is our destiny. The human being is a work in progress, and the difficult conditions we encounter may actually contribute to our growth. John Hick has referred to the conditions of our existence as portrayed by Irenaeus as "the vale of soul-making."

One essential in our growth toward God is ambiguity. God's presence is veiled from us. The world may even look as if there is no God. The veiled character of God's presence creates a space of protected freedom for us. If God's goodness and power were on display, we would be drawn to God like moths to a flame. In this way we may come to God by our own volition.

Another essential for our growth is struggle. Contending with hardships in our context strengthens us. Developing as moral beings also requires making hard moral choices. For that to happen, the world must necessarily be a place where good and evil contend. God has provided just the right

---

1. Augustine, *Enchiridion* 8.23. *Handbook on Faith, Hope, and Love*, trans. Albert Outler, Christian Classics Ethereal Library, https://www.ccel.org/ccel/augustine/enchiridion.html.

environment, a mix of both good and evil, for our growth. Good is not rewarded, and evil is not punished; otherwise we might do what is good for the reward and not for its own sake. The ambiguity and struggle necessary for our character formation are the reasons the world is the way it is. God is good to make provision for our moral formation. The world where we encounter suffering and evil is a "vale of soul-making" for us, and that is as it should be. Divine compassion accompanies us in this process.

Limitations of These Responses:
Radical Suffering / Innocent Suffering

These traditional responses are thoughtful and shed much light on the matter of suffering and evil and how it might be understood in the light of God's goodness and power. However, they do not altogether satisfy, particularly in cases of extreme suffering—what Wendy Farley has named "radical suffering."[2] This is suffering that has the power to degrade and dehumanize, including child abuse, torture, and death camps. This kind of suffering cannot be thought of as contributing to our moral formation (Irenaeus) or as deserved punishment (Augustine).

In this analysis we give special attention to the category of innocent suffering as the test case of our theodicies. For example, we might illustrate with the account in Matthew 2:1–18 of the slaughter of the innocents. Herod ordered the murder of all infants in and around Bethlehem under the age of two in hopes of eliminating the one said by the wise men to be born "king of the Jews." Traditional answers do not help when the innocent are slaughtered. This is not just the absence of some good (*privatio boni*), but the horrific presence of something genuinely evil. If their suffering is compared to the dark blue shades necessary in an overall beautiful painting, it simply is not worth it. Justice cannot abide a cosmic harmony whose edifice is maintained on the unavenged tears of tormented children.[3]Suffering as a punishment or consequence of their sin is simply not plausible in the case of these infants. Nor does the response

---

2. Wendy Farley, *Tragic Vision and Divine Compassion: A Contemporary Theodicy* (Louisville, KY: Westminster/John Knox, 1990).

3. "Imagine that you are creating a fabric of human destiny with the object of making men happy in the end, giving them peace and rest at last. Imagine that you are doing this but that it is essential and inevitable to torture to death only one tiny creature . . . in order to found that edifice on its unavenged tears. Would you consent to be the architect on those conditions? Tell me. Tell the truth." Fyodor Dostoyevsky, *The Brothers Karamazov* (1879; New York: Bantam Press, 1970).

that suffering and evil "build character" work. In some cases we might say that we learn and grow from what we endure, but these children are simply slaughtered. There is no question of their learning from this or being built up by it. Even the promise that, in the end, all will be well rings hollow. A good ending does not undo the damage. The slaughter of the innocents is irredeemably unjust, yet history is full of such actions.

Perhaps a better response is to lament with the Psalmist, "O Lord—how long?" (Ps. 6:3). Better still might be a response of protest. We should not make sense of the slaughter of the innocents; we should instead resist it with all our might. Any answers to the theodicy question that enable us to make sense of the suffering of others are problematic. They allow us to work this into a picture of what is "normal." Such answers obscure the horror, cruelty, and tragedy of suffering. They help us to bear with the suffering of others. They quiet our impulse to protest, and they sedate our motivation to resist.

The slaughter of the innocents reaches beyond the human horizon to the wider world of nature. When we widen the circle to this larger view, innocent suffering is amplified to unimaginable proportions. We can bring into view the waste and carnage of our whole evolutionary history and the untold suffering of myriad creatures along the way. The breadth and extent of this innocent suffering have caused environmental philosopher Holmes Rolston to speak of nature as "cruciform."[4] He gives an example of pelican chicks. Female pelicans usually lay two eggs, the second one two days after the first. The second chick is allowed to survive only if the first does not thrive. Its usual fate is to be driven from the nest. The parents will prevent its return, and its usual fate is to thrash about on the ground until it dies of starvation. Such a picture may be compatible with the process of natural selection as it ensures that each reproductive cycle is fruitful. However, it is not compatible with the assumptions that a good God is directly determining all the details of world process. Perhaps "direct determination of all the details" is not the best description for how God works in the world. We turn now to consider a constructive alternative.

Implications of Incarnation

We have asked the question "How can we say 'God is with us' in the face of so much suffering and evil?" Our first step is to interrogate the

---

4. Holmes Rolston, "Kenosis and Nature," in *The Work of Love: Creation as Kenosis*, ed. John Polkinghorne (Grand Rapids: Eerdmans, 2001).

question itself. What do we expect "God is with us" to look like? Are our expectations consistent with the Incarnation? The assumption behind the question of the chapter seems to be that "God is with us" would be contradicted by the continuing presence of suffering and evil. However, in the Incarnation in Jesus of Nazareth, suffering and evil did not just go away but were very much part of the picture. Jesus was not a mighty warrior who came to overthrow the oppressive powers of the Roman Empire. Jesus was not a powerful king who would make Israel great again. In many ways he was a disappointment to the popular expectations of what "God is with us" should mean. Yet in faith we affirm that, in him, God is with us. It seems this requires adjusting our assumptions. God does not come among us with all-controlling power to take charge of things and put everything right. God comes among us with a compassionate presence, in solidarity with us in our situation of suffering and evil, and manifesting power as vulnerable, suffering love.

Going back to our test case of the slaughter of the innocents, first we make a very basic claim: the slaughter of the innocents is not God's doing and not God's will—not for punishment (Augustine) and not for pedagogy (Irenaeus). In the account in Matthew 2, the slaughter of the innocents was Herod's doing.

Those who agree thus far may still pose the question "If God is all powerful, why does God not at least prevent it?" Why indeed? If God could prevent it and yet did not, the goodness of God would seem to be in question. This predicament pushes us to clarify what we mean when we say God is all powerful. To that we turn next.

What Kind of Power Does God Have?

The question is not, *how much* power does God have? The question is, *what kind* of power does God have? When we say God is omnipotent, how are we defining "potent"? Many people commonly assume that this term entails power in the mode of domination and control. This is deeply problematic. When we attach "omni" to that meaning for power and project it onto God, we end up seeing God as all-dominating and all-controlling then. Several problems arise. First, human freedom is surely compromised if God is all-controlling. Also, the theodicy problem is exacerbated. It seems that God would have the power to make all right with the world and does not use it. Can such a God be thought to be wholly good? Finally, this way of thinking about God's power has the unwanted effect of sanctioning the use of power in the mode of domination and control in the realm of human affairs. This kind of power gains a blessing by its association with the divine. There are negative social and political consequences.

Our claim throughout these chapters has been that in the Incarnation we see that God is love. If that is so, then the power we should be looking for when God is with us is power that is loving. The power of love is certainly different from (and arguably greater than) the power to dominate and control.

Charles Hartshorne, one of the chief interpreters of Whitehead and process thought, has a heavy critique of the traditional way of thinking about God's power; one of his books is titled *Omnipotence and Other Theological Mistakes*. He argues that the traditional concept of omnipotence lacks both coherence and religious viability. What is perfect power? The tradition has sometimes assumed that for God to have perfect power, God must be *able to do absolutely anything*. For example, if you start a sentence with the words "Can God . . . ," then the answer must be "yes." The coherence of such a concept of omnipotence becomes strained as it encounters instances of the omnipotence paradox. Can God create a rock so big that God cannot lift it? Can God make a square circle?

Another assumption that seems to be at work is that for God to have perfect power, God must have *all the power there is*—a monopoly on power. Hartshorne points out that the notion of God holding all the power seems an idealization of the tyrant-subject model. We do not admire tyrants in the realm of human affairs, so why project that image onto God? According to Hartshorne, this analogy is "perhaps the most shockingly bad of all theological analogies, or at least the one open to the most abuses."[5] He underscores his point with Whitehead's famous comment, "The deeper idolatry, the fashioning of God in the image of the Egyptian, Persian and Roman imperial rulers was retained. They gave unto God the properties that belonged to Caesar."[6] A divine monopoly on power as in the tyrant-subject model lacks religious viability.

An alternative to this model is available, however. God's power, which is the power of love, is generative, persuasive, and shared.

God's power is generative. We have treated power as if it is a substance or a quantifiable commodity. We view it on a scarcity model, as if it were a pie that we are dividing up and there is only so much to go around. More

---

5. Charles Hartshorne, *Man's Vision of God* (Chicago: Willett, Clark & Co., 1941), 203.

6. Alfred North Whitehead, *Process and Reality* (1929; repr., New York: Macmillan Co., 1978), 525.

for you means less for me. But what if power is not like that? What if it is more like love? Love is generative in nature. Love is such that the more you give away, the more you have. What if power is itself a relational and generative force like love? Even in human relations, when we empower others we do not thereby lose power, but may rather generate it and multiply it in our social world.

God's power is persuasive rather than coercive. In the realm of human affairs we much prefer persuasion over coercion. Why would we not make this power that we deem better and more worthy of emulation our model for understanding divine power? If what we are describing is the power of love, it is not in the nature of love to coerce and control the beloved. The power of love respects freedom and allows for mutuality and reciprocity.

God's power is shared power. We have presented a relational vision here. How would a monopoly of power make sense in a world where there are other beings, each with their own power? In a social-relational context, power must be shared power. In our discussion of creation we have claimed that the world has been granted its own authentic existence. God has made space for creaturely freedom and self-determination. Freedom is affirmed and embraced.

If God's power is generative, persuasive, and shared, we do not have to assume that whatever happens is God's will. Other wills are involved here. Evil remains a problem, a mystery, and an absurdity, but it does not have to be thought of as something that is done, willed, or controlled by God. Suffering remains a problem, but it is not just *our* problem. When we suffer, God suffers. God is in, with, and for us in our situation of suffering. It could even be said that in our suffering, God suffers more deeply than we do. God knows (and experiences) the full extent of what we suffer from external causes. God also knows the disasters we bring upon ourselves—the wreckage we sometimes make of our own lives. Added to this, God knows what could have been. Whitehead put it well; in relation to our suffering, God is "the great companion—the fellow sufferer who understands."[7] When it comes to the suffering associated with transitoriness, our situation of "perpetual perishing," our every moment is received into the divine life, and God exercises a "tender care that nothing of value be lost."[8] We might characterize God's way of being with us in our suffering and perpetual perishing as a "saving solidarity."

7. Whitehead, *Process and Reality*, 520.
8. Whitehead, *Process and Reality*, 535.

In relation to evil, God is working persuasively and powerfully to redeem and transform. It can really be said that in all things God is working for good. Whatever happens in world process—and that is largely up to us—God experiences it, grieves the wreckage we make of our possibilities, judges and transforms, and presents back to the world new and better possibilities. God's way of being with us in the face of evil might be thought of as a "redemptive resistance."

We see God's saving solidarity and redemptive resistance very clearly in the Incarnation of Jesus of Nazareth. In saving solidarity God takes on flesh. God becomes one with us—becomes one of us—suffering with us even to the point of death on the cross. In Jesus' life and ministry we see resistance to all that would hurt or destroy. He showed compassion and healing, transforming power—a redemptive resistance in the face of evil. In his resurrection we see God's life-giving power to redeem. This is the kind of power we might expect to see if God is with us.

How Is God Present and Active in World Process?

Here we argue that God is present and active in world process—*really with us*—but in ways that do not overturn our freedom or natural processes. Divine *presence* has already been discussed in earlier chapters in terms of panentheism—God in all things and all things in God. God pervades all things and yet transcends all things. This kind of presence does not compromise creation's freedom and integrity.

Divine action is the primary focus of attention here. God acts with and within ordinary means. God does not need to act supernaturally by intervention from outside world process. God does not step in here and there, now and then, to subvert natural processes. Augustine and Calvin both offer support for this point of view. In *The City of God*, Augustine argues that even what we call "miracles" are deeds of power that are *not* contrary to nature—though they may be contrary to what we *know* of nature. Calvin takes an interesting turn on this question. He suggests that what we understand to be "laws of nature" are only God's own self-consistent activity. What is "miraculous" is that God is acting in world process (everywhere and always) from within. Multiplying loaves and fishes is not qualitatively different than providing daily bread; it is just more calculated to strike the eye.

These views drawn from the tradition are already countering the external interventionist patterns of thought that have proven problematic in relation to scientific understandings of the way the world works. Much hinges upon how we understand divine action. What if we followed the lead of Augustine and Calvin and thought of God acting with and within natural process in a way that is continuous? We may affirm that God is at work for good in all things. Freedom means that there is more than one actor here, and the divine intentions can be resisted and thwarted. Sometimes in our freedom we align our actions with the divine purposes, and good is accomplished. When we see good things happening, we often say, "God is at work." It is a kind of confession of faith drawn from us. In those moments we have for a time seen through to what God is already doing everywhere and always.

The traditional doctrine of providence has affirmed that God acts in the world. This is central for Christian faith, but there is more than one way of thinking about how God acts in the world. There are theological problems with thinking that God now and then intervenes from the outside, overruling freedom or subverting natural processes. Such a view brings in its wake the unintended assertion of the ordinary absence of God. This is problematic theologically. Furthermore, if we think that God can and occasionally does act in this way, we may want to ask why God does not intervene more often—in the face of natural disasters, plagues, and human atrocities. Much suffering and evil could presumably be prevented through divine intervention. The problem of theodicy is exacerbated by this external-interventionist understanding of divine action. This model for divine working in the world is also problematic with our understanding from science about how the world works. The scientific and the theological problems both invite us to reconsider such notions of God's activity.

We are seeking a way of maintaining divine activity in world process without external, interventionist thinking. God is present and active in world process in a way that is continuous rather than discontinuous, in a way that upholds rather than violates the creation's own freedom and integrity. Is there any reason not to allow that God may act with and within natural processes? Some very interesting proposals come from scientist/theologians who are working on ways of understanding and articulating this perspective. We offer these by way of illustration.

Arthur Peacocke (biochemist, theologian, and Anglican priest) suggests that divine activity might be thought of on the model of biochemical processes, in which larger wholes are said to "influence" the parts that constitute them. Higher levels constrain and shape the patterns of constituent units in a lower level in what is termed "downward causation." An example would be the way an organism's wider environment affects its development and well-being. The world is a system-of-systems organized in levels of increasing complexity. Peacocke suggests that we think of God, who encompasses all, as acting in this way. Divine influence may influence all things "without abrogating the laws and regularities that specifically apply to them."[9] As Peacocke puts it, "God is best conceived of as the circumambient reality enclosing all existing entities, structures, and processes, and as operating in and through all while being 'more' than all. . . . God's infinity comprehends and incorporates all."[10] This provides a way of understanding God's activity in the world without recourse to external interventionist models.

John Polkinghorne (theoretical physicist, theologian, and Anglican priest) offers another such proposal. Where Peacocke envisions a kind of top-down model for divine working, Polkinghorne's model offers a bottom-up approach. Polkinghorne considers the unpredictability and uncertainty that science finds at the quantum level and also finds in chaotic systems with their sensitivity to small triggers (e.g., weather patterns). This dynamic of unpredictability and indeterminacy in physical reality, he conjectures, signals an "openness" in the system. He suggests that we might think of God's activity as a kind of "active information" working at the quantum level. Polkinghorne thinks of this as "the scientific equivalent of the immanent working of the Spirit on the inside of creation."[11]

These interesting proposals are representative of some creative work on how God may act in the world in ways that do not amount to occasional external intervention that violates natural processes. Such proposals go a long way toward thinking about how God works in the world in ways that are consistent with what we know of how the world works. They also envision God acting continuously rather than just occasionally, which, as we have said, would imply the ordinary absence of God. The God-given freedom of the creation is upheld in a way that gives an answer to how suffering and evil can arise even though God is with us and ever working for good in all things. Such reflections as these take us a step further toward an understanding of divine activity in world process that is both more credible and more faithful.

9. Arthur Peacocke, *Paths from Science towards God: The End of All Our Exploring* (Oxford: One World, 2001), 51.

10. Arthur Peacocke, "Articulating God's Presence in and to a World Unveiled by the "Sciences," in *In Whom We Live and Move and Have Our Being: Panentheistic Reflections on God's Presence in a Scientific World*, ed. Philip Clayton and Arthur Peacocke (Grand Rapids: Eerdmans, 2004), 147.

11. John Polkinghorne, *Science and Theology: An Introduction* (Philadelphia: Fortress, 1998), 89.

Creation, Concursus, *and Calling*

Implications of divine incarnation in all things and the conclusions discussed in previous chapters may yield some additional insights into how
God is with us. We look briefly here at traditional themes of creation,
concursus (accompaniment), and calling in light of the larger discussion.

Jürgen Moltmann, in his book *God in Creation*, articulates a panentheist position. He puzzles over how it can be that, if God is all in all, there
can be anything but a pantheistic dissolution of the difference between
God and creation. He argues that there is a sense in which God creates
within Godself a space for a genuine other to be.[12] He draws upon the
Jewish kabbalistic notion of *zimzum* to elaborate. *Zimzum* means "concentration and contraction, and signifies a withdrawing of oneself into
oneself."[13] It is, in a sense, a divine "making room" in God's own being
for an other, which is the creation. An important conceptual parallel for
Christian theology is the divine *kenosis* (self-giving) that takes place in the
incarnation.

God creates by "making room in Godself for the other." It seems that
the creation is a world in process that is continually changing and even
has its own self-organizing processes. God's creative work is ongoing
(*creatio continua*) as an "immanent Creator creating continuously in and
through the processes of the natural order."[14] There seems to be a "per-
petually endowed creativity."[15] In this way, the creation has capacity for
self-creation. New things come into being. The processes of emergence
of "something more" out of "nothing but." God is "in, with, and under"
all that is. For this reason we do not need to look for some gap in the
causal nexus for God to fit in and act upon the creation. Speculation on
how God acts in the world is possible, and some models are more theologically promising than others. However, we need not expect to find a
mechanism for God's acting. God is apparently more subtle than that.

Barth makes an interesting proposal concerning divine action when he
reclaims the older dogmatic concept of *concursus*, which has been present
in the Christian tradition as a way of thinking about God's ongoing creativity in the world. He renames the concept of divine *concursus* as divine
"accompanying." One element in this is the confidence that God, having

---

12. Jurgen Moltmann, *God in Creation: A New Theology of Creation and the Spirit of God* (San
Francisco: Harper and Row, 1985), 86–93.

13. Moltmann, *God in Creation*, 86.

14. Peacocke, *Paths from Science towards God*, 129.

15. Peacocke, *Paths from Science towards God*, 137.

called the creation into being, does not abandon it but is really continually present in and with the creation.[16] Another element is an affirmation that God supports the creation in its freedom. There is a divine "letting be" of the creation. God "affirms and approves and recognizes and respects the autonomous actuality and therefore the autonomous activity of the creature as such."[17] God "goes with the creature and co-operates with it. God is the Creator and Sustainer of the creature."[18] If divine *concursus*/accompanying is taken seriously, then God's action is not an overriding. Rather it seems that God "supports us all the day long," as it were, in freedom.

"God acts but does not overrule. The Spirit guides, but with a gentle respect for the integrity of creation. . . . There is a divine letting-be, a making room for the created-other, together with the acceptance of the consequences that will flow from free process and from the exercise of human free will."[19] God's accompaniment both guides and supports this self-creating creation. The one who accompanies is "always a step in advance of the free creature."[20] God is calling, leading, luring the creature toward good ends in a future that is genuinely open to the self-making and world-making of creatures. Process theology has a way of picturing this divine leading that is compelling. It maintains the reality of divine persuasive influence without coercion. Whitehead affirmed Plato's conviction "that the divine element in the world is to be conceived as a persuasive agency and not as a coercive agency. This doctrine should be looked upon as one of the greatest intellectual discoveries in the history of religion."[21]

As Hartshorne suggested, "God's influence is supreme. . . . But the direct influence of God is analogous only to the direct power of thought over thought, and of feeling over feeling, and this is the power of inspiration or suggestion."[22] God, as the Ground of Order and the Ground of Novelty, is pictured as holding before the events coming to be the (ideal) possibilities of what they may become. Whitehead speaks of these ideals as the divine "initial aims."[23] These aims are not coercive in that

16. Karl Barth, *Church Dogmatics*, III/3, *The Doctrine of Creation*, ed. G. W. Bromiley and T. F. Torrance (Edinburgh: T. and T. Clark, 1976), 91.

17. Barth, *Church Dogmatics* III/3, 92.

18. Barth, *Church Dogmatics* III/3, 93.

19. Polkinghorne, *Science and Theology*, 95.

20. Barth, *Church Dogmatics* III/3, 93.

21. Alfred North Whitehead, *Adventures of Ideas* (New York: Macmillan, 1933), 312.

22. Charles Hartshorne, *Reality as Social Process* (Glencoe, IL: Free Press, 1953), 275.

23. Whitehead, *Process and Reality*, 244.

the event may only partially incorporate them or may even reject then. At best they are "persuasive" influences. The metaphor in process thought is perception: what we see influences us but does not determine exactly what we will do.

These initial aims of God become a "lure" toward the good that is possible. Because the world is "in God," what happens in the world may enrich and actualize the divine experience, but it may also produce suffering in the divine life. Such a notion contradicts traditional assumptions that God dwells in unbroken bliss purchased by the exclusion of creaturely misery.[24] There is an assumed divine vulnerability in this give-and-take with the world.

Jay McDaniel, in his elaboration of the Whiteheadian vision, has helpful ways of thinking about this divine persuasive influence in world process. As he says, God influences creation as "an immanent, ever-adaptive, omni-invitational, Lure or Beckoning Presence."[25] All creatures experience this lure in the depths of our preconscious experience. God's initial aims are inwardly felt possibilities or goals that we ourselves must actualize and that, if they were actualized, would yield a maximal "wholeness" or "fullness of life" relative to the situation at hand.[26]

God's luring in the cosmos may be the impetus to greater complexification and diversification and the emergence of genuinely new realities. The traditional theological idea of a "principle of plenitude" illumines this apparent directionality in the evolutionary process. Like a companion or friend who inspires one to achieve the very best that is in one's power, God lures each and all toward fullest actualization, toward harmony and intensity that overcome discord and triviality. In this way, God acts persuasively within the created order at all levels—with atoms, molecules, cells, and organisms—in ways appropriate to that level.

As Whitehead says, "The world lives by its incarnation of God in itself."[27] As Lewis Ford has observed, Whitehead assumes an "incarnational universe."[28] For Whitehead, each temporal occasion embodies God and is embodied in God.[29] As we have argued, what is revealed in the divine incarnation in Jesus of Nazareth is not an exception to God's ordinary way of acting in the world but rather, because of his perfect

24. Lewis Ford, *The Lure of God* (Philadelphia: Fortress, 1978), 92.
25. Jay McDaniel, *With Roots and Wings* (Maryknoll, NY: Orbis Books, 1995), 140.
26. McDaniel, *With Roots and Wings*, 140.
27. Whitehead, *Process and Reality*, 151.
28. Ford, *Lure of God*, 51.
29. Whitehead, *Process and Reality*, 348.

responsiveness to divine initial aims, we see in him what God is intending and doing everywhere and always. God's intentions and actions for each and all become transparent in Jesus the Christ. He is their "chief exemplification." The initial aims of God that persuasively lure in the direction of the divine intentions may be another way of talking about traditional concepts such as "calling" and "vocation."

Final Thoughts

We have proposed in this chapter a way of understanding how God acts in the world. One conclusion from this approach is that freedom is real. In some ways this has been an extended reclaiming of the free-will defense, but hopefully in a more defensible form. For the free-will defense to function, we need a robust understanding of freedom. Divine power must be sufficiently subtle to allow for this. Instead of power in the mode of domination and control, we see power that is shaped by love. Freedom is the risk love takes, to honor and preserve the freedom of the beloved. With such love there is vulnerability and the risk of suffering. This decidedly different vision of God is beautifully articulated in the hymn by W. H. Vanstone, with which he closes his book titled *Love's Endeavour, Love's Expense.*

> **Love's Endeavour, Love's Expense**
> Morning glory, starlit sky,
> Leaves in springtime, swallow's flight,
> Autumn gales, tremendous seas,
> Sound and scents of summer night;
>
> Soaring music, tow'ring words,
> Art's perfection, scholar's truth,
> Joy supreme of human love,
> Memory's treasure, grace of youth;
>
> Open, Lord, are these, Thy gifts,
> Gifts of love to mind and sense;
> Hidden is love's agony,
> Love's endeavor, love's expense.
>
> Love that gives gives ever more,
> Gives with zeal, with eager hands,

Spares not, keeps not, all outpours,
Ventures all, its all expends.

Drained is love in making full;
Bound in setting others free;
Poor in making many rich;
Weak in giving power to be.

Therefore He Who Thee reveals
Hangs, O Father, on that Tree
Helpless; and the nails and thorns
Tell of what Thy love must be,

Thou art God; no monarch Thou,
Thron'd in easy state to reign;
Thou art God, Whose arms of love
Aching, spent, the world sustain.[30]

This way of thinking has many advantages theologically. One challenge that comes with it is this, what happens to the "guaranteed triumph of the good" that was part of the system of thought when God is in control of everything? It seems we have let go of that if freedom is real.

Indeed, we have let go of the guaranteed triumph of the good. There are many reasons why we might want to do that. When we look at the state of the world, does it look as if God is in control and that things are working themselves out according to a detailed blueprint in the divine mind? Or if God *is* in control and our crisis situation is temporary and allowable (for reasons known only to God), and God can fix everything in the end, then we have to ask: Why wait? We judge a person very harshly who does not prevent or put an end to the evil when they can. It seems that God is indictable for the calamities we endure in the meantime. We may well ask, what kind of God is this? We seem to let go of the *goodness* of God. With the alternative we have been presenting, at least God is good—all the time.

In the alternative proposed in this chapter, moreover, freedom is real. A consequence is that there are no guarantees of a triumph of the good in any given moment or in some final ending. What we do have is assurance

30. W. H. Vanstone, *Love's Endeavour, Love's Expense: The Response of Being to the Love of God* (1977; repr., London: Darton, Longman, and Todd, 2007), 119. Used by permission of Darton, Longman & Todd.

that God, who is loving, is working in all things for good and never gives up—no matter the wreckage we make of things. We still hold that God is all powerful but God's power is not controlling power. It is the power of love. God creates with us, accompanies us in our freedom, and calls us to ever new and better possibilities. This is the God who is *with us.* Furthermore, God is never defeated by evil[31] but overcomes it moment by moment, judging and transforming as the world's current states are received into the divine life. Whitehead puts it this way: "He saves the world as it passes into the immediacy of his own life. It is the judgment of a tenderness which loses nothing that can be saved. It is also the judgment of a wisdom which uses what in the temporal world is mere wreckage."[32]

Suffering and evil will never have the last word. If there is no triumph of the good guaranteed, there at least remains a guarantee that evil will not ever win. God is everlastingly working for good; God receives what goes on in the world into the divine life. God responds—judging, transforming, and offering back to the world new possibilities for good. Hope endures.

In some ways, hope is better than a guarantee. A guarantee invites torpor. We may say to ourselves, for example, that God will not let us destroy the Earth with nuclear annihilation or ecological irresponsibility. Then we do not have to worry about those things or take decisive action in resistance to them. Hope, on the other hand, motivates us for action. Hope may be what we need most. Even the Twenty-third Psalm—that most comforting of all psalms—does not offer a guarantee that we will not have to "walk through the valley of the shadow of death." What it promises is, "Thou art with me." God is with us in these valleys. We are made strong for the struggle that is our reality by this divine presence and shepherding through it all.

We see, in Jesus the Christ, God's saving solidarity in the face of suffering and a redemptive resistance in the face of evil. That God is active in both the solidarity and the resistance is what faith affirms. Suffering and evil are real and our response as the people of God are to bring our own solidarity and resistance to these realities. The real question for us is not, why is there suffering and evil in the world? The question is, what are we going to do about it?

---

31. For a fuller discussion of God's action in relation to the problem of evil, see my chapter "Ends and Endings," in *World without End: Christian Eschatology from a Process Perspective,* ed. Joseph Bracken (Grand Rapids: Eerdmans, 2005), 177–96.
32. Whitehead, *Process and Reality,* 525.

Mujerista (Latina womanist) theologian Ada María Isasi-Díaz pro-posed that God is with us *en la lucha*—in the struggle.[33] This word is especially needed in the present crisis. Isasi-Diaz observes that among the theories of the atonement we have discussed, some are more helpful than others in a situation of struggle. The substitutionary, sacrificial satisfac-tion theories of the atonement are not as helpful for us now, because they seem to imply that it has all already been done for us. The *Christus Vic-tor* theory of the atonement seems a bit triumphalistic under the present circumstances. Christ the exemplar or moral example seems to resonate better with us in a time of crisis such as we now face. He is the exemplar for us—the one who shows us the way to be: how to be truly human, how to exercise compassion, how to engage in transforming work. This example inspires and motivates us. We actually need to *do* some things to engage this struggle. It is the activist Jesus we need to see (and follow) in these times.

This approach is consistent with what we have said about how God acts in the world. God works in and through us. Pope Francis has made an interesting observation that moves in this same direction. Regarding prayer, he suggested that this is how prayer works: You pray that the hungry may be fed, and then you feed them.

We have engaged the question: How can we say "God is with us" in the face of so much suffering and evil? Looking through the lens of incar-nation has made it possible to argue that God is indeed with us—all of us—and especially in the face of suffering and evil. Perhaps the question is not so much whether God is with us as it is *whether we are with God* in this struggle.

33. Ada María Isasi-Díaz, *En La Lucha / In the Struggle: Elaborating Mujerista Theology* (Min-neapolis: Augsburg Fortress, 2004).

Conclusion

I am writing this conclusion in the harrowing days of the pandemic and the exposure of systemic racism and the injustices of our criminal justice system. People are peacefully protesting violence, and they are met with violence. There is complete dysfunction in the nation's highest office. One dreads to hear the morning news: what fresh disaster?

Now more than ever we need to hear and believe the good news that God is with us. This book has inquired into what that means and what difference it makes. We have framed the Incarnation in Jesus of Nazareth within a vision of God as being *really* in the world and yet more than the world. In the process, we revisited the affirmations around the Incarnation made at Chalcedon: "truly God and truly human . . . two natures in one person." We sought to reclaim these affirmations in a way that does not force a choice between Christology from above and Christology from below. The Holy Mystery of God's presence in Jesus of Nazareth remains mysterious, but some possible misunderstandings that may obscure its meaning have at least been addressed. A closer look at some biblical texts, Trinitarian theology, and process-relational approaches have aided the effort to make a more coherent interpretation.

Incarnation fundamentally changes how we think about God. God is no longer a God who is far off, but one who is close at hand—one "in whom we live and move and have our being." God is love, and the dynamic relationality between God and the world is characterized by creative-responsive love. Since God is in all things and all things are in God, God's relation with the world is internal to God, not external. This means God will suffer when God's beloved creation suffers. God leads the world in its creative advance, but all creatures have capacity for creativity and thus are co-creating with God. Genuine freedom and agency characterize the creation. The metaphor of the world as an organism is more helpful than the metaphor of the world as a mechanism for conveying its intrinsic value and vital interconnection.

When incarnation is the lens through which we look, we see a very different picture of the human being as well. Our understandings of who we are and what we are called to do are both transformed. We are created in the image of God, and thus we are called to reflect the divine image by extending God's care and creativity through our relations with one another and with the wider world of nature. We are at home in the cosmos, created from the earth. We are embodied and embedded. Human beings are not separate from or over-and-above the rest of creation. Yet we do have heightened capacities for rationality and freedom, and therefore heightened responsibility for care and creativity. The divine embrace of flesh in the Incarnation makes it clear that bodies matter. An incarnational ethics entails living in ways that care for bodies. We illustrated what that might mean by reflecting on disability discrimination and racism.

A deeper and richer understanding of the Christ event is also possible when we recenter all its aspects more fully in incarnation: birth, life and ministry, death, and resurrection. Some distortions that have characterized our understanding of the person and work of Christ can be corrected if we take this larger view. We will be able to see better how "God is with us" in Jesus of Nazareth and understand God's saving work in him more fully. Overarching themes emerge: God's solidarity with us in our situation of sin and suffering and God's resistance to all that would hurt or destroy.

When contemplating what it means to say, "God is with us," it is important to be clear on what we mean by "us." Do we mean just us Christians? Just us humans? Just us Earthlings? In each case, we commend a widening of the circle of inclusion. The God who is with us is God of all things visible and invisible. The divine embrace is very wide indeed. Incarnation is larger than we have imagined, and God is greater. The more we enlarge the circle of care and conclude that we are all in this together, the better chance we have to address the multiple interlocking crises of our day together. We are a planet in peril. We face the nuclear threat, political turbulence, economic disparity, ecological disaster, and social injustice. We need to find our way to a different kind of world, or there is no future for us. We need to find a way to become "convivial community," characterized by solidarity, sufficiency, and sustainability. It is necessary to have an enlarged understanding of "us" when we say God is with us.

How can we say God is with us in the face of so much suffering and evil? Christian tradition has many responses to this question. The question, however, may betray a presumption that God controls everything that happens in world process and can therefore fix things if God is with us. If that were the case, then indeed it looks as if God is not with us. It may be that this is a misrepresentation of the kind of power God has and exercises in world process. What if God's power is not power in the mode of domination and control, but another kind of power? What kind of power would be more consistent with our affirmation that God is love? We propose that God is all powerful, but that the kind of power God has—the power of love—is generative, persuasive, shared power. God is acting in the world in ways consistent with this kind of power. God is continually creating with the creation, accompanies it in its creaturely freedom, and is ever calling it to new and better possibilities. Freedom is real, and that means we can make a wreck of things—and we have. Nevertheless, God is continually working for good in all things. Even now God is, moment by moment, making all things new. We can live in hope. God will be all in all.

Index of Scripture

205

Index of Subjects and Names

revealing divine intention, 38
seeing God in, 9–10
seeing the human in, 8–9
suffering of, 32
teachings of, 107–10, 115
unique relationship of, with God, 114
whitewashing of, 105–6
See also Christ
Jesus and the Disinherited (Thurman),
  106–7
Jesus movement, as strategy for resisting
  oppression, 107
Jim Crow, 88, 89
John, Gospel of, theological complexity
  of, 12
John Paul II, 140
Johnson, Elizabeth, 117, 124
Jungel, Gerhard, 130
justice
  God calling for, 118
  love and, 83
  teaching for, 90–91
justification, 177
Justin Martyr, 14, 147

Kaufman, Gordon, 36n18
Keller, Catherine, 41, 158n55, 161
kenosis, 12, 193
King, Martin Luther, 98
kingdom of God
  Jesus' preaching on, 97–98, 110
  kin-dom, 98
  resurrection and, 132
King James Version, imposing dualism,
  63
Kluge (John) Center (Library of
  Congress), 169
Ku Klux Klan, 88
Kuyper, Abraham, 113

language, in chimpanzees, 68
Lao Tzu, 161
Leibniz, Gottfried, 181
Levinas, Emmanuel, 157, 158
liberation theology, 82
life satisfaction, 160
Lisbon, earthquake in (1755), 180–81

Living Buddha, Living Christ (Nhat Hanh),
  42
Logos, divine, emptying himself, 11–12
Logos Christology, 12–13, 147. *See also*
  cosmic Christology
Lomax, Mark, 98
love, power of, 188–90, 203
Love's Endeavour, Love's Expense (Vanstone), 196–97
low Christology. *See* Christology: from
  below
Lowe, Victor, 23
Luther, Martin, 8

MacNair, Rachel, 92
Manicheans, 182
Martelet, Gustave, 137
Mary (mother of God), annunciation to, 15
mass extinctions, 65
material reality, God's embrace of, 3,
  45, 60
Matthew, Gospel of, resistance narrative
  in, 106
Maximus the Confessor, 103
McDaniel, Jay, 195
McFague, Sallie, 36n18, 161
Merton, Thomas, 77, 79, 81
messianic martyr mythology, 96
metanoia, 80–81
Metz, Johann Baptist, 121–22
Middle Passage, 88
Migliore, Daniel, 129
miracles, 190
modalism, 32–33
Moltmann, Jürgen, 33, 38–39, 121, 123,
  129, 155, 156, 193
monarchical modalism, 33n5
monotheism, Trinitarian theology and, 18
moral evil, 4, 180, 181–82
moral influence theory, 110
morality, 68, 183
Muhammad, 140
mutual indwelling, 33–34
mutuality, 189

natural evil, 4, 180
natural law, 150

perfect, 188
persuasive, 189
shared, 189
precautionary principle, 170n83
preferential option for the poor, 82
Primack, Joel, 65
process panentheism, 36, 37, 43, 45
process theology
  on God leading, 194
  immortality and, 129
process thought, 10
  addressing nature's objectification,
    151–59
  in conversation with theology, 23–24
  on divine being and acting, 136
  perception in, 195
  reconsidering Creator-created divide,
    34
  shift to, from substance thinking, 24
process-panentheism, on divine embrace
  of material reality, 59
process-relational metaphysics, 152
process-relational theology, 2, 10, 30, 31,
  44–45, 145
  assuming internal God-world relation,
    32
  dynamic relationality and, 22
  panentheism in, 35. *See also*
    panentheism
  Whitehead and, 23
process-relational thinking, 22
progressivist view, 80
providence, 149–50, 191

quaking aspens, 40
quantum mechanics, 40, 153

race trauma, 82, 94–95, 108–9
racialization, 86–87
racialized violence, resistance to, 95–96
racism, 82, 107, 169–70
  incarnational ethics and, 86–97
  systemic, 91, 179, 180
radical suffering, 185–86
Rah, Soong-Chang, 87, 92
Rahner, Karl, 104, 113
Rankine, Claudia, 91

ransom theory, 110, 130–31
rationality, distortions of, 79–80
Reagan, Ronald, 143–44
reality
  interconnectedness in, 23. *See also*
    interconnectedness
  as process, 23, 31
reciprocity, 189
redemption
  disembodied, 147
  for extraterrestrials, 171
  need for, 176–77
redemptive resistance, 190
redwoods, 66–67
Reformed theology, reinforcing divine
  connection with nature, 148–51
reign of God, focus on, 9
relationality, 17, 30, 31
  central to God's image in humans, 85
  dynamic, 10
  process-relational theology and, 22
  transcendent, 37
  within the Trinity, 19, 26
relational ontology, 154
relational thinking, 22. *See also* process-
  relational thinking
religion
  politics and, 143–44
  sentiment about, present-day, 141
religious liberty, threats to, 143
religious others, love of, 142
religious pluralism, 138–39
religious violence, 141, 144
resistance
  Christ event and, 133–34
  Jesus' advocacy of, 106–9
  redemptive, 190
  resurrection as motivator for, 132
resurrection
  ambiguities around, 124–26, 128–29
  centrality of, 126–27, 130–31
  deep, 122–24
  demythologizing, 124
  eschatology and, 128–29
  as God's gift, 129
  historicity of, 125
  hope from, 132

white fragility, 92
white male European body, idealization
    of, 105
white solidarity, 92n61
white supremacy, 80
    churches' and seminaries' involvement
        in, 93
    entrenchment of, 92–93
    manifestations of, 87–89
    recognition of, 92–93
    resistance to, 91–97
Whitehead, Alfred North, 23, 24–25, 32,
    35, 37–40, 61, 105, 121, 128, 151–57,
    188, 189, 194–95, 198
Williams, Delores, 93–94, 100
Williams, Reggie, 86–87, 90–91
Wink, Walter, 109

Winters, Jennifer, 166
Wiseman, Jennifer, 164
Wolf-Chase, Grace, 170
womanists, on racial injustice, 93–97
women, secondary status of, 62
Wood, Francis, 155
Word, the, presence of, beyond Jesus,
    136–37
world, alterity of, 37
World Bank, 160
world process, 24

Yerkes Institute of Primate Studies, 68
Yom Kippur, 118–19

Zealots, 107, 108
zimzum, 193

CPSIA information can be obtained
at www.ICGtesting.com
Printed in the USA
BVHW060402161021
618916BV00009B/108